Making
Evaluation Matter

Thank you for choosing a SAGE product! If you have any comment,
observation or feedback, I would like to personally hear from you.
Please write to me at contactceo@sagepub.in

—Vivek Mehra, Managing Director and CEO,
SAGE Publications India Pvt Ltd, New Delhi

Bulk Sales

SAGE India offers special discounts for purchase of books in bulk.
We also make available special imprints and excerpts from our
books on demand.

For orders and enquiries, write to us at

Marketing Department
SAGE Publications India Pvt Ltd
B1/I-1, Mohan Cooperative Industrial Area
Mathura Road, Post Bag 7
New Delhi 110044, India
E-mail us at marketing@sagepub.in

Get to know more about SAGE, be invited to SAGE events, get on
our mailing list. Write today to marketing@sagepub.in

This book is also available as an e-book.

————————ॐ☁——————————

Making Evaluation Matter

Writings from South Asia

Edited by
Katherine Eve Hay
Shubh Kumar-Range

www.sagepublications.com
Los Angeles • London • New Delhi • Singapore • Washington DC

International Development Research Centre
Ottawa • Cairo • Montevideo • Nairobi • New Delhi

First published in 2014 by

 SAGE Publications India Pvt Ltd
B1/I-1 Mohan Cooperative Industrial Area
Mathura Road, New Delhi 110 044, India
www.sagepub.in

SAGE Publications Inc
2455 Teller Road
Thousand Oaks, California 91320, USA

SAGE Publications Ltd
1 Oliver's Yard, 55 City Road
London EC1Y 1SP, United Kingdom

SAGE Publications Asia-Pacific Pte Ltd
3 Church Street
#10-04 Samsung Hub
Singapore 049483

International
Development
Research Centre
P.O. Box 8500
Ottawa, Ontario
Canada, K1G 3H9
www.idrc.ca
info@idrc.ca

ISBN (e-book)
978-1-55250-583-0

Published by Vivek Mehra for SAGE Publications India Pvt Ltd, typeset in 10/13 Berkeley by Diligent Typesetter, Delhi and printed at Saurabh Printers Pvt Ltd, New Delhi.

Library of Congress Cataloging-in-Publication Data

Making evaluation matter : writings from South Asia / [edited by] Katherine Eve Hay and Shubh Kumar-Range.
     pages cm
   Includes bibliographical references and index.
     1. Evaluation research (Social action programs)—South Asia. 2. Social service—South Asia—Evaluation. 3. Economic development projects—South Asia—Evaluation. I. Hay, Katherine Eve. II. Kumar-Range, Shubh.
   H62.5.S64M35   001.4—dc23   2014   2014026958

ISBN: 978-93-515-0027-8 (HB)

The SAGE Team: Rudra Narayan, Saima Ghaffar, Nand Kumar Jha and Dally Verghese

Contents

List of Figures

List of Tables

List of Boxes

Preface

The idea for this volume came with the formation of the Community of Evaluators (CoE) for South Asia in 2008. The CoE's goal is to enhance the field of evaluation. That initiative brought together a group of evaluators from across South Asia interested in working together to strengthen the quality, use, and relevance of evaluation in the region.

Dedicated evaluators came together from several countries in South Asia and developed a programme of activities that resulted in several regional meetings, an active web platform, and a highly successful Evaluation Conclave series. Through these programmes and activities, the CoE has brought together hundreds of evaluators working in South Asia who were previously disconnected from each other and created a space for sharing and professionalization.

As the group began to take shape, one of the gaps it identified was that evaluators in South Asia were not documenting and sharing their evaluation experiences. This gap was limiting both advances in evaluation in South Asia and in the field internationally. So, one of the early objectives of the CoE became to document the experiences and insights of South Asian evaluation experts.

There were many ways to do this, but the CoE was ambitious and decided to work on writing articles that had the rigor and quality to be considered part of the scholarly literature in the field of development evaluation. We agreed to spearhead and steer this effort, which ultimately turned us into the editors of this volume.

An early challenge was the limited publishing experience of many evaluators—most of whom were either working with development organizations or independently. Many were previously unpublished in the evaluation literature or generally, so helping develop strong pieces that captured the deep experience of practitioners while maintaining strong quality standards and links to the existing body of evaluation literature was not an easy process. With CoE support, we organized a series of 'write shops' to begin engaging with ideas and drawing on peer support and resources. One of the challenges facing many writers and researchers working in poorly resourced settings is the prohibitive cost of access to academic journals and writings, so 'virtual' access to all major academic research collections was provided to the authors.

The 'write shops' were oriented at exploring and drawing out a number of themes, including the context of South Asia, methodological developments in evaluation, and the challenges of using evaluation. Once initial drafts were available, we gave substantive and organizational feedback to the authors. We then sent papers that were deemed strong enough for consideration in the volume out for expert peer review by international and regional evaluation experts and domain experts. Reviewers included some of the top experts in development evaluation and domain experts in several fields. Each paper was reviewed by at least three people. Often papers were only accepted after several rounds of revisions. Originally a 'blind' review, in several cases there was interest from the reviewers or authors to engage directly after the review to follow up. As the intent was to support the work and to foster connections, this was not blocked, but encouraged.

As we continued working on this effort, we became increasingly aware of the opportunity we have in this region to contribute to the literature of development evaluation. While evaluation practitioners in South Asia are using and adapting internationally accepted evaluation concepts and methods—and even developing innovative ones—this is not reflected in the literature. Attempting to help remedy this situation was a huge motivation that kept us going. We became more convinced that in order to build a strong field and practice of evaluation in the region, the quality and stature of evaluation scholarship needed to be supported, and that this volume would make a significant contribution towards that end.

This volume is a testament to the authors who persevered through this arduous process—taking time from evenings, weekends, and holidays, and going through the multiple reviews and revisions that the process entailed. As we moved forward, many noted they experienced the distinction between writing an evaluation report and writing *about* evaluation, often struggling with how to effectively relate their own learning to the larger body of thinking in a way that wrapped theoretical ideas holistically around tangible concepts.

The contributors to this volume are representative of the range of people involved in the evaluation field in South Asia. Among the group are evaluators who are embedded in large development and research organizations, who teach in university settings, who have spent their career working within government, and who work within funding agencies. We have tried to highlight and reflect the diversity of ideas that these different positions and experiences bring. The diversity within the evaluation community in South Asia is vast; among the writers in this volume, you will see many differences of views on issues of use, design, approaches, and methods. But there are also many points of convergence where they come together: on issues of quality, of use, and ultimately of 'making a difference' in improving real lives on the ground.

This richness and the diversity of these writings reflect the richness and diversity of the evaluation field. As such, this process has proved to be incredibly stimulating and useful. We have learnt a great deal, and our own thinking and work on evaluation has changed in the process.

Shubh Kumar-Range and Katherine Eve Hay
November 2012

Acknowledgements

The idea for this volume came from members of the Community of Evaluators for South Asia (CoE). Many COE members were key to making this volume a success. Khilesh Chaturvedi and the Association for Stimulating Know-How were notable drivers early on. Support from the current COE secretariat, Swasti, was also a huge help. The authors benefited immensely from the valuable comments of many reviewers from around the world and later from the peer review coordinated by SAGE. Those comments helped improve the quality of the chapters and the volume overall. We are grateful to SAGE, New Delhi, for publishing this volume and to Rudra Narayan Sharma for shepherding it within SAGE. Our appreciation also goes to Canada's International Development Research Centre (IDRC) which provided the financial support to make the volume a reality. Of special note are the efforts of many of the behind the scenes people at IDRC, including Valthsala, who kept us coordinated and on track. Bringing these voices and perspectives into the broader evaluation discourse was a collaborative effort involving many people. We are grateful for the support.

1

Introduction: Imagining Development, Imagining Evaluation

Katherine Eve Hay and Shubh Kumar-Range

> Truth is by nature self-evident. As soon as you remove the cobwebs of ignorance that surround it, it shines clear.
>
> Mahatma Gandhi

> The pure and simple truth is rarely pure and never simple.
>
> Oscar Wilde

This book is a collection of writing on evaluation from and on South Asia. Indeed, it is the first book of its kind to be published. It draws on a depth of experience from evaluators in several countries in South Asia and explores how evaluation can support better or more equitable development in the region. The intent of the book is not to establish a singular 'voice' that speaks of South Asian evaluation but to bring together different voices and perspectives to examine evaluation approaches, experiences, use, and relevance in South Asia and to begin to see what issues and questions emerge from that process.

Overview

The book has 13 chapters that explore a rich and diverse range of issues that focus on the context, use, and methodology of evaluation in South Asia.

On Context

Chapter 2, 'Evaluation for Development Results: Implications of the Governance Context in South Asia', by Shubh Kumar-Range, explores the links between governance, types of accountability, and evaluation use. It uses available data to analyse the qualities of the governance environment in South Asian countries and then examines the implications for the evaluation climate and the strategies and methods that are most likely to result in the effective use of evaluation to achieve development results. Chapter 3, 'Building the Field of Evaluation in South Asia: A Framework and Ideas', by Katherine Hay explores and develops a framework for evaluation field building. It suggests elements a robust evaluation field should include and maps these against the current situation in South Asia. The chapter then proposes strategies for field building to support and strengthen this evolution (indeed revolution) in evaluation practice and use.

In Chapter 4, 'The Importance of Context in Participatory Evaluations: Reflections from South Asia', Sonal Zaveri suggests that participatory evaluation (PE) needs to be examined and understood in the particular context of South Asia. Zaveri draws on examples to discuss some of the contextual factors related to true participation in the region. She argues that we need a more nuanced understanding of community and participation in South Asia and suggests that evaluators need to think deeply about how they use PE and to anchor it in the 'real' world, where context plays an important role in evaluation implementation and use. This idea is reinforced in Chapter 5, 'Evaluating Rights and Social Justice: Process, Politics, and Positioning in South Asia', by Veronica Magar and Pradeep Narayanan. This chapter explores how rights- and justice-oriented evaluations can lead to better and more sustainable results by analysing and addressing inequalities, discriminatory practices, and unjust power relations, which are often at the heart of most development problems. It asks: who owns evaluations? Can evaluations belong to civil society organizations and social movements? How can evaluations be owned by the poor and marginalized, so they have control of knowledge and evidence to ultimately influence the state?

On Use

A set of chapters on the use of evaluation begins with 'An Evaluation Practitioner's Journey with Utilization-focused Evaluation', Chelladurai Solomon's account (with Sarah Earl) of his own personal journey with utilization-focused evaluation (UFE), its application in Asia, and how it has transformed his evaluation practice. Solomon explains how the rigour, the systematic approach, and the 'use' value in the UFE framework have influenced how he sees and conducts evaluations. Chapter 7, 'Enhancing the Use of Evaluation: Experiences from the Field', by Manas Bhattacharyya and Khilesh Chaturvedi, also explores utilization-focused evaluation (UFE), this time through the experience of an evaluation organization. They describe how they have promoted and facilitated the use of their evaluations at eight different development organizations. They note that the most crucial question of any evaluation is whether its findings and recommendations will be used to make the necessary changes in the intervention that was evaluated. Chapter 8, 'The Importance of Understanding Context and Structures in Programme Evaluation: A Case Study from India', by Suneeta Singh, Sangita Dasgupta, and Dayanand Singh expands the exploration of evaluation use by applying an institutional and structural lens. They ask: what are the 'necessary and sufficient conditions' under which evidence from evaluation is useful for developing programmes to address developmental challenges? They use the question to identify the challenges for effective evaluation in HIV/AIDS programming for a marginalized community in India. They conclude that the evaluations did not adequately use evidence that relates to social and structural factors, even when it was widely available, thereby limiting the usefulness of the evaluations for finding effective solutions.

On Methodology

The next group of chapters looks at methodology. Chapter 9, 'The Need for Methodological Diversity in Evaluating Complex Health Interventions', by Anuska Kalita, focuses on a nutritional and health intervention aimed at reducing low birth weight of children and moves the book more directly into methodological discussions. She examines the evaluation of this complex intervention in Jharkhand, India, and describes how the evaluation design was impacted by political factors and implementation realities, in an overall context of a weak research environment. Kalita highlights the complementarity between quantitative experimental designs and qualitative analysis. She uses both to highlight social, political, and economic inequities around forest rights and tribal development programmes and their implications on food security. Kalita concludes that given the complexities in evaluating health interventions involving communities and health systems, one needs to adopt diverse research methodologies for a comprehensive understanding of effect, outcomes, and impact.

In 'Operationalizing the Capability Approach (CA) for Evaluating Small Projects'—another chapter based on case studies, this time from Nepal—Ram Chandra Khanal (Institute for Policy Studies) looks at methodological issues and innovations in evaluating poverty reduction programmes. He examines the potential for using capability approach (CA)-based tools for evaluating the management of local development projects and highlights their value in identifying sustainable poverty reduction projects relative to income-based approaches. In this case, the context is of two small local development initiatives in a rural community in Nepal. The chapter outlines the conceptual and operational challenges encountered during the study and explores the possibility of devising capability-based evaluation systems for small projects in South Asia.

Also using a methodological lens is Chapter 11, 'Impact Evaluations: Ways to Get It Right—Tips for Achieving "Impactful" Impact Evaluations' by N. Raghunathan, Siddhi Mankad, and Ravinder Kumar, which examines impact evaluations (IEs), a method that is growing in importance in South Asia. They describe how a rigorous process in planning, designing, and implementing IEs can help achieve impactful IEs. The chapter also describes potential obstacles to the evaluation process and demonstrates how a deeper knowledge of the programmatic context and complexities helps evaluators and other practitioners design better IEs in South Asia.

Finally, in Chapter 12, 'Giving Voice: Making Evaluation Contextual for Marginalized Groups in South Asia', Nazmul Ahsan Kalimullah and

Mojibur Rahman Doftori connect issues of context and marginalization to methodological issues. They argue that development is not only an issue of economic betterment but is also about improving people's sense of self-worth, self-determination, and hope for the future. They argue that evaluation can incorporate the voices of marginalized groups into policy-making and implementation and, in doing so, make development more relevant to people at the fringes of society.

A Diversity of Voices

Chapter 13, 'Voices from the Field', by Ethel Méndez concludes the book by weaving together the voices of different evaluators working in the region. The chapter draws on quotes from the evaluators interviewed by Méndez and ideas generated from meetings of over 130 South Asian evaluation stakeholders who gathered in meetings organized by the Community of Evaluators (CoE) in Kathmandu, Mumbai, Chennai, and Dhaka. Captured in this chapter, their ideas portray a strengthening field that is plagued with power imbalances and technical and theoretical challenges. Méndez also captures their ideas about how evaluation in South Asia could be improved. Complementing this chapter are Méndez's question-and-answer-inspired profiles of all of the evaluators in the book. It is hoped that this section provides an illustration of the diversity and intellectual energy that enliven the evaluation field in the region and those within it.

Themes

At a deeper level, this book paints a portrait of how the cultural, institutional, and socio-economic context in South Asia can be better integrated in evaluation. Several chapters specifically address evaluation challenges relating to conditions of social, political, and economic inequity, including poverty reduction, health, nutrition, HIV/AIDS, and rights and social justice-oriented programmes. The authors make the case that such integration will help to understand how this context shapes existing inequities and how these inequities influence the outcomes of development programmes. These influences need to be recognized and leveraged for greater understanding and can be used to support decision-making that targets more equitable and better development in the region. In this section, we draw from the chapters to pull out the different themes and connections that underlie the experiences and knowledge of those practising and thinking about evaluation in South Asia.

We examine the vast diversities and deep divisions reflected in hierarchical socio-economic realities and cultural constructs that continue to shape today's social spaces. We look at how these factors shape the challenges and opportunities faced by evaluators and how this is reflected across the chapters in the idea of evaluation as *exploring, critiquing, responding to,* and *reshaping* these divisions and inequities. Here we pull out the strategies proposed by the authors to address persistent inequities, including the examination of methods and strategies around using evaluation findings. Finally, we look across the chapters to explore what is needed for development evaluation to come of age and be taken seriously in decision-making in South Asia.

Exploring Inequities

The South Asian context is rooted in persistent and growing power imbalances and starkly hierarchical socio-economic realities. Ancient societal constructs continue to contour today's spaces, overlaid with new forms of inequities. These not only shape the development realities and challenges but also the challenges faced by evaluators.

All the chapters clearly recognize and are situated within this reality. Describing this context, Nazmul and Doftori explain that the cultural domination of powerful groups has created a plethora of inequities— including child labour, gender biases, and discrimination against people with disabilities. Zaveri notes that deep seated cultural beliefs about the role of children, women and older members of society combined with social stratifications, make a complex web of unspoken but palpable sets of norms . . . . Kumar-Range points to social development indicators for South Asia, which show that the region is falling behind all other parts of the world, including sub-Saharan Africa. Kalita draws this out when she describes the context for an evaluation conducted in Jharkhand, India, where she notes that the maternal and child health scenario was dismal; the infant mortality rate is 70, 54.5 per cent of children are underweight, 41.7 per cent of babies are low birth weight, almost 4 out of 10 women are undernourished and two-thirds of women in child-bearing ages are anaemic.

All of the authors posit that evaluation provides an opportunity for deeper examination of this context and these inequities. Hay emphasizes the role of evaluation in realizing more equitable development. Authors also point to the challenges that such persistent inequities pose in conducting evaluation. For example, as Zaveri notes, these complex hierarchies pose the challenge of first even recognizing and then working with communities within community.

Critiquing Inequities

These hierarchies, and particularly the persistent inequities that they underpin, are central to the majority of the chapters. The authors recognize that development is not adequately meeting the needs of most citizens; as Hay puts it, evaluation can be used to reinforce existing dominant systems and it can also be used to challenge them. Magar and Narayanan echo this, noting that, evaluations can be used as a tool to wield power and continue their dominance. For the authors, recognition of, and response to, inequities are essential if evaluation is to be relevant, given the issues facing the majority of the citizens of South Asia. When Bhattacharyya and Chaturvedi note that development evaluation in South Asia is important 'given the extent of poverty and marginalization', it is clear that inherent in their understanding of evaluation is that it must play a role in *addressing* that poverty and marginalization. Likewise, Magar and Narayanan note that rights and social justice evaluations are motivated by existing inequities derived from power relations, which are at the heart of development problems in South Asia. They argue that evaluation can contribute to social change and transformation.

In addition to demonstrating that evaluation provides an opportunity for deeper examination or understanding of inequities, several chapters suggest that evaluation must

- play a role in redressing inequities directly (through programme changes or in the process itself) and/or
- play a role in redressing inequities by challenging the nature of, or approach to, development more generally.

Even those chapters whose focus is largely within existing development paradigms flag this critical lens. For example, Raghunathan, Mankad, and Kumar note that evaluations should stir a debate, create chaos, or disturb the equilibrium, stimulate thinking and action, or lead to discursive changes or policy dialogue. Other chapters explicitly suggest a more radical form of evaluation—one that uses evaluation questions, evidence, and process to reject or question (rather than reinforce) existing modes of development. Such a view of evaluation suggests that it should not only explore inequities but explicitly challenge inequities. This implies a larger view of evaluation, or an explicitly political and values-based view of evaluation, one that seeks transformation and as such can be framed as inherently subversive. Nazmul and Doftori and Khanal note that the evaluation approaches they present (pluralistic and contribution approaches respectively) are a way to tackle inequities and diversities that may not be addressed adequately in mainstream development strategies or their implementation. For example, in his chapter, Khanal suggests that evaluation of a relatively simple set of projects could be a space within a larger development context to question and interrogate that context. Doing so can be seen as part of a process of articulating and shaping, critiquing, and reshaping understanding of that context.

Responding to Inequities: Methodological Choices and Options

Moving on from an interest in understanding and challenging inequities leads us to the methodological question of how one does so. The chapters introduce the reader to the broad range of evaluation methods being used in the region—including approaches that are pluralist (Kalimullah and Doftori), participatory (Zaveri and Khanal), transformatory (Magar and Narayan), use and decision-making oriented (Bhattacharyya and Chaturvedi, Solomon and Earl, and Singh, Dasgupta, and Singh), experimental (Raghunathan, Mankad, and Kumar; Kalita), and use mixed methods (Kalita).

Several methodological threads weave through the theme of examining and addressing inequities. They include the importance of qualitative and mixed methods and of the evaluation process and participatory approaches.

Evaluation design, Kalita argues, has to respond to contextual realities. She argues for more nuanced qualitative evaluation in all studies (including those using IEs). She notes that in her evaluation in

Jharkhand, while the baseline survey presented the demographic and epidemiological realities of the region, the needs, practices, and challenges that the communities face in achieving better health would only have been authentically and fully described, documented, and understood through qualitative research and mixed methodologies.

This call for qualitative approaches is echoed by other authors. Magar and Narayanan, while outlining many of the quality gaps in qualitative approaches in the region note that the qualitative-quantitative binary argument is misplaced, since mixed methods are of particular value when the evaluation is trying to solve a problem in a complex social context.

What Kalita argues—and is similarly flagged by other authors in different ways—is that qualitative research methods can help researchers and evaluators develop an understanding of the processes whereby particular outcomes come about. They can thus deepen understanding of 'what needs doing'. Mainstream development is ultimately just that— what we think 'needs doing', or how we think change will happen. As Kalita notes, qualitative methods enable us to not only test whether an intervention worked but also to test the theoretical basis of an intervention. In her case, quantitative analysis suggested that the intervention didn't work—anaemia rates for women and girls went up during the intervention. However, qualitative analysis revealed the erosion of traditional knowledge of and use of local foods among tribal groups . . . . as a result of deforestation, urbanization, 'modernization,' and 'co-option into the mainstream' and how both contribute to changing food behaviours and a decrease in the availability of food items high in iron. Qualitative analysis explained the lack of impact of the intervention. Similarly, Singh, Dasgupta, and Singh argue that evaluation is limited typically to understanding what technical outcomes were achieved, whether the institutional configurations worked, and whether the money spent was done so usefully. However, they caution that understanding these aspects alone is not sufficient for development change to take place, as they don't take into account the developing reality.

The relevance of using diverse methods and interdisciplinary analysis is echoed by several authors, including those who also use and promote experimental methods. For example, in their chapter describing how to do 'good' IEs, Raghunathan, Mankad, and Kumar also argue for the need to look for hybridization of methods that allow better understanding of social complexities and realities that cannot be explained through one- or two-dimensional enquiry and incorporate multi-dimensional 'sense-making' processes. This may seem a minor point—that all good design of evaluations of complex programmes should include mixed methods. However, with the increasing push for some methods over others, and some polarization in the evaluation field along methodological lines, it is important to flag that this argument cuts across all chapters, regardless of the particular method the author may happen to favour or use more regularly. Zaveri argues that participation needs to happen in all evaluation designs, including randomized control trial (RCT) designs, as participatory approaches are one way to try to address and redress power inequities within and through evaluation.

In challenging or critiquing inequities, the evaluation process must also refrain from replicating or reinforcing inequities. Several authors emphasize the need for the evaluation process itself to be a space to counter existing power imbalances by putting more power in the hands of those traditionally marginalized. Zaveri notes that given the existing inequities, not only is PE needed for empowerment and participation but it tends to be harder to do in these circumstances. Bhattacharyya and Chaturvedi also note that participatory processes in evaluation can help ensure actual and meaningful participation of stakeholders, which in turn can build ownership and the use of the findings, including for challenging or critiquing inequities.

Reshaping Equity: Strategies to Make Evaluation Matter at the State Level

Whether as critique or in support of mainstream development, the ability of evaluations to make a difference is shaped by the ability and interest of evaluation users to incorporate the learning offered. As Hay notes, a key premise of South-led evaluation field building is that equitable development requires greater use of evidence from evaluations in decision making. Bhattacharyya and Chaturvedi outline the emergence and internalization of UFE in part as a response to this promise and in response to other broad evaluation and development trends. Solomon, in turn, lays out what a use-oriented approach actually entails in practice. However, social asymmetries are often mirrored in governance systems—as Nazmul and Doftori note, historical development since independence from colonial powers has largely continued the traditions of 'state versus population' and the cultural domination of powerful groups. These asymmetries also raise challenges for the use of evaluation in South Asia.

Hay points out that public policy shapes the institutional context for evaluation and the room for evaluation to critique policies and programmes. As Kumar-Range notes, the qualities of the governance environment in South Asian countries have implications for the evaluation climate and the strategies and methods that are most likely to result in the effective use of evaluation to achieve development results. To be relevant, evaluators must understand and relate their work to the larger public policy and institutional context that shape development outcomes. It is important for evaluation as a field to adapt to these conditions. So what does that governance environment look like?

Kumar-Range notes that economic liberalization and its focus on efficiency and decreasing the role of government may reduce attention to or resources for monitoring and evaluation. But she also points to increasing pressure for accountability, itself a product of growing democratization, making the evaluation climate more suitable for social accountability, bottom-up, and ex-ante approaches, given the weak regulatory and related accountability structures in governments. Kumar-Range and Hay point to the growth or resurgence of nationally owned and led monitoring and evaluation systems in South Asia. Kumar-Range, and Singh, Dasgupta, and Singh note that this trend is aligned with global agreements and instruments and aimed at shifting the onus from donor-led project evaluations to evaluating development effectiveness and integrating national evaluation systems with decision-making processes.

Several of the chapters speak to the practical challenges and opportunities of using evaluations to foster change in government policies and programmes. The authors note that this requires attention on several fronts: understanding and working with the political and governance environment for development evaluation (Kumar-Range), building the field of evaluation to bring evaluation results into decision-making (Hay), and having a concrete focus on use and/or knowledge translation throughout the evaluation process (Raghunathan, Mankad, and Kumar; Solomon and Earl; Bhattacharyya and Chaturvedi; and Singh, Dasgupta, and Singh).

Some chapters examine the system from above, and others are rooted in concrete experiences within that system—mirroring evaluation itself, which is both engaged and used at the level of discourse and policies, and in the concrete functioning of programmes and projects. For example, whereas some authors argue for the need for greater understanding of the nature of the governance environment in order for evidence to actually inform change, several others illustrate this point and begin to build this understanding through case studies.

Along these lines, Raghunathan, Mankad, and Kumar note that a key challenge is inadequate dialogue between evaluators and evaluation commissioners. They describe one evaluation conducted with a State Planning Commission where they 'realized that stakeholders from different government departments had very different expectations', noting, '. . . when the ministries all finally came together at the presentation of the evaluation findings, they were clearly not on the same page. . . . So while the evaluation brought out policy-relevant findings . . . the chances of these being incorporated in policy discourse were diminished'. Similarly, Magar and Narayanan point to the need to challenge rigid terms of references (TORs) and guiding frameworks to address human rights and social justice issues and the need to be watchful as stakeholder participation can be curtailed because of cost issues.

Hay suggests that evaluators need to explore what she characterizes as multiple emerging avenues for influencing decision-making. Again, drawing from their practice, Raghunathan, Mankad, and Kumar emphasize this point. For example, in one IE for the government, the evaluation team was mandated to simply deliver the report and share the findings. However, they speak of a 'realization that we had a larger responsibility', which drove them to develop other ways of sharing and using the findings, including suggesting an alternative to the existing model of agricultural extension which they then also became involved in testing. They note simply that 'for bringing change, evidence is necessary . . . but not sufficient'.

Conversely, the use of findings by government can at times to lead to other challenges. For example, Kalita explains how evaluation findings showing a project's success led to many of the interventions in the programme being integrated into state-wide programmes. However, this made it difficult to evaluate the extent to which the intervention worked, as the universalization of the scheme effectively eliminated the control group. However, the strong message in her chapter is that given the incredibly vulnerable context and need for resources, the needs of providing improved services 'trumped' the need for keeping the study design 'clean' or 'contamination free'. Values of equity and justice come first.

Magar and Narayanan also raise cautions about assuming that use is always positive. They note that there are many negative uses of evaluation that must be guarded against, including to wield power, to depoliticize social conditions of the poor and marginalized, and to support decisions that have already been made by agencies or other stakeholders.

Connecting Practice with Theory

The chapters also serve to reinforce the importance of bridging theory and practice. During the course of producing this book and in conversation with regional evaluation practitioners, it was evident that much new learning was being generated in the course of applying and adapting accepted evaluation theories. Such adaptations not only help to contextualize existing theories but in the process also create a rich body of experience to help theoretical thinking move forward. Unless a concerted on-going effort is made to make these connections, the literature on development evaluation will become increasingly uneven. In reflecting and capturing their practice, the contributors have made that bridge and demonstrated the value of doing so. For example, Kalimullah and Doftori show how the local contexts of extreme inequity in South Asia demonstrate the need for pluralistic evaluation methods, and Zaveri's analysis shows the complex challenges involved in conducting PE that need to be further researched to improve PE practice. Khanal shows that no project is too small to benefit from conceptual clarity on larger issues of development goals and human aspirations. He demonstrates the need for theory to inform action on the ground.

Kalita also highlights a challenge that many interventions, are often defined pragmatically, according to local circumstance, rather than building on any specific theoretical approach and later points to this as both a weakness and a strength. The extent and range to which methodological approaches are being generated, modified, and used in the region is vast, though the documentation of that work remains limited. This book begins to capture some of that work, grounded in local social contexts, but much more work here is needed.

The Way Forward

Strengthening evaluation's contribution to shaping more equitable development in South Asia requires attention on several fronts: understanding and working within the political and governance environment for development evaluation, strengthening the use of existing approaches and methods and experimenting with new ones, and working to bring evaluation results into decision-making at all levels. A multi-pronged approach to evaluation field building that encompasses the use and users and producers of evaluation is required to improve the practice of evaluation in the region and its use in decision-making for better development results.

As shown in this book, documenting and promoting the range of participatory and stakeholder-oriented evaluation approaches that are being developed, tested, and applied in this region is critical. These are being generated and are grounded in local social contexts and need to be nurtured as capacity building for evaluation is promoted. This includes methodological approaches that would enable use of evaluation findings for more sound decision-making.

These writings play a small part in widening the lens on whose experiences are heard, captured, and used to shape the evaluation field. We hope and expect to see these efforts sustained, as the field continues to be strengthened and expanded.

2

Evaluation for Development Results: Implications of the Governance Context in South Asia

Shubh Kumar-Range

Background

Development evaluation examines the performance of a whole range of development efforts with the aim of enabling effective use of public resources to achieve stated goals. An interesting review by Caracelli (2000) traces how the intellectual roots of programme evaluation have evolved since the 1960s and have expanded to embrace context, its role in facilitating decision-making, and social accountability. The evaluation literature describes many pathways and approaches by which evaluation can influence the change processes towards social betterment (Henry and Mark, 2003; Johnson et al., 2009; Patton, 2008). Since governments have primary responsibility for the use and allocation of public resources, it would be reasonable to assume that they have the greatest stake in supporting and promoting development evaluation. In low-income countries, scarcity of fiscal resources for development should further increase the importance of promoting high-quality evaluations and their use. However, even casual observations suggest that this, for the most part, is not so in South Asia. Although evaluations of development programmes are conducted routinely, the widespread perception expressed by evaluators in the region is that this is a 'donor-driven' exercise and that it is inextricably linked with the national governance parameters that shape a country's evaluation-related policies (see Chapter 13, 'Voices from the Field' in this volume).

Development aid is becoming more and more a means of budgetary support to governments, with the onus for evaluations related to achieving results, accountability, and the efficient use of resources shifting to national systems. This shift in how development aid was focused began emerging at the United Nations' International Conference on Financing for Development held in Monterrey, Mexico, in March 2002,[1] where a growing consensus emerged that donors and developing countries alike needed to know that aid was being used as effectively as possible.

A new paradigm of aid as a partnership, rather than a one-way relationship between donor and recipient, was evolving and the Paris Declaration on Aid Effectiveness of 2005 accelerated the pace of change. The Paris Declaration contains 5 principles and 56 partnership commitments to improve the quality of aid. For example, under the first principle of ownership, partner countries commit to exercise leadership in developing and implementing their national development strategies, and donors commit to respect partner countries' leadership and help strengthen their capacity to exercise it. During this watershed period, attention shifted from *aid* effectiveness to *development* effectiveness and the mutual responsibility of donors and partner governments. In this process, monitoring development progress became a prerogative for all countries, and universal acceptance of Millennium Development Goals (MDGs) helped to set the pace. Accepting the MDGs meant that all countries needed to monitor their performance and resource allocation closely.

The production and use of quality evaluations in the development process are essential to achieving the desired results and using resources efficiently. Thus, achieving development results, monitoring progress, and evaluating for improved effectiveness and efficiency of resource allocation have become a cornerstone of 'good governance' and encapsulate the ideal of 'accountability'. Broad agreement reached at Monterrey for a new global partnership was matched by action for the adoption of improved policies and good governance by developing countries and the provision of increased aid and trading opportunities by rich countries (Picciotto, 2002, 2007). At the same time, the onus for and ownership of evaluations have moved to the country level. This has resulted in a marriage of the seemingly conflicting goals of trade liberalization and strong governance and is at the heart of the challenge of understanding how best to improve the conduct of evaluation and use of its results in South Asia.

In most governments, accountability has been equated traditionally with monitoring resource allocation, that is, inputs into development, with government accounting offices and finance ministries typically tasked with this. However, with the larger objective of actually achieving development results with these allocations, the relevance of documenting outcomes and understanding ways to improve efficiency of resource allocation becomes greater. It is no longer just about where the money goes but what it does. This makes evaluation and its use an integral part of accountability in good governance.

While the notion of accountability for resources has expanded, so has the concept of evaluation use. Thus, while governments may be seen as the primary 'users' of development evaluation, there is also a large role for the clients of development efforts to participate in this process and give *their* feedback to help improve services and service delivery. This represents a shift, to use Cornwall and Gaventa's (2000) phraseology, from 'users and choosers to makers and shapers'. This has been accompanied by expanded notions of social accountability— a concept that has developed relevance beyond the corporate world, where the term was coined, and has become an important aspect of all development activities.

How do these ideas of evaluation use fare in the South Asian context? This chapter explores the links between governance, types of accountability, and evaluation use. It uses available data to analyse the qualities of the governance environment in South Asian countries. It then examines the implications for the evaluation climate and the strategies and methods that are most likely to result in the effective use of evaluation to achieve development results.

Evaluation for Development Results: A Conceptual Framework

Governance and Evidence-based Decision-making

The use of evidence, including evaluation findings, for policy decision-making requires stable and transparent governance structures and procedures (Carden, 2009). Systems that depend on evidence for decision-making are also likely to be more open and accountable than those that do not, creating a demand for quality evaluations. Accountability matters for normative and ethical reasons as well as because it is a key contributor to development results. However, in liberalizing economies such as those in South Asia, incorporating evaluation results in decision-making is not easy and requires an effective evaluation policy.

Economic reforms in this region have been steadily moving from traditional top-down planned development to a more market-oriented development, with a demand for more dispersed accountability centres. Market reforms, with their roots in neoclassical economics and public choice theory, do address notions of efficiency in the delivery of services to citizens but fail to consider adequately questions of accountability. Examinations of allocative efficiency in an economy have generally not paid much attention to the choice and management of government services. Institutions that shape public management have much to do with maintaining status quo and related notions of trust, loyalty, and cultural norms—variables that do not neatly fit within theories of economic efficiency.

In addition, differences in political culture have a profound impact on how states deal with conflict and culpability. For example, variations in representative political institutions are an important influence on public servants in their handling of accountability relationships with citizens, stakeholders, and elected officials.

Conceptualizing Accountability

Accountability is a multidimensional concept and at a fundamental level addresses questions that have to do with being answerable for one's actions. In practice, accountability is referred to most commonly in terms of financial accountability—for reporting of expenditures and balance sheets. More recently, governments have been wrestling with measurement of ends rather than means in public programmes. Canada, a leader in this area, has introduced a 'results accountability model' that would 'measure the real impact of government activities on society'.[2]

Armstrong (2005, p. 1), writing from a United Nations perspective, states that in public administration, 'Accountability refers to the obligation on the part of public officials to report on the usage of public resources and answerability for failing to meet stated performance objectives'. In addition, accountability is co-dependent with transparency and integrity. The past few decades since the end of the Cold War have seen the gradual expansion of democratic governments, with broader public participation and higher expectations of social and economic participation. This, together with the spread of economic liberalization and globalization, can be seen to have increased both national- and international-level demands for public sector accountability.

In the context of governance, accountability traditionally related almost exclusively to elected representatives. In contemporary governance thinking, by contrast, the objects of accountability initiatives quite centrally, if not primarily, include non-elected public bureaucracies. This is not particularly surprising given the blurring, in recent times, of the line between the political and the administrative. An illustrative figure drawn from the World Bank's *Global Monitoring Report* (2006b) gives an overview of accountability in a national governance system (see Figure 2.1).

The enormous complexity of the public sector prevents clear accountability relationships from being defined. Who should be accountable to whom within the governance sectors? There is inevitably a tension no matter how it is set up, thereby diluting its effectiveness. Viewed from this perspective, solutions to problems of accountability may rarely be final, especially within complex administrative setups that are always changing. Accordingly, we must adopt a culture of continuous learning since these problems will never disappear. This is essential because

Figure 2.1
The National Governance System Framework

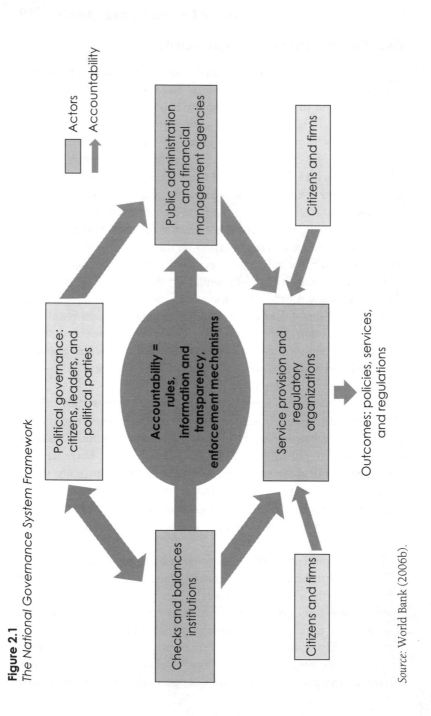

Actors

Accountability

Political governance:
citizens, leaders, and
political parties

Public administration
and financial
management agencies

Accountability =
rules,
information and
transparency,
enforcement mechanisms

Checks and balances
institutions

Service provision and
regulatory
organizations

Citizens and firms

Citizens and firms

Outcomes: policies, services,
and regulations

Source: World Bank (2006b).

a service-oriented public sector, basic to meeting the MDGs, depends on the integrity, transparency, and accountability of public institutions (Armstrong, 2005).

As federal and decentralized governance systems become the order of the day, norms and institutions of public sector management—even within a single country may not conform to a single homogeneous model. Economic liberalization that is geared to allocative efficiency and the reduction of the role of government may also serve to dilute attention for monitoring services to the population. Differences in political culture also have a profound impact on how an administrative entity deals with conflict and culpability. For example, variations in representative political institutions—be they based on consensual or more adversarial relationships between the power centres of subgroups—are an important influence on public servants in their handling of accountability relationships with citizens, stakeholders, and elected officials. While we may certainly learn from examples of public management elsewhere, we must realize that notions of accountability are deeply rooted in their respective societies. Therefore, consequences of transplanting these norms or practices to other situations will not necessarily produce the desired results.

Particularly relevant to the international development context is the definition of accountability used in the Global Accountability Project (GAP) Framework developed by One World Trust. It states that accountability refers to 'the processes through which an organization makes a commitment to respond to and balance the needs of stakeholders in its decision-making processes and activities, and delivers against this commitment' (Blagescu et al., 2005, p. 2). Evaluation is one of the four key dimensions of accountability identified in this GAP Framework—along with transparency, participation, and feedback mechanisms. Although the GAP Framework was developed to address the accountability of global organizations, it is equally applicable to government organizations. The key challenge, the organization's report says, is in 'creating a more balanced accountability, in which the voices of those most affected by an organization's activities are not overshadowed by the interests of the most powerful stakeholders. Accountability thus becomes a process that manages power imbalances . . .' (Blagescu et al., 2005, p. 20).

Balancing Accountability

There are two different approaches to accountability—*ex post* and *ex ante*—which, if exercised together, would provide a more balanced representation of stakeholder's voices and interests. Ex post (or after the fact) accountability refers to accountability exercised after a decision or action has been taken, or a project finished. Ex post approaches include traditional result-based monitoring and feedback mechanisms that occur at the end of a completed project or initiative. Ex ante (or before or during a process) accountability, in contrast, refers to accountability exercised throughout or during an action or project. It includes elements such as evaluations of actions plans or assessment tools before a project starts, stakeholder participation, and transparent processes that allow for input in defining desired results.

It is evident that to ensure accountability in providing the best possible level of service to the public, one should expect at least some degree of 'voice' with stakeholder participation and ex ante accountability. These would be in addition to instituting checks and balances and feedback mechanisms that would be part of traditional ex post accountability.

Moncrieffe (2001) elaborates on the concept of stakeholder participation as a key element of accountability in representative democracy. Social accountability and many empowerment evaluation approaches now being developed are elaborating on enhanced stakeholder participation and, thus, may also be considered to be part of ex ante accountability.

The Social Accountability Movement

Corporate social accountability began to come to the fore in the era of globalization. By 2000, audits that incorporated social, ethical, and environmental aspects had come into the mainstream of business thinking (Owen et al., 2000). As non-state actors and civil society groups began to gain credence (possibly due to a failure of governance), they represented new means of attaining accountability, often serving as a watchdog of government programmes, their management, and results. This represents an essential ingredient of social accountability-oriented evaluation in this region. In tracing the growth of social accountability in governance, with particular reference to India, Jayal (2008) observes how widely entrenched this idea had become.

At the same time, there was an emerging movement within the international development community to subscribe to a human rights-based approach to development. During the past 10 years, this human rights orientation to development has been growing. Most countries have also signed the principal international human rights covenants and have begun to modify their national legislative frameworks accordingly, in addition to supporting governance and public sector reforms for their implementation (Ackerman, 2005). Many social accountability initiatives have stemmed from this growing emphasis, including the well-known Bangalore Citizen Report Cards implemented by the Public Affairs Centre in India.

Social accountability-oriented developments in South Asia (and in the developing countries generally) can also be seen as evolving from the macroeconomic and governance challenges in the post-structural adjustment world (Cornwall and Gaventa, 2000). A recent study published by the World Bank Institute (Sirker and Cosic, 2007) demonstrates that compared with other regions, social accountability initiatives across South and Southeast Asia have a much greater element of community participation and involvement. Often, the collaboration between civil society groups and governments in many of these initiatives is striking and stands out in contrast to that in other regions.

How the Concept of Social Accountability Is Shaping Evaluation Practice

A key element of evaluation for development results involves assessing benefits received by the most affected people—those in whose interest development resources are being allocated. To focus resources, and perhaps in response to perceived insufficient accountability to those most affected, there has been growing acceptance of rights-based development, citizen participation, and social accountability requirements of both the government and private sectors, as discussed earlier. This movement has contributed to many empowerment evaluation methods and tools.

What is evident is that accountability frameworks are increasingly including a combination of ex post or 'top-down' and ex ante or 'bottom-up' approaches, which have an impact on approaches to evaluation for development results. It can safely be postulated that effective functioning of development accountability by the public sector in South Asia will require support from both ex post and ex ante evaluations with broad participation by communities—especially given the wide scale of public mismanagement that has become rampant in this region combined with the slow pace of improvement in human development indicators.[3]

We now take a closer look at governance and accountability issues and their impact on development evaluation in South Asia.

The Impact of Governance Dimensions on Evaluation Systems and Use in South Asia

The use of evaluation results is largely reliant on institutional setups that favour transparency and accountability. Such setups also foster evidence-based decision-making and create a demand for relevant and useful evaluations, which in turn support evaluation field building (See Hay's chapter 3). Good governance makes these conditions possible.

In South Asia, even with the economic liberalizations of the past two decades, governments play a large role in allocating development resources. The extent of accountability in governance, the manner in which power is exercised in the management of a country's economic and social resources for development, and the way governments design, formulate, and implement policies are all a key part of the context in which evaluations are conducted and used.

Constraints on Evaluation Use

A seminal analysis of the status of development evaluation in South Asian countries by Ahmed and Bamberger (1991) highlights these links between institutional structures and the state of evaluation. The study provides an important baseline for assessing progress and examining critical aspects of the governance–evaluation interaction. The authors noted that '[A]lthough project monitoring systems were started soon after each of the South Asian countries gained independence, the establishment of central monitoring and evaluation agencies (CMAs), paying particular attention to evaluation, is a recent development with a history of less than *five* years. So far, the evolution of the systems has been very controversial' (Ahmed and Bamberger, 1991, p. 270). The study identified a number of constraints affecting the quality and use of evaluations in national development systems in South Asian countries. Summarized below, they include challenges related to accountability structures, demand, and quality.

- *Organizational complexity in generating and using evaluations.* There was a great deal of organizational confusion; the function of evaluation was often transferred from one central agency to another, with different ministries developing parallel systems of their own. Seeing evaluation as a purely 'technical' function limited its use in decision-making. Often top policy-makers and other primary stakeholders were not connected with the evaluations, weakening an important link to an effective demand for the results.
- *Low demand for evaluations and their results.* Evaluations were a priority mainly for donor-funded programmes, with a focus on implementation rather than on development outcomes. This interest ended when these projects were completed. Consequently, little information was available on long-term operations, maintenance, and project impacts, '. . . including such questions as: are children benefiting from the schools that are funded by foreign donors? Are the health clinics still operating? Are the better roads affecting employment or agricultural production?' (Ahmed and Bamberger, 1991, p. 270). Some elaborate evaluation studies were conducted, but they had little practical use. Few of these efforts were considered cost-effective or useful by policy-makers and project managers. Often, evaluation studies were subcontracted to universities and consulting groups, took a long time to produce, and tended to be very theoretical and, thus, found to be of little use.
- *Supply-side issues for quality evaluations.* Though capacity for conducting evaluations is present, it is spread out unevenly, and much of it is latent—as evaluations mostly involve social science researchers, who may not consider themselves as evaluators as such. The professionals are dispersed and not connected to

professionalization of evaluation opportunities Monitoring data quality problems was particularly an issue, and with little feedback from the central agency to the local staff, there was no incentive to improve data collection and presentation. None of the agencies surveyed for the study had any systematic data quality-control procedures. The limited number of qualified evaluators also hindered the production of quality evaluations. There were also few training facilities available for building evaluation skills or for skill building for senior policy-makers and other potential users of evaluation results.

A great deal has changed in the past two decades, and many recent initiatives have emerged that are helping to build evaluation capacities and enhance its professionalization in this region, including building networks of professional evaluations.[4] However, these will take a sustained effort over many years to produce a clear impact. At the present time, as seen from Ethel Méndez's overview of the opinions of evaluation professionals from South Asia in this volume (see Chapter 13, 'Voices from the Field'), the predominant perception is that evaluation in this region is still predominantly donor driven and its use for serving larger developmental or accountability functions limited.

At the same time, this region has also made several important contributions to the practice of evaluation—particularly in developing bottom-up, participatory, and social accountability-oriented approaches. Bangalore's Citizen Report Cards is one example of such an approach. Despite these contributions, and a recent surge of interest in evaluation discourse in this region, the predominant impression is that, on the whole, the field has been stagnating (see Hay, Chapter 3, 'Building the Field of Evaluation: A Framework and Ideas', in this volume). Hay suggests that the field of evaluation in South Asia needs to be strengthened to promote and support the use of evaluations in decision-making. This field building also includes and is dependent on governance related to structures and practices.

A few promising recent developments should be noted. Sri Lanka in particular has been building a national accountability framework with a national monitoring and evaluation system and database. The role of that evaluation field building has played in this is important to note, with

Sri Lankan National Evaluation Association (SLEvA) having been closely associated with the monitoring and evaluation systems that are being developed in the country for tracking progress in development as well as its links with public sector resource allocation.

Governance Indicators

According to Weiss (2000), key governance attributes that generate demand for evaluations include accountability for decisions by public officials, devolution of resources to local levels, and meaningful participation by citizens in debating public policies and choices. Many efforts are being made by different organizations to assess different facets of governance at the national level, the most comprehensive being those compiled by the World Bank. These indicators have been consistently assessed over many years and, thus, offer time series look at any possible trends. The analysis that follows looks at specific governance indicators (drawn from the World Bank's Worldwide Governance Indicators [WGI]) that are most closely related to the attributes for South Asian countries that could be associated with a favourable climate for development evaluation.

WGI have been compiled by the World Bank as part of its database on 'actionable governance indicators'. The details of how these indicators are produced are given in the World Bank's report, *Governance Matters* (World Bank Institute, 2009). Compiled from a wide range of data sources, the WGI offer a time series analysis from 1996 onwards and are one of the largest publically available compilations of international data on governance. These national-level indices focus on six dimensions of governance—voice and accountability, political stability and absence of violence/terrorism, regulatory quality, rule of law, control of corruption, and general government effectiveness.

Of these, two indicators were selected for this analysis to measure governance attributes related to evaluation use and systems:

- *Regulatory quality*—defined as 'the ability of the government to provide sound policies and regulations that enable and promote private sector development' (World Bank Institute, 2009,

p. 2)—was chosen as a measure of the quality of governance
or 'top-down' systems to ensure accountability. Even though
this indicator explicitly measures Regulatory Quality in relation to private enterprise, it is expected that, to the extent the
government has clear and monitorable rules and regulations
for implementation of private sector-related policies, it would
also be reflected in public services delivery (especially as more
and more emphasis is being given worldwide on public-private
partnerships). Higher values on this indicator could signify a
national governance environment offering greater scope for the
use of ex post types of evaluations.

- *Voice and accountability*—defined as 'the extent to which a country's citizens are able to participate in selecting their government,
  as well as freedom of expression, freedom of association, and a
  free media' (World Bank Institute, 2009, p. 2)—were chosen as
  a measure of the degree of citizen participation and the capacity
  of the people to demand accountability or 'bottom-up' pressures
  that enable governments to be accountable. Higher values on this
  indicator could signify a national governance environment offering greater scope for ex ante evaluation systems.

Results show that for all South Asian countries, the scores for both
indicators tend to fall below the world median (i.e., have a percentile
rank of under 50) except for Voice and Accountability in India, where
the percentile rank rose above 50 since the mid-1990s (Table 2.1).
Regulatory Quality scores for all South Asian countries are below the
global median and, except for Afghanistan, all show a surprising downward trend since 1996. However, Afghanistan still remains one of the
lowest-performing countries on all governance indicators worldwide.
This finding suggests that top-down traditional evaluations of the ex
post type are even less likely to be utilized than they may have been
before, given the deteriorating climate for strong regulatory systems to
be in place.

Voice and Accountability scores for all South Asian countries are
also below the world median for 2008 except for India, which was at
almost the 60th percentile in 2008 and again in 2010. This could help
to explain the relative mushrooming of social accountability initiatives

Table 2.1
Government Accountability and Regulatory Quality in South Asian Countries: 1996–2010

| | Regulatory Quality | | | | | | Voice and Accountability | | | | | |
| | 1996 | | 2008 | | 2010 | | 1996 | | 2008 | | 2010 | |
	Estimate	Percentile Rank	Estimate	Percentile Rank	Estimate	Percentile Rank	Estimate	Percentile Rank	Estimate	Percentile Rank	Estimate	Percentile Rank
Afghanistan	-2.2	3	-1.58	4	-1.56	5	-1.8	2	-1.26*	11*	-1.5	8
Bangladesh	-0.2	35	-0.82†	21†	-0.86	22	-0.20	42	-0.61†	31†	-0.28*	38*
India	0.1	40	-0.21*	47*	-0.39†	39†	0.12	53	0.45*	59*	0.42	59
Nepal	-0.7	23	-0.66	27	-0.74	24	-0.10	46	-0.79†	25†	-0.53*	31*
Pakistan	-0.4	29	-0.47*	35*	-0.60†	30†	-0.70	27	-1.01†	19†	-0.82*	27*
Sri Lanka	0.46	64	-0.28†	44†	-0.21	45	-0.20	41	-0.44†	34†	-0.51	31

Source: World Bank (2006c).

Notes:

1. The governance indicators presented here reflect the statistical compilation of responses on the quality of governance given by a large number of enterprise, citizen, and expert survey respondents in industrial and developing countries, as reported by a number of survey institutes, think tanks, NGOs, and international organizations. World Bank has compiled these data since 1996 and updates it every year for about 212 countries.

2. Regulatory Quality estimates for each country are based on information from 17 sources.

3. Voice and Accountability estimates for each country are based on information from 21 sources.

4. The indicators are constructed using an unobserved components methodology described in detail in World Bank's paper (World Bank Institute, 2009).

5. The governance indicators are measured in units ranging from about −2.5 to 2.5, with higher values corresponding to better governance outcomes.

6. Percentile ranks indicate the percentage of countries worldwide that rate below the selected country. A percentile rank of 50 indicates that an equal number of countries are ranked below and above it. Thus, higher values indicate better governance ratings.

* indicates an improvement from the previous period.

† indicates a deterioration from the previous time period.

and pilots that have been taking place in India, an indication of an improvement in the governance 'context' for supporting ex ante evaluations and their use.

Status of Ex post Evaluation Systems in South Asia

There are very few regional assessments of the level of ex post evaluation use in South Asia. The analysis by Ahmed and Bamberger (1991) found very little by way of evaluation use. One of the reasons cited was over-centralization of commissioning evaluations and little connection with programme managers and their concerns.

That situation appears to have changed little since then, at least for India. According to the Planning Commission—in a response to a Right to Information (RTI) application filed by the author in January 2010 seeking information about the Commission's role in doing and using evaluations of government programmes—its Programme Evaluation Organization (PEO) conducts evaluations only when these are requested by nodal ministries/departments. These requests are considered by PEO's Development Evaluation Advisory Committee (DEAC), and if selected, a Consultative Evaluation Monitoring Committee (CEMC) is constituted to guide all aspects of the evaluation. After that, it is up to the nodal ministry/department to take actions recommended by the evaluations; the Planning Commission's only follow-up is to place the report on their website. Neither the Planning Commission nor the PEO keeps any record of any follow-up actions taken. This illustrates that there has been some decentralization away from the Planning Commission with respect to its ownership of evaluation results. Since there was no follow-up with nodal ministries/departments, the extent of the use of evaluation results is unknown.

Comparing the political context and approaches to programme evaluation in the USA with those in developing countries, Bamberger examines how evaluations are funded, controlled, conducted, and used. He concludes with two main differences: first, that donors are more in the lead in developing countries than in the USA as far as both supply and demand for evaluations are concerned, and second, the national evaluation systems that do exist in developing countries are highly centralized and give priority to the needs of ministries of finance and planning. Consequently, evaluation has remained less of a means of programme management and has limited stakeholder participation (Bamberger, 1991).

The political dimension is evident in the few notable cases in which ex post evaluations have been used for making policy reforms. These include the case of abolition of ration shops in Pakistan in 1987 and the elimination of fertilizer subsidies in Bangladesh in 1996. In both these cases, the results of the evaluations were consistent with the political and budgetary priorities in the country. In contrast, though many evaluations of the Integrated Child Development Services (ICDS) programme have been conducted in India, only selected improvements have been made, even as the political expediency of programme expansion has been emphasized.

Ex post evaluations generally require national statistical systems that can track a combination of inputs, outputs, and outcomes. These are present in varying degrees in South Asia, with systems in India being quite robust and with Sri Lanka in the process of greatly expanding its baseline and monitoring databases for development. However, although these systems are instrumental in tracking development and conducting evaluations of development efforts, their existence does not necessarily mean that evidence and evaluation are well integrated into national performance assessments and policy- and decision-making processes. Hornby and Perera (2002), in their analysis of the complexities faced by the Sri Lankan Ministry of Health when that country was undergoing health sector reform, emphasized that new forms of organizational support and learning are required for evidence-based performance management and decision-making at the policy level.

Although national monitoring and evaluation systems exist in varying degree in this region, at best they have weak links to systems of accountability. This is likely to be another reason for the growing interest in social accountability-oriented, ex ante evaluation in this region.

Status of Ex ante Evaluation Systems in South Asia

The changing context of governance in the era of globalization has strongly influenced the conditions that have led to the growth of the social accountability movement for achieving development results. We are moving from a state-centred and 'top-down' perception of development, in which citizens are recipients of state-delivered programmes, towards a market-led version of liberalized economic systems connected to global economic systems. The latter is, however, hardly effective in delivering benefits to the poor. This has provided the entry point to actors in civil society to exercise voice and influence critical aspects of social access to public resources and programmes to which they are entitled as a result of stated policies.

Social accountability initiatives empower citizens to strengthen the accountability of governments to their people. Examples of such initiatives include citizen participation in public policy-making, participatory budgeting, independent budget analysis, public expenditure tracking, citizen monitoring of the performance of public service delivery and projects, social audits, citizen advisory boards, and lobbying or advocacy campaigns. Initiatives that use collective action to reform service delivery provide clear examples of engaging in social accountability by monitoring implementation and enabling the uptake and use by the organizations or agencies running the programmes.

For example, Parmesh Shah, in a blog posted on the World Bank's website (Shah, 2009), writes about how social accountability interventions strengthen citizens' capacity to demand greater responsiveness and accountability from public officials and service providers. He provides three examples of social accountability interventions in India with large budgets that generated a series of changes *in just one year*. These include:

- a social accountability intervention in Rajasthan that gathered feedback from key stakeholders to evaluate the implementation of the National Rural Employment Guarantee Scheme (a large employment generation scheme), which led to changes in the programme's implementation and heightened beneficiaries' awareness on their entitlements;
- parental and community monitoring of school administrator and teacher performance in Andhra Pradesh, which led to a 10 per cent drop in teachers' absenteeism, a significant decrease in

school dropouts, and 100 per cent enrolment of children in eight villages; and

- a system of monitoring service delivery performance closely linked with village-level planning in Maharashtra, which led to a substantial increase in growth of children, rates of child immunization, and improved sanitation in 178 villages.

A review of South Asian social accountability initiatives listed on the South Asia Social Accountability Network (SASANET) website[5] suggests that many pilot or small-scale projects are starting up. A comparative study by Joshi (2008), examining their effectiveness in producing improvements in service delivery, considers them to be constrained by the capability and level of commitment of 'deliberative' or decision-making institutions that they seek to inform. Key results from this comparative study are summarized in Table 2.2.

Table 2.2
Mapping Citizen Participation in the Exercise of Public Authority

		Deliberative institutions (decision-making)	
		Strong citizen participation*	Weak (ineffective, unrepresentative) citizen participation
Social accountability institutions (monitoring)	Strong citizen participation	Governance Councils, Brazil (health, education, etc.)	Citizen report cards, right to information, expenditure tracking, social audits
	Weak citizen participation (selective inclusion or co-optation)	Participatory budgeting, Brazil Participatory planning, Kerala, India Bhagidari, Delhi, India	

*Strong and weak refers to the degree of participation, rather than the outcomes of such participation.

Source: Joshi (2008, p. 14).

However, social accountability schemes alone may not be adequate to bring about the desired improvements in service delivery. In her analysis, Joshi distinguishes between institutions promoting social accountability and those that are deliberative (make decisions). Each type offers different ways of participating in the exercise of public authority and each have different implications for how social accountability initiatives are likely to emerge, how they operate, and what results they produce (see Table 2.2). It is evident that some participatory institutions are stronger at creating spaces for citizen involvement in public policy decisions (participatory budgeting) and others do better at monitoring government action (social audits). It would be a mistake to assume that institutions are able to perform well on both dimensions, yet it is precisely such institutions that are most effective in using ex ante evaluations.

Jayal (2008) makes a similar conclusion, drawing from experiences from India and elaborating on the perceived and actual results from social accountability schemes. Using the examples of the use of the Right to Information Act of 2005 in India and public interest litigation (PIL), he suggests that the impact of these actions on actual development results is unclear. 'Normatively, of course, effective and responsive service delivery is to be preferred in combination with stable patterns of social accountability. But it is hard to disregard examples of political commitment and administrative competence, without much civil society activism, providing efficient public services' (Jayal, 2008, p. 108).

A study on social accountability initiatives in Asia that included case studies from India, Bangladesh, Nepal, and Pakistan (Sirker and Cosic, 2007) documents how citizens can impact development results 'by asking the right questions at the right time in the right manner, or in other words, by making their voices heard, often backed by the evidence, information and communication strategies' (Sirker and Cosic, 2007, p. vii). This study identified some cross-cutting enablers for social accountability, including responsiveness and voice, power of information, local ownership, political buy-in, and local capacity building. The authors also identified areas of concern in the sustainability or expansion of these efforts, which for the most part tend to be pilot projects. The concerns include fragility of civil society space, urban focus, challenges of adaptation and contextualization, and weak regional networking.

Conclusions

The importance of managing for development results is increasing globally, and there is a need for South Asian countries to respond by improving their development accountability systems. This is especially relevant given the low levels on social progress indicators, such as the International Food Policy Research Institute's (IFPRI) Global Hunger Index in this region. Rationalizing how evaluations and their use can contribute should be a key part of this process. A seminal analysis from the early 1990s (Ahmed and Bamberger, 1991) highlighted the low level of evaluation emphasis and use and identified the main problems of the evaluation systems in South Asian countries. Although some change—in both evaluation and governance systems—has undoubtedly taken place since then, much remains the same and a detailed follow-up assessment is overdue.

The analysis in this chapter uses the World Bank governance indicators to assess the extent to which the governance context in South Asian countries is favourable to evaluations. The indicators reflect the quality of top-down accountability systems and the strength of the citizen voice in policy decisions.

Findings suggest that most South Asian countries are facing difficulties in public sector reforms, as reflected in the stagnant or deteriorating top-down accountability systems. It is possible that this situation is contributing to the growing popularity of participatory and social accountability-oriented evaluations. The current governance context for support of either ex post or ex ante evaluations is below the global median for all countries. On the Voice and Accountability indicator, only India is faring above the global median, suggesting that promoting and using evaluation results remain an uphill task in the region. In light of this, it is not surprising that there has been a rapid growth in use of ex ante social accountability-led evaluations in India, and this appears to be related to recent governance measures such as RTI and the use of PIL that have improved the Voice and Accountability aspects of governance.

There is a need to look further at whether social accountability-led evaluations have contributed to improvements in programme-related decision-making and whether these can have a synergistic effect on regulatory quality and accountability within governance systems.

Notes

1. For details, please see www.un.org/esa/ffd/ffdconf/ and www.un.org/esa/ffd/monterrey/MonterreyConsensus.pdf
2. Policy Brief (Institute of Governance, 1999).
3. The International Food Policy Research Institute's (IFPRI) Global Hunger Index, which is based on levels of child undernourishment and mortality, shows South Asia lagging behind all other regions in the world, including Sub-Saharan Africa, since 2000 (IFPRI, 2012). According to United Nations Development Programme's (UNDP, 2010) Human Development Report, all South Asian countries rank below the global median in the Human Development Indicator (http://hdr.undp.org/en/media/HDR_2010_EN_Tables_reprint.pdf).
4. Some examples include Sri Lanka Evaluation Association (SLEvA) started in 1999 with the assistance of UNDP and UNICEF, and the Community of Evaluators (CoE) for South Asia, which was started in 2008 with assistance from International Development Research Centre (IDRC). These organizations are active in the region in promoting the professionalization and capacity development of evaluators and are working to create an enabling environment for conducting and using quality evaluations in countries of this region.
5. www.sasanet.org/

References

Ackerman, J.M. (2005). *Human rights and social accountability* (Social Development Paper 86). Washington, D.C.: World Bank.

Ahmed, V. and Bamberger, M. (1991). Monitoring and evaluating (M&E): The South Asian experience. *Public Administration and Development*, 11 (4), 269–73.

Armstrong, E. (2005). *Integrity, transparency, and accountability in public administration: Recent trends, regional and international developments and emerging issues.* New York: United Nations.

Bamberger, M. (1991). The politics of evaluation in developing countries. *Evaluation and Program Planning*, 14(4), 325–39.

Blagescu, Monica, de Las Casas, L., and Lloyd, R. (2005). *Pathways to accountability: The GAP framework.* London: One World Trust.

Caracelli, V. (2000). Evaluation use at the threshold of the twenty-first century. In E. Whitmore (ed.), *Understanding and practicing participatory evaluation: New directions for evaluation* (No. 88, pp. 99–111). San Francisco, CA: Jossey-Bass.

Carden, F. (2009). *Knowledge to policy: Making the most of development research.* Ottawa: SAGE/IDRC.

Cornwall, A. and Gaventa, J. (2000). From users and choosers to makers and shapers: Repositioning participation in public policy. *IDS Bulletin*, 31(4), 50–62.

Henry, G.T. and Mark, M.M. (2003). Beyond use: Understanding evaluations's influence on attitudes and actions. *American Journal of Evaluation*, 24(3), 293–314.

Hornby, P. and Perera, H.S.R. (2002). A development framework for promoting evidence-based policy action: Drawing on experiences in Sri Lanka. *The International Journal of Health Planning and Management*, 17(2), 165–83.

Institute of Governance. (1999, April). *Policy brief.* Ottawa, Ontario, Canada: Institute of Governance.

International Food Policy Research Institute. (2012). *Global hunger index.* Bonn, Germany: IFPRI.

Jayal, N.G. (2008). New directions in theorizing social accountability? *IDS Bulletin*, 38(6), 105–10.

Johnson, K., Greenseid, L.O., Toal, S.A., King, J.A., Lawrenz, F., and Volkov, B. (2009). Research on evaluation use: A review of the empirical literature from 1986 to 2005. *American Journal of Evaluation*, 30(3), 377–410.

Joshi, A. (2008). Producing social accountability? The impact of service delivery reforms. *IDS Bulletin*, 38(6), 10–17.

Moncrieffe, J.M. (2001). Accountability: Idea, ideals, constraints. *Democratization*, 8(3), 6–50.

Owen, D.L., Swift, T.A., Humphrey, C., and Bowerman, M. (2000). The new social audits: Accountability, managerial capture or the agenda of social champions? *European Accounting Review*, 9(1), 81–98.

Patton, M.Q. (2008). *Utilization-focused evaluation.* Thousand Oaks, CA: SAGE Publications.

Picciotto, R. (2002). Development cooperation and performance evaluation: The Monterrey challenge. In *OED: The first thirty years.* Washington, D.C.: World Bank.

———. (2007). The new environment for development evaluation. *American Journal of Evaluation*, 28(4), 509–21.

Shah, P. (2009). *How to make a billion dollars work.* Retrieved from http://web.worldbank.org/WBSITE/EXTERNAL/TOPICS/EXTSOCIALDEVELOPMENT/EXTPCENG.html. Accessed on September 2, 2011.

Sirker, K. and Cosic, S. (2007). *Empowering the marginalized: Case studies of social accountability initiatives in Asia.* Washington, D.C.: World Bank Institute.

United Nations Development Programme. (2010). *Human development report 2010—The real wealth of nations: Pathways to human development.* Geneva, Switzerland: UNDP. Retrieved from http://hdr.undp.org/en/media/HDR_2010_EN_Tables_reprint.pdf. Accessed on September 12, 2011.

Weiss, T.G. (2000). Governance, good governance and global governance: Conceptual and actual challenges. *Third World Quarterly*, 21(5), 795–814.

World Bank. (2006a). *GMR 2006 Millennium Development Goals: Strengthening mutual accountability, aid, trade, and governance*. Washington, D.C.: World Bank.

———. (2006b). *Global monitoring report*. Washington, D.C.: World Bank.

———. (2006c). *Worldwide governance indicators, 1996–2010*. Retrieved from http://data.worldbank.org/data-catalog/actionable-governance-indicators.

World Bank Institute. (2009). *Governance matters*. Information sheet. Retrieved from http://info.worldbank.org/governance/wgi/pdf/WBI_GovInd.pdf. Accessed on September 15, 2011.

3

Building the Field of Evaluation in South Asia: A Framework and Ideas

Katherine Eve Hay

Introduction

Governments and other development actors are constantly making decisions on policies, programmes, and projects. In doing so, they may weigh the opportunities and costs of acting or not acting, starting, continuing, revising, or ending any of them. Some of this decision-making is based on sound evidence or information; some on weak, absent, or faulty evidence; some on opinion; and much on a range of other factors not related to evidence at all.

Much has been written about building evaluation capacity and the need for improving the quality of evaluation to address gaps in evidence-based policy and programming. There are calls for more training, funds to support different types of evaluations or evaluations on particular issues are being established, and a range of organizations are trying to address capacity gaps. In parallel, there is an increasing call to shift evaluation use from serving donor needs to serving the needs of the countries where programmes are undertaken (Segone 2008). Such a transition will require improvements in evaluation quality, supportive institutions and structures, and significantly strengthened in-country evaluation capacity. But how will this happen? What will underpin this shift?

It would be naïve and simplistic to assume that strengthening the supply of, and the demand for, evaluation would make decision-making transparent, technocratic, rational, and linear. As Boyle et al. (1999) noted, evaluation findings may be 'drowned out' by other aspects in the political context, and, 'often for good reason' (Boyle et al., 1999, p. 5). The idea of evaluation field building developed in this chapter encompasses both the need to strengthen the quality and practice of evaluation and to broaden the space and platforms for using evaluation knowledge in decision-making. It calls for a more deeply contextualized understanding of what quality, rigor, and use should entail. In doing so it embraces, rather than ignores, the complexity of decision-making and implementation systems.

Making evaluation matter in the cycle of policy, programming, research, and evaluation that must constitute sound, evidence-based, and equitable development is not simple. This view of evaluation goes beyond measuring performance or management-oriented functions; evaluation, here, recognizes that development is not adequately meeting the needs of most citizens. This recognition brings with it a need for shifts, critiques, and democratization processes to fundamentally change the systems and institutions of decision-making and the ways that both connect with citizens. Evaluation can be used to reinforce existing and dominant development systems, discourses, and approaches; it can also be used to challenge them. Evaluation, here, is conceptualized as being part of dynamic, critical, and change-oriented processes.

Taking the case of South Asia, this chapter explores and develops a framework for evaluation field building. It suggests elements a robust evaluation field should include and maps these against the current situation in South Asia. The chapter then proposes strategies for field building to support and strengthen this evolution (indeed revolution) in evaluation practice and use.

The Field of Evaluation

What is the 'field of evaluation' and why does it matter? Before attempting to answer these questions, we first need to define and distinguish between some important concepts.

Programme and policy evaluation is the systematic application of research methods to assess programme or policy design, implementation, and effectiveness, and the processes to share and use the findings of these assessments.

Evaluation practice is the 'doing' of evaluation, **evaluation capacity** is the ability to do evaluation, and **evaluation use** is the application of evaluation to some change process.

Evaluation field building refers to the range and diversity of efforts to strengthen practice, capacity, and use. Field building includes, but is distinct from, evaluation capacity building or professionalization. Field building encompasses an understanding that these dimensions exist in a broader context that can support or weaken efforts to strengthen practice, capacity, or use. A field-building view focuses on and brings attention to ways to shift the system of elements (whether through work on various elements or on a set of interconnected elements).

The idea of field building emerged from literatures of sociology of knowledge, sociology of professions, and organizational development (see, for example, Freidson, 1970; Jacobs and Bosanac, 2006; Macdonald, 1995; Reeser et al., 1990; Wright, 2005). Much of that work relates to building professional or organizational fields (see, for example, Berry and Parasuraman, 1993). The sociology of professions literature would tell us that a field is an *area of specialized practice* carried out by trained practitioners. Among other things, members of a field have training, practice, research, and theory-based knowledge; share a common language; communicate and exchange information; and have access to education and training. They have standards of practice and the members of the field are considered credible by key constituencies. This chapter not only draws upon that work but also integrates ideas from work on building *fields of action*.

Groups may work to strengthen the capacity to do evaluation well, but without reshaping the system that surrounds evaluation, it may make little difference to the development processes that evaluation should be informing and improving. When work encompasses the institutions and settings that surround and reinforce evaluation practice, it has shifted from evaluation capacity building to the deeper and broader practice of field building.

Elements in the Field of Evaluation

Building the field of evaluation entails understanding the connections between, and co-evolution of, key elements in a field of practice. This chapter proposes a framework of evaluation field building that includes five elements: people; spaces and forums; knowledge; norms, guidelines, and standards; and institutional context (see Figure 3.1).

Figure 3.1
The Five Elements of the Evaluation Field

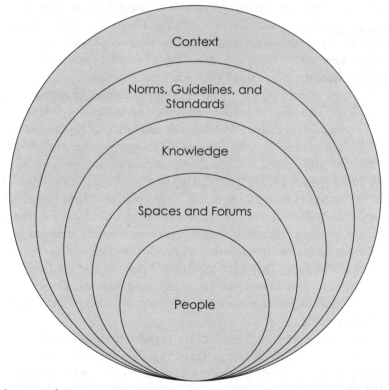

Source: Author.

1. A field has **people**—evaluators, trained practitioners, researchers, and leaders. A field also has incentives for supporting leaders.
2. A field has **spaces and forums** for building the knowledge, skills, and credentials of members. These include evaluation associations, conferences,

Figure 3.1 continued

Figure 3.1 continued

academic programmes, and vehicles for communication (e.g., newsletters, journals, websites, etc.) that facilitate collaboration, learning, and exchange.

3. A field has a **knowledge** base, or credible evidence of results, derived from research and practice on issues of relevance.
4. A field has **norms, guidelines, and standards** (including ethics) that guide professional practices.
5. A field operates in an **institutional context**, which includes public policy, financial, and other resources, as well as people, including those representing key constituencies, advocates, and other stakeholders (such as policy-makers, clients, influential leaders, community members, and others).

People

A field has trained practitioners, researchers, and leaders. A field also has incentives for supporting leaders.

Evaluators and Researchers

How does evaluation matter? Calling this 'the real evaluation gap', Carden (2007) argues: 'It is critical that the citizens, development researchers, and professionals of Southern nations lead the way in building the field of evaluation research and practice in their region' (Carden, 2007, p. 4).

Despite the efforts of evaluators and researchers all over the region, there is a lack of an identifiable mass of South Asian evaluation experts based in, and/or supporting, the evaluation work of academia, government, policy research organizations, and development organizations. At the implementation or grassroots level, and among resource groups supporting grassroots development, there are thousands of people and groups engaged in and learning from innovative and contextualized development work. Such work is often evaluative in nature. It is difficult to know the breadth and depth of this work. This work, and the evaluators who do it, are dispersed and unconnected. This is a gap, but one that also presents untapped promise. The grounded experience of such practitioners can help situate evaluation theory, methods, and application within a framework of use and practice.

A challenge is the sheer number of skilled evaluators, given the size of programmes and populations in the region. Shiva Kumar (2010) comments on the paradoxical situation of evaluation capacity in India, noting:

At a macro level, India has a reasonable (even impressive) capacity to undertake evaluations. Indeed, many well-established universities, policy think tanks, social science research institutions and colleges—both within and outside government—have a pool of experienced evaluators. However, on closer examination, we find that there simply aren't enough institutions with the capacity to conduct evaluations for a country of India's size and diversity. Also, evaluation capacity is unevenly spread across the country. (Shiva Kumar, 2010, p. 239)

Much evaluation in South Asia is done by social scientists working in particular applied research domains. They play a crucial role and this role should be strengthened. As Scriven (2001) has argued, evaluation can be understood as a 'transdiscipline' that, like statistics, is both an autonomous discipline but is also used by all other disciplines (Scriven, 2001, p. 305). However, the competencies needed to be an evaluator, while connected to the competencies required to be a social science researcher, are also different and specialized. Toulemonde (1995) proposed that evaluation professionals fit five basic criteria: they call their work 'evaluation', have mastered the range of techniques and can mix or combine them, are specially trained in evaluation, know various conceptual frameworks underpinning evaluation and can move from one to another, and devote the majority of their time to evaluation. Distinct from professionals, he suggested, these 'craftsmen' master a range of evaluation techniques in a practical and adaptive way but tend to learn evaluation on the job, whereas 'amateurs' have only a partial knowledge of evaluation theories and techniques, do not master the range of techniques, and have the tendency to use their favourite approach (Toulemonde, 1995, pp. 46–7).

These are interesting distinctions to consider in the context of South Asia. Much evaluation in the region is certainly led by 'craftsmen', but a great deal is also led by researchers who, despite often spending a large portion of their time on evaluation, do not identify themselves as evaluators (whether of the professional or specialist variety). Thus, although they draw on the theories, tools, and approaches from their various disciplinary backgrounds, they are less likely to be aware of, draw from, or contribute to the *field of evaluation*—whether as rooted within particular disciplines (such as education or public health) or development evaluation more broadly. Shiva Kumar (2010) notes, 'Professionals carrying out evaluations in South Asia . . . tend to be social science researchers, not trained evaluators' (Shiva Kumar, 2010, p. 238).

A strong field of evaluation not only requires skilled people leading evaluations but also needs evaluation researchers. South Asia is an increasingly important testing ground for evaluation research. For example, the Massachusetts Institute of Technology's (MIT) Abdul Latiff Jameel Poverty Action Lab (J-PAL) and the International Initiative on Impact Evaluation (3IE) have offices in India and are promoting impact evaluation in different ways—J-PAL conducts impact evaluations and provides training on how to do them, whereas 3IE funds impact evaluations. Similarly, many other methodologies originating from the North were tested and are now commonly used in development evaluation in South Asia (Ashford and Patkar, 2001; Chambers, 1994; Dart and Davies, 2003; Earl et al., 2001). Most of these methodologies emerged from Northern roots or have been articulated in the North. If some of these approaches have been owned, co-developed, or modified in South Asia, how did this happen? Are South Asian evaluators implementers and managers, or are they also engaging in evaluation research and theory? Clearly both are important. The point is not to suggest a false dichotomy; the connection between theory and practice leads to innovation in both. However, a lack of conceptual work on evaluation in South Asia limits the advancement of the evaluation field both in South Asia and beyond. The field of evaluation needs continued and deepened theory and practice that are rooted in contexts, needs, and cultures.

Leaders

In addition to evaluators and evaluation researchers, a strong evaluation field needs leaders. Who are the leading writers and thinkers on development evaluation and evaluation research in South Asia? And which institutes provide leadership in this area? Organizations with a mandate of, and expertise in, rigorous multi-method evaluation are few or non-existent in some countries in South Asia. The work of South Asian thought leaders is largely unseen in existing evaluation forums.

If we cannot identify the leaders, is it because they don't exist or because this leadership is nascent? Or are they there but we don't know who they are? Both the question of limited numbers and invisibility are problems, though different in nature and demanding different responses. How can local and global evaluation communities and proponents, including state and non-state actors and organizations, identify and support emerging leaders to expand their leadership roles? What would this support look like?

The limited evaluation leadership in South Asia today does not only reflect an absence of evaluation expertise. It also reflects a lack of space to share expertise, be identified as a leader, guide others, and support and inform evaluation field building. Being a leader, by definition, entails being recognized as such by others. Such recognition, in general, requires spaces or forums where those identifying themselves as evaluators can connect to strengthen the quality and practice of evaluation and to allow leadership to emerge and be articulated. Such spaces and structures are explored in the next section.

Spaces and Forums

A field has spaces and forums for building the knowledge, skills, and credentials of members. These include evaluation associations, conferences, academic programmes, and vehicles for communication (e.g., newsletters, journals, websites) that facilitate collaboration, learning, and exchange.

In the North, while recognizing the variation in different countries and contexts, important spaces where evaluation leadership, scholarship, and practice have emerged, include evaluation associations, evaluation conferences, and universities (a site for both evaluation research and training the next generation of evaluation practitioners and researchers). These provide opportunities for mentoring, sharing ideas, peer review, and networking. These are also spaces for critique and dissent. While recognizing that different models may be appropriate in South Asia, a good starting point would be to review the state of these spaces in the region.

There are no graduate programmes in evaluation in South Asia. The absence of formal curricula is a problem for the future of evaluators, evaluation researchers, and evaluation leaders in the region. There are moves being made here; for example, a number of universities in Bangladesh, India, and Sri Lanka are developing a postgraduate diploma in evaluation. This is promising, but it must be understood within the context of a university culture where there is teaching but often no, or very little, research. Can the evaluation field leap-frog this persistent challenge in

South Asia and develop a curriculum that integrates evaluation research and practice to keep it relevant, rigorous, current, and grounded in the development context? If not, can an evaluation curriculum that is not grounded in research and practice be credible or of high quality, given the distinctly applied nature of evaluation? In addition, universities are looking for marketable courses—this requires that young people see evaluation as an interesting career choice amid other options. The success of new educational opportunities in evaluation will co-evolve with other aspects of the evaluation field, as it is fundamentally connected to evaluation being perceived as relevant (and thus of interest to young people) and ultimately to the demand for evaluation and evaluators.

Professional associations have limited reach and influence, with the exception of the Sri Lankan Evaluation Association (SLEvA). The SLEvA Conference is the only recurring evaluation conference in the region. There are no other associations in the region that hold regular conferences and meetings. In Bangladesh and Afghanistan there are informal evaluation networks, but, as of yet, no formal evaluation associations. The Community of Evaluators (CoE), Nepal, has been very recently registered formally as a national organization in Nepal. The Development Evaluation Society of India and the Pakistan Evaluation Network have seemed largely inactive or limited to a few individuals over the past several years, though both may be showing some signs of revival.

There are some regional initiatives in place. The CoE, a South Asian initiative of evaluators (see http://www.communityofevaluators.org for more information), held a very successful regional evaluation conclave in 2010 with more than 300 participants and it had to close registration for the event. Given the high demand, it is planning a subsequent event in 2013. However, even the most promising initiatives can be still be characterized as being at least partly donor initiated or dependent. For example, the CoE started its life as a donor-funded project and continues to rely on such funding. In general, there is a lack of peer-assisted and on-going training forums for evaluators to deepen their expertise and contacts in the region. Certainly, given the scale and number of evaluations and practicing evaluators in the region, the spaces for them to connect, improve their practice, and deepen their skills are inadequate.

In addition to having spaces for collaboration, networking, and learning, a field has forums for articulating theory, practice, and knowledge. There is currently an absence of forums or incentives for sharing work, publishing in general, or publishing in local languages, in South Asia. Combined with the absence of university programmes and curricula, the result is a lack of documentation and publishing by South Asian experts, based in South Asia, on evaluation research and practice, and a glaring absence of South Asian research in social science research journals generally (Arunachalam, 2009). In this context, efforts like the United Nations Children Fund's (UNICEF) support to an evaluation journal in South Asia (Williams and Sankar, 2008) are important; however, only one issue of the journal was produced. A new initiative to create the *South Asian Journal of Evaluation in Practice* is being taken forward by Sambodhi (an Indian evaluation research and training organization). One issue of the journal has been produced, but the journal is struggling with getting high-quality submissions. Even if we take non-evaluation-specific journals where key issues of public policy are discussed and raised and examine the extent to which evaluation results are shared, there remains an absence of reporting and writing on evaluation research and findings.

Knowledge

A field has a knowledge base, or credible evidence of results, derived from research and practice on issues of relevance.

Is evaluation producing credible evidence and knowledge in South Asia, either through the practice of evaluation and/or evaluation research? There are two dimensions to this issue of credibility: the first is the *soundness* of the knowledge that is being produced, and the second is the *relevance* of that knowledge to development questions and priorities. Relevance relates inextricably to use. Rigorous evaluations on questions of little concern or evaluation findings relevant to key issues that are not used (whether to inform discourse or practice) are of little value.

On the first dimension, *soundness*, there appears to be no published research on the quality of evaluation in, or within, South Asia. That said, policy-makers regularly complain that work is not high quality (Hay and Sudarshan, 2010), even though those judgments may be made on a limited set of criteria and a limited understanding of different methodologies and may be overly influenced by the reputation of the individual or group conducting the evaluation. Writing on South Asia, Shiva Kumar

(2010) notes, 'Evaluations typically get judged as "good" or "bad" on the basis of statistical rigor—not recognizing that a good evaluation is not the same thing as a well-designed survey' (Shiva Kumar, 2010, p. 239).

On the second dimension, *relevance*, the past few years have seen renewed interest in evaluation from state and non-state actors. However, discussions and anecdotal evidence from several countries in the region suggest that while there is discourse on the importance of evaluation, there is also a great deal of scepticism or even cynicism about the role evaluation is playing. The picture may actually be one of gradually declining confidence in development evaluation, a growing or continued weakening of public sector evaluation institutions, poor and declining evaluation quality, and limited evaluation use and uptake (Basnyat, 2009; Goyal, 2009; Khan, 2008; Pal, 2009; Tudawe and Samranayake, 2008). Is evaluation irrelevant?

There is a flurry of evaluation research happening in South Asia, much of it led by Northern academics and largely driven by external incentive structures (such as publishing in academic journals in the North or external funding competitions). Although this research may meet standard criteria for excellence or research quality, is anyone using these findings to shape policies and programmes? Whose questions are being addressed? For evaluation to be relevant, an expanded evaluation knowledge base is required to assess which interventions are working and whether assumptions behind development policies and programmes are valid. This knowledge base is dependent, at least in part, on demand from users of evaluation findings in the system (see section titled 'Institutional Context' in this chapter).

Norms, Guidelines, and Standards

A field has norms, guidelines, and standards (including ethics) that guide professional practices.

Evaluation organizations traditionally have played a role in setting standards of practice and quality. In South Asia, groups such as the United Nations Evaluation Group (UNEG), various evaluation associations, and others have documented guidelines, norms, and standards to be followed in conducting evaluations. However, most countries in the region do not have such guidelines, or, if they do, they are not adhered to (Shiva Kumar, 2010).

Institutional Context

A field operates in an institutional context, which includes public policy and financial and other resources, as well as people, including those representing key constituencies, advocates, and other stakeholders (such as policy-makers, clients, influential leaders, community members, and others).

Public policy relates to the ways in which decisions are made, the decisions themselves, the role evidence plays in decision-making, and openness to evidence and critique. A much greater emphasis needs to be placed on understanding institutions or the 'rules of the game' that govern evaluation use and, more broadly, the use of evidence in South Asia. What would supportive public policy around evaluation look like?

A supportive institutional setting would include governments that are open to evidence, particularly critical evidence. Shiva Kumar (2010) writes: 'A tradition of evaluation is yet to permeate the administrative, bureaucratic, and political cultures of the South Asian countries. Many managers are fearful of evaluation; they see it as an audit or a fault-finding exercise' (Shiva Kumar, 2010, p. 239). This raises the question of whether the space for evidence, critique, and debate on development programming and policies is growing or shrinking in South Asia.

Elsewhere, I have suggested that South Asia has gone through two phases of development evaluation corresponding to the major development paradigms of planned development and liberalization (Hay, 2010). Centralized planning and the evaluation systems designed to support those planning processes were an important feature of postcolonial governments in South Asia. These evaluation systems, though eroded in many cases, are one of the institutional structures through which evaluation connects with planning, policies, programmes, and research. Looking at the evaluation field in various South Asian countries, the recent surge in evaluation meetings, discussions, and activities may reflect a surge in interest yet may also partially camouflage, despite some notable improvements, the declining or stagnant state of evaluation overall. As Prof. Abhijit Sen of the Indian Planning Commission noted in a plenary address at the Evaluation Conclave held in New Delhi in 2010, India does have a long tradition of evaluation, but despite commitments made three years ago for a thorough restructuring of the evaluation system in India, nothing has happened to make those changes. A further three years since that statement, there has been arguably little further change.

For example, one of the proposed new structures, an Independent Evaluation office, is still not operational. Boyle et al. (1999, p. 11) noted that the institutionalization of evaluation in public administration 'needs a number of years of sustained intervention . . . to arrive at a position where evaluation practice is a formal, recognized, and utilized part of the decision-making process of government and public organizations'. Although published more than a decade ago, their observation still resonates, particularly on the technical questions on the institutionalization of evaluation. So why has progress been so slow? Boyle et al. (1999) highlight four elements they consider foundational for institutionalization: sound data systems, social science traditions, a cadre of trained evaluators, and good governance (and specifically, low levels of corruption). No country in South Asia has all of these elements in place. This suggests that field building must include, but transcend, government. In contexts where governments may be weak, closed to evidence, and increasingly autocratic, unstable, or corrupt, it would seem critical to focus demand-side efforts on other champions and users of evaluation. Even in cases where governments are receptive, there is no guarantee that gains in institutionalization will not be lost or eroded when there is a change in power.

While it is essential to strengthen evaluation in public administration, a field-building approach would emphasize strengthening evaluation in public policy. Public policy provides a broader framework and opens alternative approaches if public administrations do not prioritize evaluation. For example, the changing role of social movements and the judiciary in pushing for evidence-based policy-making in South Asia provides new opportunities for institutionalization efforts. There have been several instances where social movements have protested against issues such as corruption and the courts have stepped in to legislate evaluative work (whether formal evaluations, commissions, or fact-finding missions). Changes and expansion in the nature of movements, including through the growing use of social media, and the increasing role of the judiciary in pushing governments to act, suggest a need to expand thinking on evaluation demanders and to consider and target civil society players, the judiciary, and social movements as potential evaluation users. Evaluation needs to serve governments, donors, local decision-makers, and citizens, particularly those citizens most needing the gains of development. A movement in this direction, for example, could connect evaluation to right-to-information campaigns, accountability and anti-corruption movements, and gender- and rights-based movements. Such shifts could expand the questions evaluation is exploring and deepen demand for making evaluations more publicly accessible and available.

Evaluation field-building strategies that work with multiple platforms and players probably make sense everywhere, but particularly in contexts where governance is weak, fluctuating, and corrupt. Weiss's (2009) understanding of policy windows is helpful here. Some windows of use are closing just as others may be opening. For example, government may increasingly request particular types of data to address management questions (an opening window) while the use of evaluation to critique policies and programmes or as a tool for democratic dialogue may be declining (a closing window). Many policy-makers not only complain about the quality of evaluation but also shield politically important programmes from the lens of evaluation or are resistant to learning from evaluation.

Work in and on the institutional setting should be towards increasingly open and supportive policies and cultures of evaluation. Such shifts are by nature negotiated, involve power, and require strategy and responsiveness to 'open windows' by policy entrepreneurs and advocates. This work is arguably one of the functions to which leaders in evaluation, as they emerge, can contribute. Development is not neutral or technocratic, and neither is evaluation field building. Field building will require astute strategizing, alliance building, and entrepreneurship.

Evaluation Field Building as a System

The previous sections of this chapter described the five key elements of the field of evaluation; however, the different parts of the field interact as a system. Some parts can create a positive push on others; other parts create a weakening pull or drag on other elements of the field. Writing on philanthropic field building, Hirschhorn and Gilmore (2004, p. 32) note that, 'institutions surrounding the focal practice . . . strengthen the practice if their goals reinforce one another'.

Each part of the system has an impact on the other parts. Take the case of university programmes in evaluation, for example. Demand and supply for such programmes occur within a broader set of changes in university environments, employment opportunities for evaluators, pulls from other sectors and disciplines for faculty and students, and so on, all of which create incentives and disincentives for this field-building activity. While the example highlights a scenario of positive push factors, elements of the system also create drag or weaken other elements. The parts of the system co-evolve within broader contexts that are also co-evolving.

Building the Field

Recognizing that there is no 'best practice' blueprint to follow from North or South on evaluation field building, the interesting question that follows is: what unique mix of evaluation field building could lead to evaluation leadership, quality, and innovation in South Asia? The elements of the evaluation field relate to each other in different ways, and these relationships should inform and guide field-building efforts.

At the core of field building are people: evaluators, researchers, trainers, users, and advocates. Together they create demand for and bodies of evidence that are shared through evaluation, policy, and programme forums. They come together in spaces of learning and sharing to teach, to use evaluation, and to create norms and standards. They work within contexts and with stakeholders that are supportive, or not supportive, and as they work they influence those contexts.

Strengthening human capacity and skills is foundational to field-building efforts. For example, if the capacity of leaders and organizations is built, they can then take on other aspects of field building—such as developing norms and trying to influence policy stakeholders. However, different elements of the field need to be concurrently strengthened, as isolated individuals with increased skills and ability will only have limited effect if other elements are not also being strengthened. For example, work to develop advocacy strategies and to advocate for appropriate public policy changes would perhaps be best done by strengthened networks of evaluators, researchers, and social activists. Work to develop norms and standards and apply those standards is perhaps best supported through creating or strengthening networks and associations of evaluators that can craft and promote those standards. Certain aspects of field building are best addressed by those working in, and members of, the field itself.

Strategies for Building the Field in South Asia

We must start where we are. Strengthening a core set of evaluators and evaluation researchers, and the spaces and structures to support their work, is an important starting point from which other elements of the evaluation field can connect. Strengthening the people involved in evaluation could include capacity-building programmes, graduate curricula, and executive training. This work could encompass prospecting for, identifying, engaging with, and creating incentives to encourage and reward leaders—including connecting with researchers and social scientists from various fields to draw them into the field of evaluation. There are multiple evaluation craftspersons (to use Toulemonde's language) flourishing in the region. However, they are dispersed, isolated, and often disconnected from broader debates, systems, and theory building. In order to learn more systematically from their work and to integrate their evaluation experience and knowledge into the broader field of evaluation in South Asia, there is a need to develop networking opportunities, associations, and communities of practice.

In the context of evaluation field building, the idea of spaces for learning goes beyond an instrumentalist approach that sees the overall goal as improving evaluation for donors. It sees the overall goal as helping researchers and evaluation practitioners to build evaluation communities, culture, theory, and practice in support of local, national, and regional development strategies and programmes. Field building entails experimentation and indigenous innovation, building on the best ideas available, but creating something better. Evaluation field building should include support for open communities of practice and experimentation with ways to accelerate learning across, and from, bottom-up processes. It could also include supporting writing; the exchange of ideas at events, meetings, networks, and conferences; and fostering structures to support information exchange and problem solving within and across myriad professional platforms such as meetings, listservs, or virtual spaces.

Working on strengthening specific elements of the field where there are opening windows will help build other aspects of the field. For example, strengthening the capacity of Southern evaluators through their involvement in evaluations will contribute, by extension, new knowledge to the field.

Support and strategies for building the field should recognize and reflect the multiple timelines involved in development and development research. There are the immediate problems and challenges—where quality evaluation can help to distinguish what is working from what is not and bring new evidence to bear on pressing policy and programming questions. Evaluators and researchers must bring the tools, skills, and practice of evaluation to bear on these questions for field-building work to be relevant. Building new knowledge around understanding the complexities related to change processes or how systems shift can be applied to persistent challenges in the medium term. Finally, building and supporting leadership and structures of evaluation practice in the long term (in parallel with, and connected to, the short- and medium-term strategies) build the future ability of evaluators to respond to pressing development problems and development needs in their countries.

In strategizing about field building, frameworks of evaluation supply and demand are conceptually helpful. However, they can oversimplify and tend not to distinguish between different types of demand and supply and the way elements of the evaluation field influence both. Field-building efforts should resist a technocratic understanding of supply or demand and, instead, see both as abstractions that are connected, in flux, and part of broader social settings that are themselves in flux. Integrating this systems perspective into field-building work implies that instead of, for example, asking 'whether an appropriate balance means working equally on both sides of the equation or whether to focus first on one side of the equation or other' (Boyle et al., 1999, p. 13), field building should be approached developmentally, recognizing that some doors will open and some will close. Field-building efforts need to analyse how contexts are shifting, remain nimble, and seek opportunities and 'quick wins,' while also working towards longer-term, often incremental, change. Such an approach recognizes that the work of institutionalization is never complete, is not linear, and is unlikely to follow a consistently upward trajectory. Building on this recognition strengthens our ability to plan for and learn from field-building efforts more thoughtfully. Developmental evaluation (Patton, 2010) may provide opportunities for understanding and evaluating evaluation field-building efforts.

Making a Difference

Evaluating field building should include building a knowledge base about how evaluation can make or is making a difference. Field building is ultimately about strengthening evaluation systems and practice to the point where they can effectively address development problems. This requires willingness to open dialogue about evidence, deep commitment to learning what is working, and comfort with exposing what is not. Evaluation use is the most difficult part. Despite asserting the value of evaluation, donors and governments are not using evaluation effectively, nor have they invested adequately in building the field of evaluation. The specific road maps will vary in different contexts, but key next steps for all those engaged in evaluation field building will include creating a long-term vision, sustained efforts on multiple fronts, and experimenting and learning from what works and what does not.

References

Arunachalam, S. (2009). *Social science research in Asia: An analysis of the published journal literature*. Retrieved from http://www.rcuk.ac.uk/RCUK-prod/assets/documents/india/socialscienceresearchinsouthasia.pdf. Accessed on January 10th, 2014.

Ashford, G. and Patkar, S. (2001). *The positive path: Using appreciative inquiry in rural Indian communities*. Winnipeg, Manitoba, Canada: International Institute for Sustainable Development.

Basnyat, B.B. (2009). *Status and challenges of impact evaluation in Nepal*. Paper presented at the Perspectives on Impact Evaluation Conference, Cairo, Egypt.

Berry, L.L. and Parasuraman, A. (1993). Building a new academic field—The case of services marketing. *Journal of Retailing*, 69(1), 13–60.

Boyle, R., Lemaire, D., and Rist, R.C. (1999). Introduction. In R. Boyle and D. Lemaire (Eds.), *Building effective evaluation capacity: Lessons from practice* (pp.1–22). New Brunswick, NJ: Transaction Publishers.

Carden, F. (2007). The real evaluation gap. *Alliance Magazine*, 12(4), 4.

Chambers, R. (1994). The origins and practice of participatory rural appraisal. *World Development*, 22(7), 953–69.

Dart, J.J. and Davies, R.J. (2003). A dialogical, story-based evaluation tool: The most significant change technique. *American Journal of Evaluation*, 24(2), 137–55.

Earl, S., Carden, F., and Smutylo, T. (2001). *Outcome mapping: Building learning and reflection into development programs*. Ottawa, Ontario, Canada: International Development Research Centre.

Freidson, E. (1970). *Profession of medicine: A study of the sociology of applied knowledge*. Chicago: University of Chicago Press.

Goyal, R.S. (2009). *Evaluation capacity building in south Asia: Experiences, lessons learned and way forward*. Paper presented at the Perspectives on Impact Evaluation conference, Cairo, Egypt.

Hay, K. (2010). Evaluation field building in South Asia: Reflections, anecdotes, and questions. *American Journal of Evaluation*, 31(2), 222–31.

Hay, K. and Sudarshan, R. (2010). Making research matter in South Asia. *Economic and Political Weekly*, XLV(3), 34.

Hirschhorn, L. and Gilmore, T.N. (2004). *Ideas in philanthropic field building: Where they come from and how they are translated into actions.Practice Matters: The Improving Philanthropy Project (6)*. Retrieved from http://foundationcenter. org/gainknowledge/research/pdf/practicematters_06_execsum.pdf. Accessed on 10th January, 2014.

Jacobs, M. and Bosanac, S.E. (2006). *The professionalization of work*. Whitby, Ontario, Canada: de Sitter Publications.

Khan, K. (2008). Evaluation challenges in Pakistan and establishment of Pakistan Evaluation Network (PEN). In B. Williams and M. Sankar (Eds.), *Evaluation South Asia* (pp. 69–78). Kathmandu, Nepal: UNICEF.

Macdonald, K.M. (1995). *The sociology of the professions*. London: SAGE Publications..

Pal, S.P. (2009). *Status of development evaluation in India—An overview*. Paper presented at the Perspectives on Impact Evaluation conference, Cairo, Egypt.

Patton, M. (2010). *Developmental evaluation: Applying complexity concepts to enhance innovation and use*. New York: Guilford Press.

Reeser, L., Cherrey, L., and Epstein, I. (1990). *Professionalization and activism in social work*. New York: Columbia University Press.

Scriven, M. (2001). Evaluation future: Tense. *American Journal of Evaluation*, 22(3), 301–7.

Segone, M. (2008a). Evidence-based policy making and the role of monitoring and evaluation within the new aid environment. In M. Segone (Ed.), *Bridging the gap: The role of monitoring and evaluation in evidence-based policy making* (pp.16–45). New York: UNICEF.

———. (2008b). *Bridging the gap: The role of monitoring and evaluation in evidence-based policy making*. New York: UNICEF.

Sen, A. (2010). *Plenary address*. Evaluation Conclave held in New Delhi, India.

Shiva Kumar, A.K. (2010). A comment on 'Evaluation field building in South Asia: Reflections, anecdotes, and questions'. *American Journal of Evaluation*, 31(2), 238–40.

Toulemonde, J. (1995). The emergence of an evaluation profession in European countries: The case of structural policies. *Knowledge, Technology & Policy*, 8(3), 43–54.

Tudawe, I. and Samranayake, M. (2008). Civil society partnership in promoting an evaluation culture in the development process—Experience of the Sri Lanka Evaluation Association (SLEvA). In B. Williams and M. Sankar (Eds.), *Evaluation South Asia* (pp. 61–8). Kathmandu, Nepal: UNICEF.

Weiss, C. (2009). Forward. In F. Carden, *Knowledge to policy*. Ottawa, Ontario, Canada: International Development Research Centre.

Williams, B. and Sankar, M. (Eds.). (2008). *Evaluation South Asia*. Kathmandu, Nepal: UNICEF. Retrieved 5 January 2009 from http://www.unicef.org/rosa/ROSA_Evaluation_Journal.pdf

Wright, D. (2005). *The professionalization of history in English*. Toronto, Ontario, Canada: University of Toronto Press.

4

The Importance of Context in Participatory Evaluations: Reflections from South Asia

Sonal Zaveri

Introduction

Understanding what 'participation' means in the context of an evaluation is fundamental to designing and implementing evaluations that challenge rather than perpetuate existing social structures, hierarchies, and systems. Evaluations cannot be deemed participatory just because the evaluator talks to or engages with the community during the process of data gathering or sharing findings. Nor is participation in evaluation confined to and defined by the use of various methods and tools. Participation necessarily includes communication with and involvement of those who are being evaluated, and it is important in designing and implementing participatory evaluations (PE) to ask *what* is being evaluated, *with whom*, *how*, and *why*. These questions are not purely theoretical but are embedded in the context in which the PE is carried out. The way an evaluator understands how context—the socio-cultural, political, and prevailing evaluative climate—influences and is influenced by these participatory processes will shape not only how PE is designed and implemented but, more important, how it is *used to change existing social inequities*.

This chapter begins with a description of participation typologies and how they address (or do not address) context; it then examines specific contextual factors in South Asia and discusses how the intersection of contextual factors and participation can influence evaluative processes. The chapter builds on examples from South Asia (India, Pakistan, Sri Lanka, Afghanistan, Bangladesh, and Nepal) to describe how contextual factors play an important role in both the use and influence of PE and offers an analytical framework that can be used in different regions and communities. The chapter argues that evaluators, by paying closer attention to contextual factors, can ensure that PE not only evaluates project results but also contributes to addressing and challenging social inequities. It also raises questions about the dilemmas and challenges evaluators face in addressing context in PE.

Understanding Participation

The underlying assumption of participation in evaluation is that the voice of the community, towards which programmes are directed, is important and needs to be heard (Chambers, 1997; Feuerstein, 1986). Due to this close link to communication, a great deal of attention in PE was directed towards how to unlock the 'voice' of the community. Conventionally, evaluation was the preserve of the educated, involved very technical subject matter, and required competencies only an expert could have. The push towards participatory evaluation (PE) resulted in an emphasis on the 'how', spawning a variety of tools, methods, and approaches with less emphasis on paper and pencil and more on visual, spatial, and oral forms of communication, so that even the illiterate could participate in the evaluation process. Although manuals described in detail how a certain participatory tool or method could be used and training programmes provided skill building, how these tools were used varied greatly in practice, shaped by who administered the tools and the prevailing contextual factors at play in the community. This experience of differences in implementing PE resulted in tools being adapted and evaluators accepting that some of them possessed better facilitative skills than did others. Although variations in skill may have accounted for some of the differences, a deeper analysis and reflection indicated that there were a number of contextual factors at play, which had their influence not only within the communities and among the people evaluated, but also on the mind-set of the evaluator.

Along with a focus on *how* to conduct PE, there emerged the need to understand *who* participated and how much. Clearly, a person engaging in the participative process influences and is influenced by others.

To understand these interactive processes, various participatory typologies (Arnstein, 1969; Hart, 1992) were developed to explain the nature and depth of communication. Typically, the typologies described different levels of communication and participation, varying from non-participation to heightened participation. At the highest level, participation meant 'citizen control', whereas the lowest levels of participation included manipulation, decoration, and/or tokenism and were referred to as non-participation. The levels clearly defined 'who' participates and 'how' and were useful in describing how an adult participates with children, how an authority figure participates with those who report to him or her, how government and civil society communicate with each other, and even how an evaluator relates to those being evaluated. The typologies explained how those in differing power roles could communicate, ranging from the most to the least participative. However, they could not explain *why* such levels existed and what could be done to alter these power positions. The people who occupied these power positions (or did not) were doing so within a certain political and sociocultural context. When participatory processes are used in evaluation, it becomes imperative to recognize these contexts, as they influence the positions occupied by both the evaluator and the evaluated. It is important, therefore, for evaluators to reflect on how context implicitly and explicitly influences the use of PE and to recognize that context is not static but continually evolving—a dynamic backdrop influencing the who, how, and what of PE.

Why we conduct PE has also received considerable attention. Participation in evaluation has been valued for gathering data and information, building ownership around the use of findings, as well as for collective learning and dialogic processes that address the underlying social and political causes that influence the intervention or programme being evaluated. In the latter emphasis on sociopolitical causes, there is an implicit acceptance that context has a profound influence. Frameworks to explain the purposes of PE can be found in Cousins and Whitmore's (1998) three-dimensional model, which includes degree of participation, range of stakeholder involvement, and control of the process by stakeholders and evaluators. They also made a useful distinction between practical participatory evaluation (P-PE) and transformative participatory evaluation (T-PE).

P-PE arose out of a more Northern context, where the concept of democratic participation was not unknown and PE was a means to find out from various sources closer to the project under evaluation what worked and what did not (Brisolara, 1998). In practice, such evaluations give greater decision-making power to programme personnel than to key stakeholders (Smith, 1999), although there has been some argument to extend involvement to clients and beneficiaries as well (Weiss, 1998).

T-PE on the other hand looks at the evaluative process as useful for empowering and transforming society. It has a clear identified role in societies where the poor—being constrained by traditions, cultures, and power differentials—have no say in interpreting the impact of various development efforts, even though these development projects are designed for them and directly influence their lives. According to T-PE, the social constructs of the community are equally if not more important than the evaluator's in interpreting the results. Although evaluators may need to share knowledge and guide the community to use the tools of evaluation, T-PE worked when they consciously stepped back with a willingness to learn from the people (Porter and de Wet, 2009; Suarez-Balcazar and Harper, 2003).

T-PEs emerged out of the approaches popularized by Paolo Friere in the *Pedagogy of the Oppressed* (1972), which encouraged the voice of the poor and dispossessed. According to Friere, 'dialogue' or the conversations with others critically analysing the world, 'praxis' or the process of reflection and action, and 'conscientization' or the critical awareness of one's social reality to uncover real problems and actual needs defined *true participation*. It is a question of giving a 'voice' to those who do not have one or are not heard; the process of *engagement* in a participatory process is itself seen as a transformative experience. The process is inherently political, as T-PE promotes social action for change and transforms power relationships to empower the marginalized (Burke, 1998; Chambers, 1997; Mertens, 1999). These writings illustrate how important participation is in addressing the power imbalances and inequities, particularly because evaluations have an *inherent* power imbalance between the givers of resources—be it a donor or government—and the recipients, and less acknowledged, between the evaluator (whose report can influence future funding or implementation) and those being evaluated.

Both P-PE and T-PE *themselves* have evolved in response to *their own contexts*, such as differences in the North/South philosophical approaches to PE (Brisolara, 1998). The process is also influenced by how evaluators coming from a different context conduct PE and how they affect the participatory processes of the community being evaluated. Self-reflection by evaluators about their own contextual framework and the differing context of the project being evaluated enables awareness and encourages a more sensitive handling of the PE process.

PE that is transformative emphasizes self-reflection and critical dialogue (communication) about whether the project has been effective and whether there have been any changes in people and/or situations and *why*. The discussion about participation necessarily addresses empowerment. Empowerment is defined generally as gaining power over one's resources and decision-making. Participation becomes both a means and an end to empowerment and the process of self-evaluation is itself empowering (Jupp and Ali, 2010). However, power is also linked to the social and cultural conditions in which people live and is a zero-sum affair—for one to get power someone else has to lose it (Kreisberg, 1992). Either way, participation in evaluation must also simultaneously address our understanding of empowerment at the individual level and at the societal level. A further challenge is that the meaning of participation and empowerment itself varies in different sociocultural systems and political contexts and is linked to local value and belief systems (World Bank, 2002).

Context

Contextual factors have clearly influenced the *how*, *who*, and *why* of participation in evaluation, shaping not only the design and implementation of PE but also the interpretation of the findings and their use. This section provides a description of some of these contextual factors and discusses their influence on participative processes. There are many ways to look at context, such as the legal, environmental, and economic climate, and the religious ethos; for this chapter, I will address three contextual factors or climates—the sociocultural, the political, and the prevailing evaluative climate—and discuss how they influence participation in evaluation in South Asia.

Sociocultural

South Asia is home to hierarchical social structures that reflect deep-seated cultural beliefs about the role of children, women, and older members of society. In addition, there are stratifications of caste, kinship, and creed. Family and community affiliations further contribute to this complex web of unspoken but palpable sets of norms around communication and socialization. One of the ways in which these ideas have been organized (among others that coexist in the Indian subcontinent) is the cultural notion of dharma/dhamma (loosely defined as duty) prevalent in Hindu and Buddhist traditions, primarily in India, Nepal, and Sri Lanka. Dharma envisions an organic society where participating members are interdependent and their roles complementary. The concept of dharma is very different from the concept of rights. Based on traditions that in some ways reinforce the contextual divides of caste, gender, and position, dharma also, in some (but not all) ways, provides a 'space' to modify them. Social institutions are legitimate, not because of contractual obligation, but because of their dharma; suggestions for reform are not to question their existence but to bring them closer to the ideal, the dharma. In this context, social conflict arises because of *adharma* (*not* adhering to the true principles of dharma), and Gandhi's concept of trusteeship for the rich—that they need to spend their wealth for the welfare of the poor—espoused this belief. This underlying concept has implications in much of South Asia, as social reform is not about abolishing hierarchical structures or rejecting the values on which they are based but about changing the individuals in positions of authority so that they realize their responsibility to contribute to the common good (Kakar, 1978, p. 41).

Sainath (1996, pp. 71, 76) has vividly captured the unquestioned hierarchical constructs in his case studies of the poorest of the poor and their interaction with authority figures—primarily the government—describing how the rights of the poor had been violated without thought and with impunity. One example cited by Sainath describes the 'success' of cash compensation for land acquired from tribal communities for the 'national interest'. He describes how India's National Policy for Rehabilitation of Persons Displaced as a Consequence of Acquisition of Land accepts that land would be acquired (mostly from tribal people) to ensure growth and that this '. . . brings in its wake hardships to the persons whose lands contribute to the process of growth'. He describes the government's attitude as one where '. . . they [the displaced] will not be consulted but band aids will be supplied free'. He claims that more than 26 million Indians were affected by this policy, all in the name of successful development. Touted as a successful programme of development, in reality, it failed on several fronts when reviewed with a contextual lens. Land compensation was in cash or the provision of alternative land, which did not respect traditional forms of ownership or address underlying social inequities. The policy did not have a prescribed way to address compensation for the acquisition of large tracts of land owned collectively for hundreds of years by the tribal community because collective ownership was not recognized. The government norms (ownership papers) did not coincide with the tribal understanding of collective ownership of property, and the compensation received was not at all adequate. Furthermore, the compensation exacerbated the marginalization of women. Women in India do not have access to either land or cash because of cultural factors; the monies received were not accessible to women, and hence, in spite of compensation, there was no change in their own or their children's well-being. In this situation, no challenge was made to existing hierarchical and gender exclusion norms. Although the land compensation scheme was deemed a success, it did not address the context in which land was owned and in fact exacerbated the poverty of tribal populations, all because the indicators of success did not even address contextual understanding of ownership and compensation.

Gender and age also play an important role in South Asian societies. Women do not have the same decision-making power as men do, even when they contribute economically (Hoque and Itohara, 2009), and among women, those of higher status (such as the mother-in-law) enjoy greater power (Agarwal, 2010). After three decades of an integrated child development programme for children below the age of five years across India, a study found that boys continued to be favoured with a greater uptake of nutrition services than girls (National Institute of Public Cooperation and Child Development, 2006). Social structures can serve as impediments, with gatekeepers (mother-in-law as well as male authority figures) blocking the way for behaviour change and decisions about birthing, birth control, spacing of children, immunization, and other issues.

In Bangladesh, 'successive governments design and plan projects with support from donors and consultants but they tend to ignore grassroots people's participation' (Munshi et al., 2011, p. 8). In another paper in the same Action Aid Learning Document series, the authors describe how entrenched hierarchical and gender inequities affect the full participation of all community members. For example, '[w]omen are not encouraged to take part in the planning and budgeting process. Even the Union Parishad (UP or district council) members who are females play their role as silent audience' and 'the hard-core poor get deprived from the results of government schemes. . . . Getting supports and services from the UPs depend[s] mostly on the wills of the chairmen and members' (Ashraf et al., 2011, p. 22). To overcome these inequities, a social audit approach,[1] responsive to the sociocultural context of the community, was initiated. The social audit members were a collective, with wide community representation including influencers (journalists, retired government officials) and special representation of the poor and women. The paper notes that the social audit team was expected to stay away from initiating or participating in quarrels or arguments and instead expected to try to maintain good relationships among all parties. The social audit process created a democratic space for people to devolve their power through a decentralized mechanism. In the examples above, women were encouraged to participate in the UP budgeting discussions through personal and social communication; members were also given instructions about women's participation, and the UP committees were encouraged to be more accountable and responsible to the needs of all members of the community. The social audit process describes a grassroots contextual approach (collective and non-confrontational) to address inequities. The authors cite examples of how the social audit process increased the accountability of doctors in primary health centres and headmasters in schools. Brokers (usually male) would manipulate women coming for family planning advice at the primary health centre, but through the social audit process, women learned to directly approach the doctors (usually male) and ask for a nurse to be present at their session with the doctor. Similarly, a school headmaster (of a higher class and caste) refused to talk to poorer guardians, and social audit groups were able to address this grievance. Poor people are often excluded from their own entitlements because they are powerless. When looking at the success or failure of a programme, evaluations must assess the contribution of contextual factors towards outcome.

Sociopolitical

Most countries in South Asia have adopted democracy as their political orientation, though there may be variations regarding the extent to which democratic processes are followed. Bangladesh has had a parliamentary system since 1991, though democratic processes are fragile (Ahsan, 2005). Nepal is just emerging from a monarchy-centric political system, and the oldest democracies of South Asia, India and Pakistan, are just 60 years old. Most countries in the region have experienced civil disobedience movements with active participation from the polity. Dialogue, discourse, and community mobilization are not new. Decentralization has also fostered the move towards greater community and grassroots involvement in democratic processes. For example, India (through the 73rd Amendment in 1992), Nepal, and Bangladesh have village-level committees that have the authority and resources to make local decisions.

However, the democratic structures and arrangements are influenced heavily by traditional political and power dynamics (Johnson, 2003). Within democratic structures at the village level, representation is dominated by the traditionally powerful upper castes of society, usually male. Women, though present, do not participate. One study found that the *number* of women present at community meetings was critical and determined whether they spoke and contributed to the proceedings (Agarwal, 2010). Recognizing that women are underrepresented in political affairs, a number of countries in the region—such as India, Bangladesh, and Nepal—have tried to rectify the situation by establishing quotas for women. Nevertheless, Asia is plagued by gender stereotyping that suggests that the woman's world is 'inside' and the man's is 'outside' (Hoque and Itohara, 2008). In one sense, the sociopolitical context provides the systems and structures that promote grassroots participation, but it is also constrained by the stratification of caste, age, and gender that automatically excludes or limits full participation in all aspects of the democratic process. Such limitations also constrain the extent to which PE can question the social power dynamics and inhibit the transformative change that is within arm's reach.

Evaluative Climate

The current call for greater recipient- (country-based) as opposed to donor-led evaluation recognizes that donors have been in control of what and how to evaluate (Segone, 2009). It is recognized that much of the innovation with participatory methodologies has come and is coming from the South—from Asia, Latin America, and Africa (Chambers, 2009)—as opposed to from the North or from donors. Nevertheless, the current emphasis on rigor and impact evaluation has challenged the contribution of PE. PE practitioners have responded by saying that qualitative participatory methods can generate numbers and statistics and by doing so not only add rigor but also 'make the realities and experiences of poor people count more' (Chambers, 2009, p. 1). Evaluators who propose rigor in impact evaluation (such as assessing change by comparing one group that received the intervention with another that did not at different points of time, commonly known as randomized control trials or RCT) also accept the role of qualitative tools that characterize a more participative approach in evaluation.

However, the current debate on the usefulness of impact evaluation is not so much about what is evaluated and how, but *why* one evaluates. Those who promote impact evaluations have a very different view than those who practise PE. A clear understanding of the different contexts of these evaluations comes by asking the question, 'Why do we evaluate?' Chambers et al. (2009, pp. 4, 8) cite Dean Karlan as saying that RCT is used for three reasons: 'to know where to spend limited resources, to know how to improve programs, and to motivate those with money to give or invest more'. However, they think that 'the starting point for an evaluation is to ask why it is being conducted, who will benefit, and what impact will the evaluation itself have and how'. They go on to say that it is important to ask about the 'political economy of the evaluation or who would gain, who would lose and how, and especially how the findings were intended or predicted to make a difference'. The context and worldview of the evaluator clearly drive the methods, tools, and type of evaluation conducted.

The current thrust towards recipient-led or country-led evaluations is promoted side by side with a more results-based and impact-oriented approach to evaluation. A closer look indicates that there is no paradigm shift, only a transfer of control to another power elite, in this case at the country level. As pointed out previously, donors, evaluators, and thought leaders from the North, with their own contextual underpinnings, are influencing ideas about how Southern evaluation field building should take place.

The evaluative climate in South Asia has also been evolving, and it is important to understand the historical context in which the change is taking place. The first wave of evaluation in the post-independence, postcolonial era (except for Nepal) was designed to serve government planning. Economists designed evaluation to assess whether activities had been implemented as per plan. Less attention was placed on the contextual factors that influenced the way in which the programmes unfolded at the grassroots. The second wave was to serve donors (Hay, 2010). Donors built the capacity of recipients (South Asians) to evaluate against donor criteria for donor needs (Carden, 2010). This second wave continued to pay little attention to contextual factors, particularly in terms of their influence on evaluative processes. It is also important to note that the administrative and political culture of South Asia lacks a tradition of evaluation, with many managers fearful of evaluation, seeing it as an audit or fault-finding exercise (Shiva Kumar, 2010). This political and social context (the hierarchical model of fear of being reprimanded by their superiors and the acceptance of donor diktats) permeates the evaluative climate, influencing the context in which PE takes place.

The next section maps how these three contextual factors—sociocultural, political, and evaluative climate—matter in the design, implementation, and use of PE. It answers questions related to *why* it is important to address the contextual factors, *whom* to involve in the participative process, and *how*. It concludes by suggesting possible ways to improve how contextual factors are addressed and the practice of PE overall.

This analysis will be useful to evaluators in thinking through how they address context in their evaluations and what steps they can take to improve the process.

Context and Practice

Sociocultural Context and the Practice of PE

Communities have to be involved if PE is to be transformative and empowering. 'Like every other word, "community" has a history of effective use—and simplistic misuse' (Lotz, 1998, as cited in Ramirez, 2008). There are a number of factors that inform an understanding of community in the context of South Asia. First, social structures in South Asia are complex, drawn across kinship, ethnic, religious, and caste strata, over which lie distinctions of gender, wealth, and other stratifications. Hence, community exists only as a notion and perhaps its most distinguishing feature is what it is not: it is *not* government and *not* a donor organization. There are, therefore, 'communities within community', indicating the diversity not only in representation but also in power structures. Understanding and addressing the sociocultural context in PE can ensure that different sections of the community can have dialogue on existing structures and systems, thus providing a roadmap for critiquing and challenging various inequalities that exist.

In a similar way, the concept of 'context' differs in its definition and application across different approaches to evaluation. In impact evaluation, for example, context is recognized as important but has a different connotation and use from the concept of context employed in PE. According to White (2009), understanding context helps to anticipate impact (treatment effect) heterogeneity and helps generalization. Anticipated heterogeneity is important, since it helps to determine sampling size and probability analysis. Understanding context helps generalization by isolating the contextual factors that led to the outcome (degree of success) of the treatment. The understanding of 'context' in impact evaluation has affected the current evaluative climate, which poses a fundamental conundrum: that one's understanding of 'context' itself is dependent on one's own worldview. PE and impact evaluation may both use the word 'context', but they use it to refer to very different issues, dramatically affecting *how* evaluations are designed, implemented, and used.

The meaning of participation may vary—from a simple counting of how to increase uptake to more complex processes of engagement that lead to changes in existing social and power structures in communities. O'Reilly (2010) describes a latrine marketing programme that encouraged women to participate, based on the assumption that their participation would lead to better uptake and acceptance of latrines. Participation was viewed as a simple, practical problem—the toilets were not being used—and the solution was to increase women's participation in the projects. However, the programme failed to understand the social meanings attached to latrines and the 'cultural reasons' for use and non-use. Social inequalities were not questioned through, for example, conversations with men to consider women's choices for latrine sitting at the household level, and therefore, there was no opportunity to spark a wider discussion about gender-based differences in access to space in the family compound and beyond. By not doing so, and though participative processes were used to assess women's uptake of latrine sitting, an opportunity was lost to challenge the established and deep-rooted sociocultural definition of 'spaces' occupied by men and women.

Evaluations that assess the impact of development programmes that encourage participation by women would benefit by assessing not only the uptake or reach of a programme but also how and to what extent power relationships between men and women have changed. Many cultural barriers may affect responses; for example, women participating in the evaluation may not talk candidly to a male evaluator or vice versa. Who asks the questions and who is present in the dialogue may affect the quantity and quality of responses received during data collection.

Communities represent multiple constituencies, some of whose interests may conflict with others. PE must take into consideration these cultural nuances. Some communities may themselves be exploitative, such as brothel keepers and sex worker's lovers who want to introduce the children to sex work (Zaveri, 2008). Village communities have ostracized trafficked children who have returned to Nepal because they have brought shame and poverty with them. While girls typically have low status at birth, they enjoy a higher status when they, like sons, send home money (even if it is from the brothels). However, if a girl returns HIV-positive, the family and community often shun her, for she now brings a triple shame: one for being a girl, another for the loss of income, and a third for bringing shame to the family. While repatriation of affected children can be touted as an indicator of success, this would also indicate that the sociocultural nuances and the context have not been addressed. PE would therefore need to address the sociocultural factors affecting why and how girls are considered a 'burden' and assess programme success by the extent to which these gendered differences were addressed (CARAM Asia, 2002; Poudel and Carryer, 2000).

As various types of collectivization—such as kinship groups, caste groupings, extended family structures, and social-traditional networks (families linked by kinship and marriage)—are common to the region, community-based implementation is likely to implicitly follow these homogeneous groupings. PE would need to have a closer look at not only *who* participates but also the *heterogeneity* of those participating in programmes.

Sociopolitical Contexts and the Practice of PE

Implementing a democratic, transformative PE may easily be jeopardized in practice, even though a variety of methods and tools such as participatory rural appraisal (PRA), focused group discussions, and key stakeholders' interviews are used. Cornwall (2002, p. 10) refers to participation as 'creating spaces where there were previously none, about making room for different opinions to be heard where previously there were very limited opportunities for public involvement, and about enabling people to occupy spaces that were previously denied to them'. She points out that so much attention is placed on the methodologies of participation that less attention is paid to what actually happens in practice, who takes part, on what basis, and with what resources. Social and cultural barriers may block the democratic and egalitarian process of collecting data and engaging the true beneficiaries to participate in the evaluation. How we identify the critical stakeholders becomes a key step in PEs. Men, more powerful individuals, or those belonging to a higher-caste group are the most likely to be included as key stakeholders in evaluations of development programmes, as they are also the most literate, articulate, available, and 'visible'. Formal social groups (women's groups, youth groups) and political groups (village committees) at the community level are also likely to be dominated by the same upper-caste and higher-income groups. Community involvement in PE, which is contingent on identifying key stakeholders, can be skewed inadvertently in favour of the most powerful. Also, if intermediary non-governmental organizations (NGOs) are involved in assisting in the evaluation exercise, key stakeholders identified are likely to be those in positions of power who have assisted the NGOs or are easily available (perhaps for all evaluations!).

Since identification of stakeholders is key in PE, it is important for evaluators interested in addressing sociopolitical contextual factors to spell out how the stakeholders are identified as well as to make explicit who is *not* included, who is invited and did not attend, and why (Ramirez, 2008). These defining characteristics of the stakeholder group are equally important for planners designing projects and need to be clearly reported.

However, even if we do identify the truly disadvantaged and marginalized, it is quite likely that they may be present but *not contribute* in the discussions, deferring to the most senior and higher-status persons present, mimicking the traditional hierarchical structures present in communities. Hart and Rajbhandary (2003) describe an evaluation in Nepal where children had learned about children's rights in their clubs, but those participating in the evaluation of their children's clubs waited until their leader spoke first, reflecting the Nepali custom of respecting the older or more influential persons in the group. Also, women and children participants often feel that they have nothing of significance to contribute; other studies have shown that if adolescents are girls, their voices are not heard—they do not participate in any decision-making process, and even when they do, there is minimal acceptance of their opinions (Rahman et al., 2007).

It is also important to be aware that participation can be tokenism. I evaluated a child trafficking prevention programme in India, where a *youth* (above the age of 24 years!) was nominated as a *child* member of the vigilance committee to represent the children. The organization, however, reported that adolescent membership in the vigilance committee was an indicator of rights-based programming. Rights-based programming ensures that people and institutions that are in power are accountable and will fulfil their responsibilities towards those with less power. Rights holders (in this case the children) can demand their rights; be involved in political, economic, and social decisions; and through this process, change power relationships (Theis, 2003). However, when we consider the influence of context, culturally, it is disrespectful to speak before older persons, and so, in practice the contribution of the youth in representing the views of children is questionable.

In the same evaluation, I met the village child protection vigilance committees—comprising several influential persons, including the village's health worker, a teacher, and the village head—and by and large, they represented the politically powerful and the ones with higher status. The question was to what extent the committee really understood the vulnerabilities that lured the very poor and socially marginalized children and families into being exploited and trafficked. In terms of social distance, they were as far away as the evaluator (myself) was in understanding the context.

The practice of T-PE can therefore be non-egalitarian and unrepresentative of either a beneficiary or a community perspective and may actually reflect the perspective of the elite members of the community, defeating its intended purpose.

Even in cases where a process of collectivization and empowerment is being studied, it is possible for the donor's own political context to influence the interpretation of the findings so that results seen as being indicative of exploitation may also be seen, from a different perspective, as representative of empowerment. HIV prevention programmes in South Asia have successfully collectivized sex workers, even though they were marginalized and doubly vulnerable—first, as women, and second, for working in the taboo world of sex. Participatory evaluations in Bangladesh and India indicated how sex workers had challenged the authority of the police who harassed them and developed guidelines so that they could practise their trade without fear and exploitation (Ghose et al., 2008). In the political context of South Asia, this was a significant achievement using the tools that were available in the region—collectives—to develop pressure groups. However, the Bush administration under the President's Emergency Plan for AIDS Relief (PEPFAR)[2] interpreted from its own sociopolitical context that the training, empowerment, and collective action of sex workers was 'promoting prostitution' (Center for Health and Gender Equity, 2008, p. 4). One of the organizations that refused to sign the pledge stated, 'We're working with these sex workers, we're telling them that if they use condoms, men will be saved from HIV. . . . You're asking them to help you fight HIV. And in the same breath you are telling them that they are terrible people and that you're against them. It just doesn't make sense' (Meena Sheshu, as quoted in Kaplan, 2006).

A heightened awareness of how sociopolitical contexts influence evaluations will make evaluators more vigilant in their practice of PE. For example, donors and governments often appoint NGOs as link partners with grassroots organizations; their role is to manage funds and provide technical support to the smaller community-based organizations. When these link NGOs accompany the evaluator to translate or manage the logistics, it is possible that the interviewees will not share their views candidly (especially critical ones) because it is considered impolite to do so to an outsider (the evaluator) or because it is disrespectful of the efforts made by the NGO/intermediary for the programme under evaluation. The community may also consider the NGO's 'status' to be closer to the donor. A deeper understanding of the subtle sociopolitical context will enable evaluators to decide who should accompany them to the community, who should participate in data gathering, and how 'confidential spaces' may need to be created for the PE process to be truly and openly participative.

When PE is conducted, one needs also to understand the 'conspiracy' of participation that permeates the evaluation process. If the evaluation proves that the intervention is not working, it can mean that the funding will stop, bringing loss of benefits to the beneficiaries, clients, or community, as well as to the intermediary organization and/or the NGO. If the NGO has a long-established reputation, it is even more difficult to critique. The NGO's status, which it enjoys, constitutes a barrier for authentic participative data gathering, as a critique would upset the status quo balance in the community. The pressure then is to *always* indicate that the intervention has worked in some fashion or other, which inhibits an evaluative opportunity to address the various barriers that block quality implementation.

Evaluative Climate and the Practice of PE

Even where PE is recognized and practised, it is important to focus on how it intends to address existing social inequities. Measures used may *look* participatory, but a closer examination indicates how they are used to *control and manage processes* (Craig and Porter, 1997). The questions and concerns of evaluation participants are not considered, which makes it less meaningful and valuable for participants to engage in evaluative thinking and reduces the evaluation process to only visible outputs, without any focus on the deeper contextual and social changes that have taken place. The role of donors in setting the evaluation agenda is vividly captured by Patel and Bartlett (2009), who argue that participation is often framed by the priorities of the evaluator or commissioner of the evaluation so that only those questions of interest to the commissioner are addressed, albeit in a 'participatory' way. They describe a World Bank evaluation of a programme to resettle pavement dwellers that was considered very successful, but failed to address a basic contributing factor—the Society for Promotion of Area Resource Centers'[3] many years of work in participation and empowerment with the pavement dwellers, especially women, had transformed their ability to react to and act on new development demands, *only* one of which was the resettlement. From this point of view, the participation of women pavement dwellers in the evaluation was tokenism because none of the structural issues that were of interest to the women were addressed.

The emphasis on programme outputs, results, or outcomes may not adequately address factors that influence overall social impact. PE, however, with a closer look at contextual factors, can help unravel barriers and constraints. For example, the number of children's clubs is an outcome indicator of children's empowerment, the clubs being formed after a period of collectivization led by a spontaneous demand for more formal structures. Nevertheless, in South Asian societies, children will generally do what adults want, so the establishment of children's clubs may not represent the empowerment of children so much as the degree of adult authority and control. Sometimes, even when clubs are formed democratically, the programmes and activities represent adult needs, subtly undermining the process of participation (Hart and Rajbhandary, 2003). In such evaluations, it is critical to understand the cultural context and factors at play in order to assess whether empowerment has truly taken place.

Although impact evaluations are useful, they may overlook opportunities to better understand the different contexts (sociocultural and political) that influence evaluation findings. More important, such evaluations do not question *why* and *how* such interventions do or do not address deeper social inequities. In the long run, these questions are important catalysts for structural societal change.

The dominant emphasis on impact evaluation is perhaps taking us towards an understanding (or a lack of focus on context) that will *also* inform and influence what is possible in PEs. For example, an Abdul Lateef Jameel Poverty Action Lab (2007) report about cheap and effective ways to change adolescent sexual behaviour in Kenya discussed how providing two school uniforms to girls for three years at a cost of US$12 resulted in reduced dropout rates and teenage childbirths. The evaluator visited and checked with the school several times a year and corroborated with home visits on the incidence of dropouts and teenage childbirths— a proxy indicator for unsafe sexual practices. The girls reported whether they had had any childbirths and the evaluator checked with hospital records as well. The evaluation used an RCT design and reported with confidence that US$12 towards uniforms will prevent dropouts and teenage childbirths. However, the evaluation missed an opportunity to explore what *other* factors may have affected the girls' attendance. Was the school uniform the *only* reason for the findings, or could it be that these girls received social and community attention and support for their attendance? Were the teachers taking greater care of the girls in their studies or were the teachers in the schools merely better than others? The design assumed that having a control group did not warrant asking these questions to explain the findings, nor (and more importantly) was it seen as important for the girls or their families or their teachers to understand, debate, or explore how and why attendance had improved and what significance it had for them.

A study in Nepal (Zaveri et al., 1997) evaluated the outcome of the hygiene checklist introduced in the Child-to-Child school programmes sponsored by Save the Children.[4] The hygiene checklist had been developed by children and was administered by them with teachers acting only as facilitators. To understand how the checklist had contributed to good health, discussions were held with families, teachers, and principals, and a number of child participatory tools were used with children. Children did a before-after discussion, ranked the disease prevalence using VIPP[5] cards before and after the school health programme, plotted communication maps, and drew what they perceived as a healthy child. An analysis of the responses to these various methods indicated how the hygiene checklist had contributed to better health, absence of disease, and greater community support for the role of children in health promotion. Because of the hygiene checklist, parents helped in cleanliness and ensured that food was cooked on time and, as a result, children were cleaner, more punctual, and more regular with school attendance. This led them to study better, which motivated the teachers to teach better, ultimately leading to lower incidence of disease, better acceptance of the importance of education, and better teaching standards. The communities became very supportive of the schools as well. The PE process was able to unravel how children became agents of change and how family and community structures contributed to the process.

Participatory evaluations that engage people in understanding what has happened are even more important in the current landscape, where there are multiple projects with multiple donors being implemented in the same community. Because of the increasing degree of 'projectization' among donors (committing to short-term projects of one or two years with very specific targets), inputs overlap or add on to others already underway in communities. NGOs that manage projects find it advantageous, as they are able to build on and coordinate services or capacities initiated in former or concurrent projects. However, in terms of evaluation, donor insistence on outputs and outcomes to indicate attribution for *their* project inputs is at best a 'convenient truth'. The outcome and impact of projects may result from a combination of factors—different projects and contexts that interact in ways that are not even the scope of a specific project evaluation. That we often look for what we want to find has been reported in structured experiments as well (Lehrer, 2010). Often, unintended outcomes may also be overlooked, especially if they are negative. A review of programmes that enabled poor, including HIV-positive women, to join and benefit from self-help groups (micro-credit groups) found that children did not necessarily benefit because they would work after school, even coming home during the school break to work on the income-generating business. However, the project did not assess outcomes using the 'child's lens context', missing analysis on child labour, children's right to play, and girls' work in the assessment of the project (Zaveri, 2008). In terms of evaluative practice, the insistence on assessing impact may overlook the need to examine the context in which programmes function and may result in evaluative practices such as PE becoming less popular and 'acceptable' and underlying contextual factors that influence or perpetuate inequities not being identified or addressed.

Even in the practice of PE, addressing the context means asking the right questions—the how's and the whys—and being observant; who speaks is as important as who does not speak, what is *not* said is as important as what is said, and what activity has *not* happened is as important as what has happened. A visit to a community centre hosting a livelihood programme may reveal that the sewing machines have all been stacked against the wall—a clear indication of non-use.

It is often the very small changes in behaviour or a situation that matter and that need to be documented. When change takes place, people pay attention to the larger changes but tend to overlook the smaller changes that, over time, will contribute to the larger change. In South Asian societies, addressing historical inequities is difficult even where participative programme approaches are followed. Understanding this context, evaluations need to observe the small changes, the 'spirit of change' (Crishna, 2007) visible to the evaluator who understands the culture and context. Not reporting on and documenting these changes can lead to erroneously describing a project as 'not working' (leading to a halt in funding for the next cycle) because a statistical difference was not found in the data analysis, when in fact a positive, though nascent, change had already begun. Because these small and contextually (though not statistically) significant changes are not considered, evaluations may actually report that a project has not worked, when in fact it has. The evaluator's own contextual background and orientation are often a contributing factor to this interpretation. There are many 'small' examples of contextual change—such as an increase in attendance at community meetings, a few girls beginning to attend a life-skills programme, the village committee taking on the nutrition requirements of a couple of orphaned children, and a teacher talking to parents about good health when they come to pick up their children from school—which may indicate a larger and important shift in process.

Conclusion

It is disturbing that there is so little discussion about what we mean by participation and why it is important in the context of South Asian countries that are home to many forms of inequity. The discussion in this chapter is a call for greater reflection and understanding of how and why contextual factors—the sociocultural, the political, and the evaluative climate for both the evaluator and the evaluation process—can lead to transformative changes and address the socially inequitable norms, systems, and structures that impede the conduct of a truly participatory evaluation. The chapter urges evaluators to address these contextual factors to maximize the potential of PE to transform societies. By placing people first, evaluators agree to learn about and understand the social, cultural, and political context in which they work and live and, through a deeper self-reflection, address how their own contextual orientation has an impact on the evaluative process.

Notes

1. A social audit is a participatory approach used to identify the gaps and loopholes and sensitize the duty bearers to ensure quality services. Through this initiative, a number of volunteer groups, comprised of community people, carry out a thorough observation and analysis of the programmes planned and implemented by government at the local level. Data are gathered, reports are shared with relevant stakeholders, and advocacy for corrective measures is initiated. This approach ensures transparency and a culture of accountability.
2. PEPFAR or The U.S. President's Emergency Plan for AIDS Relief, introduced in 2003 by then-president George W. Bush, represented the largest commitment in history by any nation to combat a single disease. Fifteen 'focus' countries received the funding, but all organizations that received PEPFAR funding to work in these countries had to have a policy that explicitly opposed prostitution and sex trafficking. This policy was known as the anti-prostitution pledge, http://www.pepfarwatch.org/the_issues/anti_prostitution_pledge/. In 2008, PEPFAR was reauthorized for US$48 billion over five years (2009 to 2013) without any change in the anti-prostitution pledge.
3. Society for Promotion of Area Resource Centres (SPARC), an advocacy group for pavement dwellers in Mumbai, was founded in 1984 by Sheela Patel.
4. See http://www.child-to-child.org/ctcworldwide_past/nepal.htm

5. VIPP refers to the use of multi-coloured, multi-shaped, and multi-sized movable cards to express ideas.

References

Abdul Lateef Jameel Poverty Action Lab. (2007, February). *Cheap and effective ways to change adolescents' sexual behavior* (JPAL Policy Briefcase, No. 3). Cambridge, MA: Massachusetts Institute of Technology.

Agarwal, B. (2010). Does women's proportional strength affect their participation? Governing local forests in South Asia. *World Development*, 38(1), 98–112.

Ahsan, S. (2005). Bangladesh since 1971: How far has it come? *Asian Affairs*, 36(2), 149–57.

Arnstein, S. (1969, July). A ladder of citizen participation. *AIP Journal*, 35(4), 216–24.

Ashraf, A.B., Miah, A.S.M.J., and Khan, M.B.B.R. (2011). Participatory plans and budget: Experience from Union Parishads in Bangladesh. In R. Bin Sattar (ed.), *Learning document series 9–10* (pp. 13–26). Dhaka, Bangladesh: Impact Assessment & Shared Learning, ActionAid Bangladesh.

Brisolara, S. (1998). The history of participatory evaluation and current debates in the field. In E. Whitmore (ed.), *Understanding and practicing participatory evaluation: New directions for evaluation* (No. 80, pp. 25–41). San Francisco, CA: Jossey-Bass.

Burke, B. (1998). Evaluating for a change: Reflections on participatory methodology. In E. Whitmore (ed.), *Understanding and practicing participatory evaluation: New directions for evaluation* (No. 80, pp. 43–56). San Francisco, CA: Jossey-Bass.

CARAM Asia. (2002). *The forgotten spaces: Mobility and HIV vulnerability in the Asia Pacific*. Kuala Lumpur, Malaysia: CARAM Asia.

Carden, F. (2010). Introduction to the Forum on Evaluation Field Building in South Asia. *American Journal of Evaluation*, 31(2), 219–21.

Center for Health and Gender Equity. (2008). *Implications of US policy restrictions for HIV programs aimed at sex workers*. Takoma Park, MD: CHANGE.

———. 2003. *PEPFAR watch: Anti-prostitution pledge*. Retrieved from http://www.pepfarwatch.org/the_issues/anti_prostitution_pledge/. Accessed on June 16, 2014.

Chambers, R. (1997). *Whose reality counts? Putting the first last*. London: IT Publications.

———. (2009). So that the poor count more: Using participatory methods for impact evaluation. *Journal of Development Effectiveness*, 1(3), 243–6.

Chambers, R., Karlan, D., Ravallion, M., and Rogers, P. (2009). *Designing impact evaluations: Different perspectives* (3ie Working Paper No. 4). New Delhi, India: International Initiative for Impact Evaluation (3ie).

Cornwall, A. (2002). Making spaces, changing places: Situating participation in development (IDS Working Paper, Vol. 170). Sussex, UK: Institute for Development Studies.

Cousins, J. and Whitmore, E. (1998). Framing participatory evaluation. In E. Whitmore (ed.), *Understanding and practicing participatory evaluation: New directions for evaluation* (No. 80, pp. 5–23). San Francisco, CA: Jossey-Bass.

Craig, D. and Porter, D. (1997). Framing participation. *Development in Practice*, 7(3), 229–36.

Crishna, B. (2007). Participatory evaluation (I)—Sharing lessons from fieldwork in Asia. *Child: Care, Health & Development*, 33(3), 217–23.

Feuerstein, M-T. (1986). *Partners in evaluation: Evaluating development and community programmes with participants*. London: Macmillan.

Friere, P. (1972). *Pedagogy of the oppressed*. London: Penguin Education.

Ghose, T., Swendeman, D., George, S., and Chowdhury, D. (2008). Mobilizing collective identity to reduce HIV risk among sex workers in Sonagachi, India: The boundaries, consciousness, negotiation framework. *Social Science & Medicine*, 67(2), 311–20.

Hart, R. (1992). *Children's participation: From tokenism to citizenship* (Innocenti Essays No.4). Florence, Italy: UNICEF.

Hart, R. and Rajbhandary, J. (2003). Using participatory methods to further the democratic goals of children's organizations. In K. Sabo (ed.), *Youth participatory evaluation—A field in the making: New directions for evaluation* (No. 98, pp. 61–76). San Francisco, CA: Jossey-Bass.

Hay, K. (2010). Evaluation field building in South Asia: Reflections, anecdotes, and questions *American Journal of Evaluation*, 3(2), 222–31.

Hoque, M. and Itohara, Y. (2008). Participation and decision making role of rural women in economic activities: A comparative study for members and non-members of the micro-credit organizations in Bangladesh. *Journal of Social Sciences*, 4(3), 229–36.

———. (2009). Women empowerment through participation in micro-credit programme: A case study from Bangladesh. *Journal of Social Sciences*, 5(3), 244–50.

Johnson, C. (2003). *Decentralization in India: Poverty, politics, and Panchayati Raj* (Working Paper 199). London: ODI.

Jupp, D. and Ali, S. (2010). *Measuring empowerment? Ask them*. Stockholm, Sweden: Swedish International Development Corporation Agency.

Kakar, S. (1978). *The inner world*. New Delhi: Oxford University Press.

Kaplan, E. (2006, 14 March). Pledges and punishment: Interview with Meena Seshu. *AlterNet*. Retrieved from http://www.alternet.org/story/33284/pledges_and_punishment. Accessed on June 16, 2014.

Kreisberg, S. (1992). *Transforming power: Domination, empowerment and education*. Albany, NY: State University of New York Press.

Lehrer, J. (2010, 13 December). The truth wears off: Is there something wrong with the scientific method? *The New Yorker*. Retrieved from http://www.

newyorker.com/reporting/2010/12/13/101213fa_fact_lehrer#ixzz1AdUH. Accessed on June 16, 2014.

Lotz, J. (1998). *The Lichen Factor: The quest for community development in Canada.* Sydney, Australia: UCCB Press. As quoted in Ramirez, R. (2008). A mediation on meaningful participation. *The Journal of Community Informatics,* 4(3).

Mertens, D.M. (1999). Inclusive evaluation: Implications of transformative theory for evaluation. *American Journal of Evaluation,* 20(1), 1–14.

Munshi, A.A., Miah, A.S.M.J., and Khandaker, L.K. (2011). Social audit: An effective way of downward accountability. In R. Bin Sattar (ed.), *Learning document series* (No. 9–10, pp. 1–12). Dhaka, Bangladesh: Impact Assessment & Shared Learning, ActionAid Bangladesh.

National Institute of Public Cooperation and Child Development. (2006). *Three decades of ICDS: An appraisal.* New Delhi, India: World Bank.

O'Reilly, K. (2010). Combining sanitation and women's participation in water supply: An example from Rajasthan. *Development in Practice,* 20(1), 45–56.

Patel, S. and Bartlett, S. (2009). Reflections on innovation, assessment, and social change: A SPARC case study. *Development in Practice,* 19(1), 3–15.

Porter, S. and de Wet, J. (2009). Who will guard the guardians? Amartya Sen's contribution to development evaluation. *Development in Practice,* 19(3), 288–99.

Poudel, P. and Carryer, J. (2000). Girl-trafficking, HIV/AIDS, and the position of women in Nepal. *Gender and Development,* 8(2), 74–9.

Rahman, M.M., Kabir, M., and Shahidullah, M. (2007). Participation of adolescents in household decision-making process in Bangladesh. *Indian Journal of Community Medicine,* 32(2), 123–7.

Ramirez, R. (2008). A 'meditation' on meaningful participation. *The Journal of Community Informatics,* 4(3). http://ci-journal.net/index.php/ciej/article/view/390/424.

Sainath, P. (1996). *Everybody loves a good drought.* New Delhi, India: Penguin Books.

Segone, M. (2009). Enhancing evidence-based policy making through country-led monitoring and evaluation systems. In M. Segone (Ed.), *Country-led monitoring and evaluation system: Better Evidence, better policies, better development results* (pp. 17–32). Geneva, Switzerland: UNICEF.

Smith, M.F. (1999). Participatory evaluation: Not working or not tested? *American Journal of Evaluation,* 20(2), 295–308.

Suarez-Balcazar, Y. and Harper, G.W. (2003). Community-based approaches to empowerment and participatory evaluation. *Journal of Prevention & Intervention in the Community,* 26(2), 1–4.

Theis, Joachim. (2003) Rights-based monitoring and evaluation: A discussion paper, Save the Children.

Weiss, C.H. (1998). Have we learned anything new about the use of evaluation? *American Journal of Evaluation,* 19(1), 21–33.

White, H. (2009). Theory-based impact evaluation: principles and practice. *Journal of Development Effectiveness*, 1(3), 271–84.

World Bank. (2002). *Empowerment and poverty reduction: A sourcebook.* Washington, DC: World Bank.

Zaveri, S. (2008). *Economic strengthening and children affected by HIV/AIDS in Asia: Role of communities.* Prepared for Joint Learning Initiative on Children and AIDS. Retrieved from http://www.ovcsupport.net.wc01.cfdynamics.com/libsys/Admin/d/DocumentHandler.ashx?id=863. : http://www.ovcsupport.net/s/library.php?ld=947. Accessed on December 2012.

Zaveri, S., Poudyal, U.R., and Carnegie, R. (1997). *Learning from children: A review of child-to-child activities of Save the Children Fund (UK) in Nepal.* Kathmandu, Nepal: Save the Children Fund (UK).

5

Evaluation Rights and Social Justice: Process, Politics, and Positioning in South Asia

Veronica Magar and
Pradeep Narayanan

As with rights and social justice (RSJ) programmes, RSJ evaluations can lead to better and more sustainable results by analysing and addressing inequalities, discriminatory practices, and unjust power relationships, which are often at the heart of most development problems. Specifically, RSJ programmes set the achievement of human rights as a development objective (UN High Commission for Human Rights, 1993). In so doing, they are held accountable for adhering to human rights treaties and universal interpretations of social justice. RSJ evaluation examines *uses* of findings, as well as evaluation processes, in terms of their contribution to the transformation of programmes, individuals, institutions, and communities. By transformation, we mean a shift in perspective that leads to action representing ideals held in human rights and social justice agreements and ideals. This is accomplished largely by facilitating participatory and reflexive evaluation processes with a range of diverse stakeholders. As with RSJ programmes, RSJ evaluations aim to further the rights and justice agenda, irrespective of whether the programme has that in its core agenda or not.

One unique aspect of RSJ-oriented evaluations is the focus on 'use'. Using evaluations as opportunities to construct and share knowledge may seem obvious. However, in day-to-day practice, evaluations often serve different purposes—that is, to politicize or depoliticize the social conditions of poor and marginalized people. There have been instances where evaluations have been misused to regulate neoliberal interests through grantees. These evaluations have had the unfortunate consequence of hampering the state's power or ambit of influence. For example, a report published by the World Bank (Bamberger and Kirk, 2009, pp. 7–8) claims that 'Impact evaluations are (also) used as a *political tool* to provide support for decisions that agencies have already decided upon or would like to make, to mobilize political support for high profile or controversial programmes and to provide political or managerial accountability'. While it is true that many evaluation exercises are not utilized, a number of them are used to obtain 'already pre-determined purposes' (pp. 7–8), giving external agencies extraordinary influence over national programmes and the state at large. This raises conceptual and operational questions about evaluation processes, politics, and positioning in the South Asian context where people's movements have been instrumental in social change. Who owns evaluations? Can evaluations belong to civil society organizations and social movements? How can evaluations be owned by the poor and marginalized, so they have control of knowledge and evidence to ultimately influence the state? What do we mean by participation in evaluation in South Asia?

In her discussion on theories commensurate with the transformational paradigm, Mertens (2008) provides guiding principles in terms of belief systems, including:

- axiology, which emphasizes human rights and social justice;
- ontology, which rejects cultural relativism and acknowledges the influence and consequences of power and privilege in what is deemed real;
- epistemology, which advocates culturally competent relationships between researchers/evaluators and community members; and
- methodology, which employs culturally appropriate mixed methods tied to social action.

RSJ Evaluations in South Asia: Exploring Challenges and Opportunities

While RSJ principles are imperative to ensuring good governance and democracy, evaluators in the South Asia region face several challenges when conducting such evaluations. To better understand these challenges, and the ways they can be overcome, 15 evaluators—representing a range of non-governmental organizations (NGOs) and academic, research, and evaluation institutes across South Asia—convened at the Evaluation Conclave 2010, in Delhi, India. With the aim of exploring the obstacles, challenges, and opportunities that arise during such evaluations in the South Asian context, the convening evaluators shared their own evaluation experiences and findings during a series of facilitated discussions and meetings.

Reflecting the opinions of the evaluators at the conclave, this chapter argues that, within the South Asian context, RSJ evaluations should remain within the scope and reach of the poor and marginalized to use to achieve sociopolitical rights and justice ends. Specifically, programme beneficiaries should have access to evaluation processes and findings and the means and capacity to use the findings. It argues for a common set of principles based on diverse methodologies and approaches that are not only rigorous but are also able to map out and highlight inequities, challenge power disparities, and be used for transformational purposes. The authors draw upon examples in their own evaluation practice in South Asia to illustrate key points and contribute to global discussions.

Defining RSJ Evaluations

Like all evaluations, RSJ evaluations use systematic methods to collect, analyse, and use information to understand programmes and policies, but they also capture inequities, exclusion, and violations of rights, whether or not this goal is implicit in the project objectives. While many programmes aim to foster social and political change, an RSJ lens can be applied to any intervention, even if these aims are not stated project objectives. While a range of methodologies can be used to carry this out, the authors argue that such evaluations should go beyond the purely objective to include measures of change that contribute to the collective struggle central to the programme aims. In the sense, the analysis of benefits of the project would also include an examination of how the benefits align with the rights of the marginalized. For example, in an evaluation of a micro-finance programme for women, irrespective of the objective of evaluation, an RSJ approach will include whether the programme perpetuates any practices of patriarchy directly or indirectly, whether or not this a stated goal of the programme.

Compared with other approaches, participatory and transformative evaluation approaches are better aligned to RSJ evaluation. This is because they engage stakeholders in learning and consciousness-raising processes. Rather than merely a collection of tools or a list of techniques, participatory and transformative approaches consist of a set of principles informing processes, which increase learning and empowerment (Harnar, 2012). While the results and recommendations of evaluation findings are considered important with participatory and transformative evaluation approaches, the processes are perhaps valued more, since it is through the processes that participants learn. Cousins and Whitmore (1998) emphasize intrinsic approaches of inquiry, which, unlike instrumental participation,[1] generate greater consciousness among people, thus building confidence in their ability to create change. Such inquiry, like other reflective participatory interventions, will itself be transformative for the project stakeholders as well as the intended beneficiaries.

RSJ evaluations require an evaluation model that contributes to social change, such as transformative participatory evaluation (T-PE). T-PE builds on participatory evaluation (PE) by engaging stakeholders representing culturally diverse groups to achieve social change and justice goals (Mertens, 2008). T-PE uses participatory inquiry that encourages collective knowledge creation (Burke, 1998; Mertens, 2008; Meyer et al., 1998). As with participatory action research, T-PE includes reflective practice exercises throughout the project cycle, which help stakeholders explore programme strengths and challenges and modify their actions accordingly. A second key concept that defines T-PE is the instrumental role of human agency in knowledge creation—through dialogue, knowledge use, and information sharing (Harnar, 2012). As knowledge informs the evaluation, its creators are empowered by seeing their knowledge at use (Brisolara, 1998; Cousins and Whitmore, 1998; Harnar, 2012; Sabo, 1999). Social change through empowerment is the hallmark of transformative evaluation. If programmes claim to 'empower' individuals, agency must be apparent within the context of collective agency. Indeed, empowerment cannot happen in isolation. Accordingly, collective empowerment is enacted at the policy level, largely through social movements, networks, coalitions, and campaigns.

Challenges in RSJ Evaluation

The South Asian evaluators at the 2010 Evaluation Conclave reported that they enjoy being able to conduct RSJ evaluations since they are consistent with their value system. However, several challenges keep evaluators from delivering strong evaluation products. Robust evaluation **frameworks** that are both relevant and precise in light of RSJ ideals are neither obvious nor implicit in the programmes being evaluated. Moreover, many evaluators face barriers in both applying effective evaluation approaches and in ensuring use. For example, trying to 'measure' abstract RSJ concepts runs the risk of oversimplifying them, as described in the examples below. At the same time, evaluations often lack adequate and consistent **rigour**, which compromises credibility and may have an impact on programme resourcing and evaluation. That is, donors are increasingly hesitant to get into challenging territory to measure abstract but necessary variables, for these would require a greater investment in designing the methodology itself. Lack of resources force evaluators to continue with simplistic variables, which do not do justice or adequately reflect the concept or variable being examined. Perhaps most challenging is ensuring evaluation **use** by engaging programme participants as well as civil society and other key stakeholders.

Findings, Frameworks, and Evaluator Responsibilities: Practicalities of Changing Practice

The 15 participants agreed that a given programme being evaluated will have its own theory of change and an assessment frame as stated in the logical project framework (log frame). These frames may or may not

adhere to notions of human rights and social justice. An example provided by a participant was an evaluation of a women's empowerment
programme that included indicators such as the number of self-help
groups (SHGs) formed, but it did not include indicators that assessed the
role of micro-finance programmes overall in defining women's empowerment, especially indicators related to the incidence of suicide among
families that are part of a micro-finance programme. The indicators
used, for example, might not reveal that many families feeling trapped by
monthly dues often experience family violence and even suicide. Therefore, there is a need for evaluators to challenge evaluation frameworks
to ensure RSJ principles and concepts are brought to the fore. As with
this example of empowerment mismeasurement, many projects overuse
the term 'empowerment'. If a project claims to empower communities,
the key components of an empowerment theory should exist in the
evaluation framework. For example, concepts such as 'individual and
collective agency' are often absent in programmes that aim to empower
communities. An evaluation framework claiming to measure empowerment would have to take 'power' into account in relation to a person's
or group's agency (Gaventa, 2006), whether or not it is in the programme objectives.

Evaluators should assume responsibility for challenging guiding
frameworks that are inadequate in measuring constructs they claimed
to have changed, as in the case of empowerment and agency. The evaluator may consider aligning values and concepts through the process of
agreeing on a 'terms of reference' with the contracting agency. Although
participants expressed valid concerns about their ideas being rejected,
most agreed that managers welcome evaluators' expert advice and are
willing to negotiate conceptual and practical changes.

Use of Standardized Frames

Some evaluators asserted that using predetermined and non-flexible
standardized frames with communities is antithetical to participation
because such frames restrict community voices. In such cases, participation is reduced to information extraction from communities rather than
collective learning across the community. For example, in many closed-
ended schedules, the choices provided do not reflect the real intent of
response from community members. For example, in one study on HIV
communities, we went with a frame where we defined the rights in the

context of health alone. However, the targeted population—sex workers—considered other rights—such as those of safety, dignity, and participation in governance—to be more significant. In a large-scale evaluation, where there is a need for a standard analytical frame, often the real community issues cease to get a space. In this kind of scenario, the participation of communities becomes tokenistic, in the sense that it is used to fit the frame of evaluators.

A standard frame actually assumes one single pathway of change. While useful in aggregating, it risks imposing measures upon communities whose responses would be varied otherwise. For example, when supporting women's empowerment in the SHG model, a standard evaluation frame excludes recognition of both other forms of economic empowerment and any negative effects on women's rights. It may also lead to questionable or biased conclusions. With the standard frame, it is more likely that negative effects will go unnoticed because they are not explicitly included. A husband may want his wife to be in an SHG since it will benefit the family, but she may refuse to join an SHG, since she may have learned in the local woman's collective that joining an SHG will trap her. The women's collective project would consider her empowered, having made such an informed decision. The SHG project, on the other hand, would consider her disempowered.

Elusive Empowerment Measures

Evaluators agreed that it is challenging to change mainstream evaluation thinking to include critical thinking frameworks. This places evaluators in a difficult position when they wish to wriggle such frameworks into the discourse and practice.

Neither programme implementers nor evaluators analyse RSJ adequately, since different power contestations are not included in a way that affirms political transformation. Some of the evaluators reported that without examining power structures, evaluations are not used effectively in these contexts. Empowerment is recognized insofar as it can be measured by quantifiable outcomes, which mistakenly leads agencies to define transformation in narrow terms—usually with economic indicators, such as increasing household income or microcredit saving.

Perhaps empowerment cannot be measured only in quantifiable terms common across all contexts. The assumption that indicators need to be SMART—that is, specific, measurable, attainable, relevant, and time bound—may actually be *not so smart*, since they tend to oversimplify complex concepts ensconced within layered meanings that are specific to the various unique and irregular situations in which programmes are situated. By not capturing the complexities, marginalization experienced by vulnerable populations is actually masked.

Empowerment is often measured inadequately through misplaced proxy behavioural indicators. An HIV/AIDS prevention programme, for example, may report that sex workers 'are empowered to use condoms'—where condom use is an indicator of their empowerment. Similarly, a 50-rupee-a-month payment by SHG members is understood erroneously to be a measure of collective power and control. Women who are empowered should be able to negotiate more than just condoms and monthly transmittals. Ironically, studies show that both sex workers and SHG members are likely to experience higher levels of abuse and little increase in decision-making opportunities at household levels as condom use and SHG contributions increase (Mohindra et al., 2008; Pettifor et al., 2010; Wee et al., 2004). Empowerment and participation are integral to overcoming obstacles associated with poverty and development (UN General Assembly, 2009).

Most of the evaluators argued that while there is a need for aggregation, scaling up, and adequate sample size, we should be careful not to obscure the real context. Clarity around context can be achieved by using mixed methods and allowing the qualitative data ground the quantitative findings to illuminate the nuances and detail.

Evaluation Methodology: Rigour and Credibility

RSJ evaluators raised methodological concerns related to rigour and scale. Although participatory tools and activities are quite advanced in South Asia, qualitative research using both participatory and extractive practices is often flawed. The actual problem may lie in the fact that rigorous techniques and processes are more challenging to apply with qualitative methods, and therefore, these methods are often substandard. More specifically, qualitative studies and evaluations tend to pay less attention to precision and accuracy and rely more on anecdotal evidence directed by the evaluator, as evidenced by the experience of one evaluator, who said:

I once pulled myself off a very important five-year review of a government programme focusing on gender and social exclusion because the lead partner did not want to use an analytical framework and said, 'C'mon you know you end up saying what you want to anyway.'

As a result of quality issues with qualitative research and ways quantitative evaluation dominates the field of evaluation, evaluators at the conclave noted that these findings are seen by the managers with whom they work as of little use. Instead of dismissing qualitative methods and, thereby, mixed methods, it would be better to ensure qualitative studies are conducted with adequate rigour so they become more legitimate in the eyes of donors, programme implementers, and the evaluation community.

Participants also expressed methodological concerns—specifically a loss of robustness—over the process of scaling and standardizing, particularly when conducting large-scale PE. Scaling and standardizing make it difficult to capture the community dynamics specific to each locale as well as the variation in opinions within a community. To the surprise of many, disagreements among community members about crucial issues do exist. In the women's rights community, for example, differing views on sex work exist. Some feminists see it as 'a right', others as 'violence'. Similarly, some addiction activists believe drug users should be denied citizen rights, and others uphold the rights of all citizens, regardless of their drug use. These differing views are contextual. Evaluations often present communities' views as homogeneous.

In terms of methodological challenges, it is also difficult to assign numerical value to a set of processes and outcomes. However, it is possible to do so working with the community. One of the authors, for example, conducted an evaluation to measure community group strength and community ownership of a programme. The evaluator facilitated community dialogues to develop the indicators, which corresponded to a continuum of progress (see Tables 5.1 and 5.2). For example, in the context of an NGO facilitating the formation and strengthening of a community-based organization (CBO), a scale[2] was developed to assign numeric value to responses about the transitioning of lead roles from NGO to community leadership (see Table 5.1).

Table 5.1
Scale Used to Measure Status of Leadership Transition

Lead role (Who is taking lead role in different actions by the community collective?)	NGO official	NGO-employed community members	Community member/leader voluntarily
Numeric value assigned	1	2	4
Reason	Leadership is still with NGO staff	Community members are able to take leadership role but still have the support of NGO management	Dependency on NGO has become almost negligible
Process of developing the numeric value	Relative weights were assigned in a discussion organized with community leaders, who have been leading the groups for a minimum of three years, on the basis of agreeing on a continuum, which maps the progress of a CBO in terms of its independent existence.		
Limitation	It is difficult to substantiate why we are assigning value of 1 to Category 1, but it is not difficult to state that Category 3 should get a better score than Category 1.		
Principle	The principles followed are of participation and transparency. The values were assigned after consultation with the community. The rationale for the value assigned is stated upfront while presenting the analysis.		

Source: Table prepared for this paper based on tools used by Praxis for Community Mobilisation Monitoring Project of Avahan programme.

The numeric value was assigned through a discussion with community leaders who had been leading the groups for at least three years. Values were assigned such that they assumed relative weights on the basis of an agreed continuum of progress in terms of the CBO's independent existence. While the intrinsic value for a response cannot be justified, the relative weights are not difficult to justify. What is important is the principle of participation and transparency. There was community participation in assigning values, which were also shared during the presentation of the analysis to the community.

Table 5.2 shows the process and definitions used to assign numeric value in a different situation where the goal was to assess community engagement on rights and entitlements.

RSJ evaluations rely on a variety of methodologies, including qualitative, quantitative, and participatory approaches. However, most participants felt that in the context of RSJ evaluations, theories of change are difficult to define and, hence, require constructivist approaches,[3] often considered too 'soft' by those who commission evaluations, as

Table 5.2
Scale Used to Measure Community Engagement

Engagement by community groups on different rights and entitlements	Community members in the governing body are aware of different aspects of rights, provisions of law, and the knowledge on responsible duty-bearers	Community leaders are not only aware but are also able to cite examples where they have actually engaged with corresponding authorities on rights and entitlements	Through collective actions, community members have actually been able to claim entitlements for members through a sustained process
Numeric value assigned	1	2	4
Reason	Community has been able to get to know about details on rights, probably through a set of training or exposures.	While community members are able to use the knowledge to initiate collective action on such issues, they have yet to see results in their favour. Results here are in terms of creating platforms with authorities.	The activity is entirely in the community domain. Community leaders are able to create platforms with authorities
Process of developing the numeric value	The relative weights were assigned in a discussion organized with community leaders, who have been leading the groups for a minimum of three years, the basis of significance of the question.		

Source: Table prepared for this chapter based on tools used by Praxis for Community Mobilisation Monitoring Project of Avahan Programme.

they are considered to be too open to 'anecdotal interpretation'. Since knowledge is constructed from experiences and internalized by learners, participatory methods are most useful in explaining the issues of RSJ from multiple perspectives, especially those not compatible with evaluator's analysis framework. However, those commissioning evaluations often dismiss constructivist approaches because of a seeming lack of appropriate rigour. Many of the evaluators argued that quantitative measures are considered more robust by those in the social development industry—including donors, international and domestic NGOs, corporations, and universities. The authors believe, however, that the qualitative-quantitative binary argument is misplaced, since mixed methods are of particular value when the evaluation is trying to solve a problem in a complex social context (Mertens, 2003, 2008, 2010; Teddlie and Tashakkori, 2009). Mixed methods can be used to answer questions that are difficult or impossible to answer using a single method.

In most cases, if an evaluation aimed to understand collective action and collective ownership, the evaluators deliberately focused on group responses rather than individual responses. Group, rather than individual, interviews were undertaken. The challenge in the group interview process, however, is to both aggregate *and* capture multiple views. For example, one of the group members may know about their rights and entitlements, whereas others may not.

The group interviews provide a space for members to discuss different interpretations of the facts, before responding conclusively. For instance, a lead role can be understood in terms of planning, auctioning, or mobilizing; group discussion allows members to explore these nuances. The assessment frame is very much dialogic rather than directive.

Not only can the group interview approach be compatible with the programme intent—to support community mobilization, for example—it can also be important in measuring the strength of the group and their collective understanding about specific issues. Not surprisingly, one participant's team faced major challenges in measuring group agency in a collective action project. This was largely because terms such as 'mobilization', 'ownership', 'vision', 'democracy', and 'collective leadership' were considered too abstract and, therefore, too difficult to measure using only individual interviews.

Evaluation Use

Stakeholder Engagement

Evaluators at the workshop noted that managers often do not enable evaluators to involve stakeholders—both from implementing organizations and the project beneficiaries themselves—in evaluation processes. Specifically, more involved participatory approaches that enhance knowledge construction and sharing are, at times, considered to be a drain on human and financial resources. As a result, evaluation processes generally focus only on results and miss opportunities to promote organizational and grassroots engagement, learning, and collective agency. According to Patton (1997, p. 90), evaluation *process use* describes changes in thinking and behaviour—at the individual, programme, and/or organizational level—because of one's participation in an evaluation, irrespective of the evaluation results. Such changes are necessary for transformation, which is the aim of most RSJ programmes.

The authors believe that evaluators generally fail to include difficult-to-reach communities in identifying equity-related issues in achieving RSJ aims. According to one participant, evaluators do not ensure that the 'silent ones', the ones who aren't normally able to make their views known, are involved or heard. One PE exercise discussed at the conclave workshop identified key health equity gaps in a national programme aiming to improve child health and nutrition measures. The participatory review demonstrated that although the programme was considered a great success, since statistically significant changes were demonstrated across most of the outcome measures, these encouraging changes benefited only an elite cadre of villagers; families living in particular locations (usually represented by lower caste, tribal, and religious minority groups) were consistently excluded from essential programme services. What this exercise did that a quantitative survey could not do was to engage community stakeholders in order to understand their situation and take action in collaboration with the programme-implementing agency. What ensued was a series of programme changes to which implementing field staff and communities were committed to enacting.

Some evaluators noted that with a cross-sectional survey-based study, the steps of reporting findings, making an analysis, and deriving inferences are done sequentially, one after the other. The views of community find a place only at the reporting stage, where community members represent only one of a larger set of stakeholder respondents. An analysis team, often without community representation, conducts the analysis and derives inferences. A survey, because of standardization and regardless of length, will not be able to elicit different context scenarios. Similarly, many evaluators do not include participants in case study analyses or other qualitative designs. Lack of engagement in the various stages of evaluation—from setting the questions, analysing the data, and using the findings—is common. Participatory and transformatory tools allow communities to present their own scenarios of success and failure and are particularly well matched to RSJ evaluations by soliciting solutions to overcome barriers. Community, and especially beneficiary, observations and suggestions complement the inferences derived from an analysis of findings and are an integral aspect of any evaluation.

Engaging Community Social Organizations and Social Movements: Effective Use of Evaluation Findings

According to Merten's guiding principles of evaluation within RSJ contexts (presented at the beginning of this chapter), evaluation use and processes are political. Using (or not using) evaluations to support RSJ, reject cultural relativism, and acknowledge power and privilege is political and must be tied to social action. In this context, evaluators must consider expanding the pool of evaluation users—in addition to programme managers and participants (whether or not they are directly involved in the evaluation), social movements have a key role to play in RSJ agendas and, along with communities, groups representing women, dalits, and the most poor, should have access to evaluation findings. Indeed, in addition to limited *process use* opportunities, as described previously, evaluators generally do not engage activists and social movement reformers in the use of evaluation findings. Since national independence struggles across the region began, social movements have contributed to social and political change on all levels in South Asia. This is largely because they aim to remove authority from the centres of power by creating decentralized and democratized structures and systems.[4] Yet applied researchers and evaluators remain distant from the needs of social movement actors, perhaps in part to remain impartial and in part because they do not see it as their mandate.

Not surprisingly, many of the evaluators agreed that reports have limited use and are directed generally towards managers and donors and not towards civil society organizations and social movements (through networks and coalitions) as primary users. In addition to the value and importance of sharing positive findings, negative findings have important implications that social movements can leverage. For example, large-scale programmes often produce unintended harmful effects, such as those described previously where improving health service delivery also reinforced existing inequities. Social movement actors should have opportunities to engage with both positive and negative findings. Most evaluators agreed that sharing evaluation findings with social movements is an untapped avenue for generating effective use of the findings.

However, it is also important to differentiate between NGOs and social movements. NGOs, and civil society in general, may not be associated with a social movement affected by a programme policy with unintended adverse effects for the poor and/or marginalized. Many evaluators agreed that NGOs often play harmful rather than mediating roles, since they are often more loyal to their donors than to the people they are serving. Evaluators must be clear about their allegiance. To do this, they must know the context.

Most successful social movements run with very limited resources, largely in the spirit of volunteerism. Civil society representatives have a right to information produced by evaluations. Recently in India, for example, civil society organizations addressed the National AIDS Control Organization of the government to commission evaluations and studies to prepare for their next five-year plan.[5] For the most part, however, evaluator experience with RSJ evaluations shows a lack of engagement with broader community social organizations (CSOs) or community members. One evaluator commented:

> I conducted a country-wide evaluation on women's empowerment and violence against women, as part of a larger food security programme. We found that while women's empowerment improve[d] around some empowerment measures, the focus of this programme excluded men. As a result, lacking any responsive intervention with the men, project field staff relied on quick (slipshod) wins—that is, to threaten errant men with laws to ensure their compliance. The newly formed women's collectives misrepresented the law. As a result, many men were falsely arrested, jailed, and intimidated.
>
> Unwittingly, these flawed practices did not lead to the kind of dignifying social change that the implementing agency had actually intended. While

I had informal discussions with leading activists, since they were involved since the design phase, there was no formal engagement with CSOs and the women's movement at large. There was a missed opportunity to engage in a broader debate on shifting movement-focus away from preoccupation with law reform and more on changing social norms. While I engaged with women's movement leader, informally, there was no formal way [to share] the findings . . . with women's movement stakeholders.

Most participants reported that limited evaluation skills have an impact on how evaluation is used to address RSJ issues in the South Asia region. RSJ evaluation requires an additional set of evaluation skills. In addition to structured training opportunities, most felt that reflective adult learning techniques—learning by doing and reflexive feedback—are the most effective ways to learn such methodologies. Co-creating knowledge is critical to this end. According to one participant:

While Praxis Institute of Participatory Practices [an organization committed to building capacity around participatory methods] has been organizing workshops on participatory monitoring and evaluation, every project that it undertakes gives new challenges. There is definitely not a single blueprint for participatory methodologies, but there is a set of principles for institutionalizing participation in the programme. These are ones that you learn through doing. Several sets of standard participatory tools now exist. These get used by many organizations. In my mind, they defy the principle of participation. Instead of learning by doing, you learn by copying. Final sets of tools should evolve with the community in their own contexts. Due to constraints of time and need for aggregation, evaluators too often impose standardized tools on the community, which negates the practice of experiential learning and co-creating knowledge.

As this quote illustrates, evaluating RSJ requires continuous engagement with stakeholders as well as oneself. The evaluator must balance the need to use standardized tools with the need to use tools and approaches that are flexible and responsive to community needs.

Ways Forward

At the 2010 Evaluation Conclave, evaluators explored what could help move the evaluation field forward, with a focus on RSJ, in South Asia.

They identified two areas of change: (i) evaluation culture, approaches, and principles, and (ii) building capacity to use an appropriate combination of mixed methods.

Evaluation Culture, Approaches, and Principles: Doing Justice to RSJ

Evaluators should convene to develop community-based platforms that encourage engagement with governments and donors. To this end, a culture of evaluation by those commissioning evaluations might be cultivated by developing T-PE guidelines and principles, based on home-grown approaches. These can be developed and promoted as standards (not prototypes), which could be used to advocate for certain non-negotiable components. On the basis of discussions with evaluators at the conclave, we identified three key evaluation principles consistent with Mertens' beliefs described earlier. These include ensuring that marginalized groups are visible and that their voices are heard within evaluation processes, from the design stage to analysis and dissemination; identifying social justice dimensions in the analytical and guiding framework; and ensuring rigorous methodologies, with frameworks and questions that include multiple inputs, contexts, and stakeholder groups (with no one excluded). What is perhaps an addition to Mertens' rendering is the need to find a balance between rigour and reflexivity (see Box 5.1). This, we feel, is important, since RSJ evaluations also need to demonstrate impact and behavioural changes (or lack of) in order to be appropriately accountable to communities.

Box 5.1: Key Evaluation Principles

1. Ensure that marginalized groups are visible and that their voices are heard within evaluation processes, from the design stage to analysis and discussion.
2. Identify social justice dimensions in the analytical and guiding framework.
3. Ensure rigorous methodologies, with frameworks and questions that include multiple inputs, contexts, and stakeholder groups (with no one excluded).
4. Find a balance between rigour and reflexivity.

Debating What Success Looks Like

Similarly, the evaluator is responsible for ensuring an appropriate mix of methodologies that are both rigorous and clear from the design stage. Evaluators should place their values and beliefs upfront in a transparent manner, expressing the subjective nature of the work, while also balancing enquiry with advocacy. Evaluators should remain accountable to communities by selecting appropriate stakeholders to participate and sharing findings. Sharing objectionable findings with managers and donors can be difficult. Unwelcome findings should be handled in a way that offers those being evaluated—project managers, donors, and other stakeholders—a way to learn from the project's or programme's challenges or mistakes. Communication, both written and oral, is critical to this end. Including and mentoring project managers throughout evaluation processes as team members is perhaps the best way this is accomplished. It requires reflection and empathy on the part of the evaluator as well, who needs to be motivated and willing to keep connected, while preserving enough distance to remain committed to the findings.

Often, an evaluator has to define the success of a programme to be able to evaluate it. Different stakeholders may define success in different ways. Donors might have one set of indicators of success, whereas an implementing organization might have another set. On the other hand, the beneficiary community members may actually see the success of a programme as being dependent on a very different set of indicators. The evaluator needs to forefront community-identified indicators while bringing all stakeholders on board and finding alignment across communities, managers, and donors.

Process strategies to enhance use require that, together with evaluators, programme managers identify stakeholders, beyond immediate users, who are directly involved with the programme. By sharing findings with key social movement representatives, evaluations can provide knowledge and evidence that can be used to transform systems of injustice.

Building Capacity: RSJ Evaluation Capacity and Demand in South Asia

The evaluators at the conclave recommended building local evaluation capacity to be able to maintain and reflect the complexity of programmes, contexts, and measures, keeping in mind the linkage between narratives and results. This would strengthen evaluation practice in the region and would be reflected in principles and practices specific to South Asian contexts. Many tools have been developed and continue to evolve in the region; these can be evaluated and, based on their rigour and grounding in critical theory, integrated into best practices. In this way, they could be used outside a limited group of practitioners to influence the global evaluation discourse. Most participatory theories are developed and disseminated from the North to the South. Yet most participatory practice has emerged from the South and from South Asia in particular. Building and sharing this participatory practice and expertise would expand the existing vertical learning (local experiences with communities on the ground shared with evaluators) to develop horizontal learning opportunities (in which knowledge is constructed and shared among colleagues in South Asia and across the globe).

Creating Demand for Change

What we have learned from RSJ evaluators is perhaps not new but will require deliberate action if it is to be used to strengthen and develop the field. Interpreting changes in people's actions and accomplishments is more than the application of the 'right' method. It includes ensuring that new knowledge is used for future programming through a broad understanding about people's right to access and participation in evaluations. Evaluation should be repositioned so that communities and other stakeholders play a more central role. To this end, evaluators and the development industry at large should create a demand for transformative evaluation, within RSJ contexts, to bring about change. Many conclave participants felt that evaluators 'have a moral responsibility to make that happen'. It was felt that transformatory evaluation practices would not only thrive but be also strengthened by use in the 'fertile ground' that exists in south Asia. Accordingly, such practices could be fine-tuned while systematically building local capacity.

Evaluators leading RSJ evaluations must be grounded in political notions of RSJ. An important aspect of being politicized is not only seeing and experiencing inequities through an analytical lens but also feeling duty-bound to take action. Together with other politicized people, these evaluators are committed to transformative social change. This requires evaluators to be reflective *and* to take a stand on relevant issues and commit to transformative social change.

Notes

1. Instrumental participation is where 'participants contribute services or financial contributions, [and] is used by development providers to reduce costs, and by the participants to gain access to a service'. Transformative participation is where 'participants determine their own needs and priorities and take collective action to achieve these, [and] is seen by either party as a means of empowerment' (White, 1996, pp. 6–15). With respect to evaluation, while an instrumental participation of inquiry restricts participants to provide just information, the transformative approach provides participants a say in the objective of evaluation as well as the analysis of findings.
2. The scale referred to here is called COPI, that is, Community Ownership and Preparedness Index. For further details on this measurement, see Narayanan et al. (2012).
3. Constructivism is a theory of learning in which humans generate knowledge and meaning from an interaction between their experiences and their ideas.
4. See, for example, deepening decentralization in states such as Kerala, India, to transfer decision-making to the village level.
5. The National AIDS Control Organisation has five-year programme called National AIDS Control Programme (NACP). In 2011, it launched the consultation for evolving NACP-4.

References

Bamberger, M. and Kirk, A. (2009). *Making smart policy—Using impact evaluation for policy making: Case studies on evaluations that influenced policy: Doing impact evaluation series* (No. 14). Washington, D.C.: World Bank (PREM).

Brisolara, S. (1998). The history of participatory evaluation and current debates in the field. In E. Whitmore (ed.), *Understanding and practicing participatory evaluation: New directions for evaluation* (No. 80, pp. 25–41). San Francisco, CA: Jossey-Bass.

Burke, B. (1998). Evaluating for a change: Reflections on participatory methodology. In E. Whitmore (ed.), *Understanding and practicing participatory evaluation: New directions for evaluation* (No. 80, pp. 43–56). San Francisco, CA: Jossey-Bass.

Cousins, J.B. and Whitmore, E. (1998). Framing participatory evaluation. In E. Whitmore (ed.), *Understanding and practicing participatory evaluation: New directions for evaluation* (No. 80, pp. 5–23). San Francisco, CA: Jossey-Bass.

Gaventa, J. (2006). Finding the spaces for change: A power analysis. *IDS Bulletin*, 37(6), 23–33.

Harnar, M.A. (2012). *Theory building through praxis discourse: A theory-and-practice-informed model of transformative participatory evaluation* (Doctoral dissertation, Claremont Graduate University). Retrieved from http://scholarship. claremont.edu/cgu_etd/57. Accessed on June 16, 2014.

Mertens, D.M. (2003). Mixed methods and the politics of human research: The transformative-emancipatory perspective. In A. Tashakkori and C. Teddlie (eds), *Handbook of mixed methods in social and behavioral research* (pp. 135–64). Thousand Oaks, CA: SAGE Publications.

———. (2008). *Transformative research and evaluation*. New York: Guilford.

———. (2010). *Research and evaluation in education and psychology: Integrating diversity with quantitative, qualitative and mixed methods. Thousand Oaks, CA: SAGE Publications.*

Meyer, L.H., Park, H.S., Grenot-Scheyer, M., Schwartz, I., and Harry, B. (1998). Participatory research: New approaches to the research to practice dilemma. *Research and Practice for Persons with Severe Disabilities*, 23(3), 165–77.

Mohindra, K.S., Haddad, S., and Narayana, D. (2008). Can microcredit help improve the health of poor women? Some findings from a cross-sectional study in Kerala, India. *International Journal for Equity in Health*, 7(2).

Patton, M.Q. (1997). *Utilization-focused evaluation: The new century text* (3rd ed.). Thousand Oaks, CA: SAGE Publications..

Pettifor, A., Turner, A.N., Swezey, T., Khan, M., Raharinivo, M.S., Randrianasolo, B., Penmar-Aguilar, A., Van Damme, K., Jamieson, D.J., and Behets, F. (2010). Perceived control over condom use among sex workers in Madagascar: A cohort study. *BMC Women's Health*, 10(1), 4.

Pradeep Narayanan. (2012). Embedding Social Transformative Approach within Monitoring and Evaluation (M&E), Reflecting Gender Equality and Human Rights in Evaluation, UNWOMEN.

Sabo, K. (1999). *Young people's involvement in evaluating the programs that serve them*. Digital dissertations, UMI.

Suarez-Herrera, J.C., Springett, J., and Kagan, C. (2009). Critical connections between participatory evaluation, organizational learning, and intentional change in pluralistic organizations. *Evaluation*, 15(3), 321–42. Retrieved from http://umontreal.academia.edu/JoseCarlosSuarezHerrera/Papers/1253197/ Critical_Connections_between_Participatory_Evaluation_Organizational_ Learning_and_Intentional_Change_in_Pluralistic_Organizations. Accessed on January 31, 2014.

Teddlie, C. and Tashakkori, A. (eds). (2009). *Foundations of mixed methods research: Integrating quantitative and qualitative approaches in the social and behavioral sciences*. Thousand Oaks, CA: SAGE Publications.

Thomas, T., Narayanan, P., Wheeler, T., Kiran, U., Joseph, M.J., and Ramanathan, T.V. (2012). Design of a Community Ownership and Preparedness Index: Using data to inform the capacity development of community-based groups. *Journal of Epidemiology and Community Health*, 66(Suppl. 2), ii26–ii33.

UN Development Programme. (2000). *United Nations Millennium Declaration*. Retrieved 2 January 2008 from http://www.un.org/millennium/declaration/ares552e.pdf.

UN General Assembly. (2009). *Report of the Secretary General: Legal empowerment of the poor and the eradication of poverty*. New York: UN.

UN High Commission for Human Rights. (1993). *Vienna Declaration and Program of Action*. World Conference on Human Rights, General Assembly (A/CONF.157/23). New York: UN.

Wee, S., Barrett, M.E., Lian, W.M., Jayabaskar, T., and Chan, K.W.R. (2004). Determinants of inconsistent condom use with female sex workers among men attending the STD clinic in Singapore. *Sexually Transmitted Infections*, 80(4), 310–14.

White, S. (1996). Depoliticising development: The uses and abuses of participation. *Development in Practice*, 6(1), 6–15.

6

An Evaluation Practitioner's Journey with Utilization-focused Evaluation

Chelladurai Solomon and
Sarah Earl

Introduction

Much is being written about specific evaluation methodologies, frameworks, and tools in an effort to build evaluation theory and practice in general. This chapter is an account of my (Chelladurai Solomon) journey, as an evaluation practitioner, with utilization-focused evaluation (UFE), its application in information and communication technology for development (ICT4D) in Asia, and how it has transformed my evaluation practice. The purpose of the chapter is to share my learning experience to benefit evaluation practitioners as well as to help build the field of evaluation, specifically in an Asian context. The rigour and systematic approach and the 'use' value in the UFE framework have influenced how I see evaluation and how I approach terms of reference (TORs) for any evaluation exercise. In my experience, the UFE framework helps to fill the gaps experienced by evaluation practitioners in this part of the world.

This chapter deals largely with my experience during the period 2010–2011, with the Developing Evaluation Capacity in ICT4D (DECI) research project[1] and draws on other evaluation and research experiences I have had in Asia. It starts with an introduction profiling my background in evaluation and then moves on to capture the context of the action research project test-driving UFE, the findings on my role as a mentor and the dynamics of that role, the challenges encountered through the process of implementing UFE, and the resulting change in my perspective. The chapter concludes with thoughts on the mentoring role in UFE, the DECI approach to this role, and what other evaluators can expect when learning UFE.

Pulled into the Social Development Sector

With an academic background in sociology and management, I started my career as a management person in social development projects implemented by non-governmental organizations (NGOs) and international non-governmental organizations (INGOs) in South Asia, and especially in India. Gradually, I got pulled completely into the social development sector and developed a fascination for 'management expertise' in that sector. My two decades of experience in the sector were as researcher, strategic programme planner, and evaluator. The research was in the areas of grassroots governance—Panchayat Raj in India; human rights—child labourers in sericulture; indigenous people—socio-economic status of the scavenging community in India, land rights, and dalits; and livelihood—the National Rural Employment Guarantee Scheme and its implementation. As a prerequisite, I had always ensured that I was engaged in research projects that were not purely academic exercises but that led to action—supporting the development of strategic programmes and projects benefiting particular groups of marginalized people.

Monitoring and evaluation of development projects came along with the research experience, and for the past 15 years, evaluation has become my professional focus, especially in South Asia. During these years, I was involved in the evaluations of projects that ranged from livelihood development to tsunami rehabilitation.

I have been associated with the Community of Evaluators (CoE), South Asia, since its inception in 2008. The CoE is a network of evaluators from South Asia, and its goal is to advance evaluation theory and practice in the region. My increasing involvement with its activities has expanded and strengthened my learning in evaluation and my contribution to evaluation field building in South Asia.

Context: Grasping the 12 Steps of UFE

UFE is a 12-step process for conducting evaluations with a focus on 'use', first described by Dr Michael Quinn Patton in his seminal book, *Utilization-focused Evaluation*. Patton is an independent organizational development and evaluation consultant and a former president of the American Evaluation Association.

While I was able to grasp the 12 steps of UFE, it was only after completing the year-long process of mentoring with the five Pan Asia Networking (PAN) projects of the International Development Research Centre (IDRC)/ DECI that the UFE concept and framework sunk in and I was able to comprehend completely the real impact of UFE. Both the process and outcome have been rewarding. As I continue to use UFE, the 12 steps of UFE have become the guideposts for moving an evaluation process forward. The following is a summary of the 12 steps as paraphrased by DECI:

- Step 1 is ascertaining **organizational readiness**. It is the primary evaluation of a client's commitment to doing useful evaluation within the UFE framework, the readiness to spend time and resources, and the willingness to enhance the readiness.
- Step 2 is assessing the **evaluator's readiness and capability.** This step looks at the match between the evaluator's knowledge, belief in the UFE philosophy, and skills, and what will be needed in the evaluation.
- Step 3 is the **identification of the primary intended users/user groups.** These would be the people who have the primary stake in the evaluation and are interested and knowledgeable about the programme and are open, credible, influential, reachable, ready to take ownership of the process and available for interactions.

- Step 4 is a **situational analysis** of the people and context. This involves looking at the particular context for the evaluation, including the organization's previous experiences in evaluation, its clarity on programme goals and objectives, the barriers and factors that might contribute to success, the on-going timeline of the organization, and the consequences of omitting any particular group or person when identifying the primary intended users.

- Step 5 is the **identification of primary intended uses**. This step looks at how the evaluation could contribute to programme improvement, making major decisions about the programme, and generating knowledge.

- Step 6 is **focusing evaluation** to ensure that all high-priority questions identified by the primary intended users and uses are addressed in the evaluation design.

- Step 7 is **designing the evaluation.** This step looks at the evaluation design and methodology and ensures that they match the intended use, are appropriate to the questions being asked, will generate credible and valid results, and are practical, cost-effective, ethical, and professional.

- Step 8 is **simulating use.** Before the data are collected, potential use is simulated with fabricated findings, almost real enough to provide a meaningful learning experience for primary intended users. After engaging in the simulation, the primary intended users can make an explicit decision to proceed with the evaluation design.

- Step 9 is **data collection**. It involves primary intended users in the data collection process and interim findings in order to maintain their interest and ownership in the evaluation.

- Step 10 is **data analysis**. This step involves organizing data to make it understandable and relevant to primary intended users, to involve users actively in interpreting findings and generating recommendations, and to examine the findings and their implications from various perspectives, with the focus on primary intended uses by primary intended users.

- Step 11 is **facilitation of use.** This step is crucial because use does not always happen naturally. This step helps the intended users use the findings and *learn from the process* in intended ways, examine potential uses and users beyond those intended and originally targeted (dissemination), decide on dissemination mechanisms and avenues consistent with intended uses and additional desired uses, and identify possible misuses and plan action to assure appropriate uses.

- Step 12 is **meta-evaluation**. This is a follow-up to determine the extent to which intended use by intended users was achieved, the extent to which additional uses or users were served beyond those initially targeted, and to determine and learn from any misuses or unintended consequences of the evaluation.

Teaming with DECI

Experimenting with UFE through DECI from 2010 to 2011 has been yet another opportunity for my learning. The highlight has been identifying an evaluation framework for maximizing the 'use' value of evaluation findings. DECI was a challenging and learning experience for each person in the five-member team.

DECI has six objectives:

1. The first is to provide technical assistance to researchers towards improving their evaluation knowledge and skills. Researchers receive training and mentoring in UFE and particular method(s) that respond to their evaluation questions.
2. The second is to introduce regional evaluation consultants (called evaluation mentors) to the concepts and practices of UFE by mentoring evaluations of on-going ICT4D projects.
3. The third is to develop a UFE workshop curriculum and test it across different ICT4D project settings.
4. The fourth is to contribute towards the completion of UFE evaluations of designated PAN projects.
5. The fifth is to develop an approach to monitoring and evaluation capacity development with possible uses in other regions or thematic areas.
6. The sixth is to communicate the DECI findings in the form of a short primer directed mainly at evaluation professionals.

In its working model, DECI designed the role of 'mentors' as facilitators from and within Asia, who have Asian experience in evaluation and who will work closely and accompany the evaluators of the DECI project partners in their evaluation. The mentors work from a distance and are not located on site, but the evaluators were placed within the organization. The mentors were also expected to work in conjunction with the two consultants based in Canada and the five-member team as a whole. Most important, the mentors were expected to apply their previous experience in evaluation, to use their evaluative thinking, and to adapt themselves to the role of 'mentor'. It was yet another challenge, but in the end the mentorship model contributed significantly to the completion of the process. The mentor both challenged and supported the evaluator in carrying out the 12 steps of UFE in their projects. The mentorship role (which I played) and the model have also been a great influence in my evaluation practice post-DECI, and I consider the UFE framework to be exceptionally appropriate to evaluation practice in Asia.

DECI Project Partners

DECI worked with five PAN ICT4D projects[2]; they were research and grant-providing umbrella projects in ICT4D and were funded by IDRC, Canada. In DECI, I was assigned to mentor two projects: the Pan-Asian Collaboration for Evidence-based eHealth Adoption and Application (PANACeA) and Strengthening ICT4D Research Capacity in Asia (SIRCA). PANACeA[3] is a network of health researchers and institutions that conduct collaborative research on e-health applications in the Asian context. The members of the network are from a number of developing countries in Asia. The three key use areas for the formative evaluation of the network using the UFE approach were collaboration and team network development, capacity building, and knowledge management.

The second project, SIRCA,[4] is also a capacity-building organization for ICT4D in Asian countries. Its goals include enhancing research capacity in the region, creating a space for discussions and knowledge sharing on ICT4D, and promoting greater awareness and linkages among emerging ICT4D researchers in Asia. Three key evaluation and use areas in the organization were identified for an in-depth evaluation using UFE approach: the grant review process, the mentorship programme, and the capacity-building activities such as workshops and conferences.

DECI–UFE Start-up

To start the process, DECI introduced the five-member team to UFE in a hands-on workshop, navigating through it by capturing the evaluation experiences of each team member and helping us to learn the UFE framework step by step. The workshop helped us gain knowledge about UFE and understand the distinct differences between UFE and other evaluation methodologies. 'UFE offers both a philosophy of evaluation and a practical framework for designing and conducting evaluations' (Patton, 2008, p. 36). UFE is also a decision-making framework for enhancing the utility and actual use of evaluations. 'Use' here means 'how real people in the real world apply evaluation findings and experience the evaluation process' (Patton, 2008, p. 37). We—the DECI team—and the five project partners had to work through the crucial factors of the UFE framework: the 'use' value, the primary users, and the primary intended uses. It was quite exciting for me to realize that the entire UFE framework and process was designed to facilitate evaluations being targeted to use.

Initial Feelings

When I was first selected to be part of the five-member team, I was anxious. I had limited knowledge of the UFE framework, little experience of mentoring an evaluator, and was not sure how I was going to adapt myself to the requirement. It was also challenging to be learning *and* delivering what was expected of me at the same time—that is, learning the framework and process of UFE and emulating and delivering the practice as a mentor to the evaluators to help guide and oversee the completion of the evaluation and its use.

At the very beginning, I had a lot to balance: face-to-face interactions with the project directors, project managers, potential primary users, and evaluators for both of the projects I was mentoring; viewing the set of slides on UFE and the 12 steps prepared by DECI; and initiating discussions and clarifying steps and processes for both myself and my mentees. As we proceeded through the steps, there were bilateral and tripartite interactions—between the mentors and evaluators; the mentors, evaluators, and consultants; and within the DECI team. Towards the end of the steps, there was opportunity for the mentor to have a second set of face-to-face interactions. During the middle and towards the end of the process, there were other opportunities for learning and sharing, including a panel discussion and a workshop on DECI-UFE, and the Evaluation Conclave 2010—South Asia and Sri Lanka Evaluation Association (SLEvA), where some of the consultants, mentors, evaluators, and primary users presented what they had learned and the challenges they encountered. Throughout the DECI experience, there was learning, relearning, sharing with one another, documenting, and careful and thoughtful navigation through the whole process of applying the UFE framework to each of the DECI projects.

Traditional Role of the Evaluation Practitioner in Asia

In evaluation, an evaluator is seen traditionally as a facilitator, not as a leader or decision-maker. Being an evaluation practitioner myself, I often wondered whether I was open to new learning. How far was I willing to go beyond the traditional confines of evaluation practice? Did I just go in, do the evaluation, and get out? How useful have my evaluation services been to the development projects or programmes? How did I perceive and influence the 'uses' of my services? Have my skills in facilitating evaluation grown with the focus on use?

From my observations in the evaluation practice in India/South Asia, the role of the evaluator has been constricted to that of data collector, interpreter, analyser, and reporter. We follow self-guided values and ethics in evaluation, in the absence of a standard designed suitably for India or Asia. There are gaps in our competencies, performance, and methodological rigour, as well as in getting the stakeholders actively involved, being accountable to the process, and showing sensitivity to the local culture. I have been witness to all the various scenarios. The Director of the Association of Rural Education and Development Service (AREDS), an NGO in Tamil Nadu, India, which celebrated 30 years of service, said during an interview that along with the changing scenario in development came a new generation of personnel or evaluation practitioners who never knew the history of development in the region or country or of the implementing agencies. They (the evaluators) had a very narrow point of view, limited to the immediate situation of the particular project under scrutiny, and only considered the project's effectiveness, efficiency, and impact in terms of the predetermined time frame, which led to disconnected findings, abrupt conclusions, and no follow-up on the evaluation findings.

Many evaluation practitioners, including me, probably belong to this generation of evaluators, evaluation experts, or professionals. I have been in evaluation practice for a long time in India and South Asia and have dealt with NGOs, government agencies, international and bilateral development bodies, and a variety of development projects. I can say now that it has been useful to have been exposed to different debates and deliberations on current evaluation practices, including the DECI–UFE research project—which has had a great influence on my thinking and practice. The next section explores the specifics of what I found to be the key findings of my experience with the DECI–UFE project. The findings are drawn from the reflection processes of the DECI team members engaged in, interviews for an evaluation conclave panel discussion organized in India, and the finalized case studies (based on the 12-step UFE process) for each of the DECI projects.

Findings

Highlights

The project partners felt at the outset that UFE focused more on the **individual** than on the organization as the owner of the process and the evaluation findings. There were long debates and arguments among the project partners during the process of identifying the primary users (Step 3 of UFE): why should the primary user be only an individual (or individuals) from the organization? An individual-focused process would go against the democratic functioning in a network type of organization. However, as the process went along and once it reached Step 11 of UFE—facilitation of use—the project partners realized why the preferred primary user was the individual or individuals instead of the organization. The interactions between the evaluator and primary users of the evaluation made it a participatory process.

The programme managers, evaluators, and primary users also felt that the 12 steps/processes of UFE were **complex**. At the beginning of the project, DECI provided opportunities for the programme managers, primary users, and evaluators to develop an overall understanding of the UFE process through its mentors and face-to-face interactions and discussions about the 12 steps. The evaluators were also able to access Patton's (2008) book on UFE. The perceived complexity became simplified through the process, as the participants were able to focus more on the process, methodology, and rigour of the steps.

The UFE process with PANACeA highlighted other aspects of the process. The first involved the **use of findings** (Step 5) and the **facilitation of the use** (Step 11), which are not included or are ignored in many other approaches to evaluation. The second was the focus on the **primary user** (Step 3). The evaluator underlined that it is people who make up organizations and that UFE **personalizes the evaluation**, which helps people take responsibility. At first, the organization did not understand that the primary users were important. There was a change in the individual who was the primary user and yet management felt this did not matter, as position of the primary user—senior manager— remained the same. However, the individual did make a difference, and the proof of this was that the intended 'use' did change when the user changed. The new primary user reviewed what the previous primary user had stated as the area worth evaluating, and she did not agree. The earlier primary user focused on service, but the current one felt that the mentorship programme should be one of the focus areas. The third aspect was the **participatory approach** in UFE: it kept the primary users informed and involved, minimized communication gaps, and avoided surprises. The primary user was aware of the methods, plan, design, and key evaluation question. The fourth aspect highlighted was the **flexibility** inherent in the UFE approach—that is, the ability to organize things in a way that worked for the situation—which helped to get the primary user and other stakeholders involved. The standard set of principles and steps allow anyone with a research capacity to follow them and function as evaluators as well. As I went along, the 12 defined steps of UFE helped to get my thinking straight and helped me to sort out the evaluation processes; it helped me to focus on many things in the evaluation process. This led to **evaluative thinking** in the organization, which showed a capacity-building outcome. This supported Patton's claim that the evaluator can work herself out of a job, if they become that good!

The identification of **primary intended uses** (Step 5) was the highlight in the SIRCA UFE I mentored. The primary intended users added evaluation uses related to their own fields and context; this step resulted in a list of varied uses covering the different aspects of the project. These primary users considered this step crucial to achieving the essence of UFE. The primary users felt that the identified uses were a strong motivating factor for them to use the evaluation once it was completed. This step allowed them to achieve a sense of ownership for the evaluation findings, since they were the ones who would use them in their own different ways. The second highlight for the primary user was **focusing the evaluation** (Step 6)—the primary intended users finalized the high-priority and key evaluation questions on the basis of primary-intended-use categories. The primary users modified, prioritized, and gave their reasons, which corresponded to the targeted uses of evaluation. All these things not only reinforced a sense of ownership and utility but also helped to make the evaluation manageable. The third highlight was the **simulation exercise** (Step 8), though it was carried out a bit late, that is, during data collection (because the evaluator was unfamiliar with UFE and was guided towards this step later by the mentors). This included some simulated findings and some actual interview responses with two to three varied responses on each key evaluation question. These were checked with available users to ascertain whether the simulated database on the key evaluation questions focused on the use as foreseen by the primary intended users. Because of the simulation exercise, the primary intended users brought in a modification to key evaluation questions to ensure the answers fulfilled a particular 'use' as foreseen by the primary intended users.

About the Appropriateness of UFE in the Asian Context

I have watched the evaluation ethos change over the years in conjunction with changes in the nature of development programmes or project collaboration. From long-term integrated development partnerships to specific and time-bound project partnerships, from volunteerism to professionalism, and from change-focused to fund-focused project initiatives.

The outcome of my recent interviews with a number of state- and national-level NGO and INGO representatives from South Asia documenting their perceptions about evaluation in development suggests that evaluation has been perceived with a sense of 'fear'—the understanding was that it was commissioned to disengage projects or discontinue funds for projects. In most cases, evaluation has been a ritual, a mandatory exercise. However, the perceptions about, and attitudes towards, evaluation differed among donors, implementers, evaluation managers, and beneficiaries. Wherever there was a positive attitude towards evaluation, there was learning from and a higher degree of use of the evaluation findings. In these cases, the findings often led to far-reaching changes and generated more energy and impetus in the projects. Through an evaluation that I undertook in 2006, a European NGO that co-funded hundreds of small development initiatives across India uncovered a weak link—insufficient coordination—in the process used for the desired benefit to reach the intended beneficiaries. The NGO worked on the finding, took a series of actions to address the weak link, and is gradually succeeding in plugging the gap.

I had also observed that the methodology and tools used in most of the evaluations in South Asia in general tended to focus on quantitative aspects, and the interviews with the NGO and INGO representatives confirmed my conclusions. For example, the project-end evaluation of a housing project of an NGO in India was geared more to finding out whether the houses were built than to finding out whether the families in the houses were happy! The evaluation tools neither opened up the minds of the stakeholders for new learning nor got them involved enough in the evaluation process to take ownership of the findings. The participation of the major stakeholders was undervalued or overruled by the limited time allocated for the evaluation of the project: they were expected to cover 1,500 beneficiary children or households across a district in 15 to 20 days, which included everything from reviewing relevant documents to finalizing the evaluation report. The scope of such evaluations normally included the management of the implementation and the results. The evaluation was rushed—from preparing the TOR through following the methods and reporting procedures prescribed therein.

In my experience, evaluation findings seldom reached beyond the commissioners of evaluation, donors, and implementing organizations. The evaluation findings were hardly put into 'use', and there was always resistance to change among donors as well as implementers. In many cases, the evaluation findings were beyond the capacity of the organization to put into 'use'. None of the stakeholders took total ownership for the evaluation findings. According to an NGO director in Cambodia, the attitude of most NGOs was, 'It wasn't that I wanted the evaluation for my learning, but that the donor wanted the evaluation, and let me see what I could learn from it.'

I have been a member and lead facilitator of evaluations where we used mostly participatory evaluation, mixed methods, or a custom-made methodological frame used by European Union or larger INGOs like Oxfam-Novib. The core evaluation methods/tools used in these evaluations were sampling, semi-structured interviews, case studies, key informant interviews, anecdote investigation, focus group discussions, simple ranking, strengths-weaknesses-opportunities-threats (SWOT) analysis, organization scans (customized and simplified), role plays/ social games for identifying changes in beneficiaries' lives or perceptions, and so on. These methodologies and tools have been useful in evaluating key questions in the areas of livelihood development, indigenous people's empowerment, human rights interventions, grassroots governance, and so on. UFE does not prescribe particular methods; it is methodologically neutral and the data collection methods/tools used with other approaches (listed above) can be used in a UFE to collect the type of data needed to respond to the evaluation purpose and questions. However, the highlight of my experience with the UFE framework was that it brought **greater ownership** and a **higher degree of use value** to the evaluation findings. UFE is very relevant in development evaluation in South Asian context. Why and how it is relevant is explored in the remainder of the chapter.

About What Makes a Good Evaluator in UFE?

All through my experience as an evaluator, I swung into action right after formalizing an evaluation, guided by the TOR and the appropriate methodology chosen to go with the work. I relied on my knowledge of evaluation theories, methods, and tools, and my years of experience in evaluation practice. It is a challenging task to be an evaluator—either internal or external.

However, *should* the evaluator be internal or external, and what did I learn about this from my experience with DECI-UFE? As the UFE framework deters rigidity and emphasizes being flexible in several aspects, I found it comfortable to work with. The framework is suggestive and guides an evaluator but does not prescribe whether the evaluator should be internal or external. Rather, it examines the pros and cons of each and then explains the crucial characteristics that need to be considered when choosing the evaluator.

In his book on UFE, Patton (2008, p. 216) cites a classic 1975 article on evaluation use by Davis and Salasin that asserts that evaluators were involved inevitably in facilitating change and that 'any change model should . . . generally accommodate rather than manipulate the view of the persons involved'. Patton points out that 'respectful utilization-focused evaluators do not use their expertise to intimidate or manipulate intended users' (p. 216). Patton explores the debate further:

> [E]xternal evaluators are valuable precisely because they are outside the organization. . . . the external status permits them to be more independent, objective, and credible than internal evaluators. Internal evaluators are suspect because, it is presumed, they can be manipulated more easily by administrators to justify decisions or pressured to present positive findings. . . . Of course, external evaluators who want future evaluation contracts are also subject to pressure to produce positive findings. (p. 217)

Patton's point is that the valid and crucial factor for choosing evaluators to conduct UFE is their ability to be good facilitators. These are evaluators who will not fall into the temptations of making themselves the primary decision-makers; identifying vague, passive audiences as users; targeting organizations as users; focusing on decisions instead of decision-makers; assuming the evaluation's funder is the primary stakeholder; waiting until the findings are in to identify intended users and intended uses; seeing themselves as being above the messiness of people and politics; being co-opted by powerful stakeholders; or identifying primary intended users but not involving them meaningfully (Patton, 2008, p. 90).

The two project partners (PANACeA and SIRCA) to which I was assigned as mentor for the UFE did not have much of a discussion about whether the evaluator should be internal or external. Rather, they went by the knowledge, skills, attitude, experience, and availability of the persons appointed as evaluators for a period of about a year. It so happened that SIRCA's appointed evaluator was external to the project and PANACeA's appointed evaluator was internal to the project. Both were experienced evaluators and handled the UFE process well until the end. Both developed good insights and understanding of UFE and the 12 steps. However, PANACeA's internal evaluator was expected to deliver the findings independently as an evaluation expert, which created extra pressure.

As a mentor, I interacted closely with both evaluators and initially thought that an external evaluator was most appropriate for the UFE process. However, to my surprise the external evaluator, who experienced the whole process, felt the opposite. She thought that the evaluator should *not* be an outsider but a trusted facilitator and part of the team. She asked to sit in regular bi-weekly project meetings; the project team was at first hesitant, so she did not sit in but tried nevertheless not to be an outsider, though in some ways she still was.

About How It Feels to Be a 'Mentor' in UFE?

As a result of the DECI–UFE process, I learned a great deal about being a mentor. While talking about mentors during a mid-course reflection within our DECI team, we joked that mentorship is 'moaching', coining the word by combining mentorship (trouble shooting with the learner as a peer) and coaching (introducing a learner to an established procedure). We wrestled with the meaning and implications of the word 'mentor' because there was a temptation to fall into the trap of being a coach rather than a mentor.

Patton wrote a lot about the role of the evaluator, both internal and external, but he never dealt with the role of 'mentor' in his book. The flexibility of the UFE framework stimulated DECI to come out with the innovative role of a mentor in the research project experimenting with UFE methodology with their IDRC partners. It would have been more complex for DECI to hire a different evaluator for each of the five projects and to be able to send them to the project locations to facilitate the evaluation. The idea of mentors evolved for both practical and creative reasons—one of the objectives of DECI was to train regional evaluators in UFE by doing it, and budget restrictions meant each project had to fund the evaluation itself.

I am of the opinion that introducing this new dimension worked and helped to bring out valuable findings from the research. The DECI team worked together at different levels. At the end, we realized that we had five mentors in DECI who guided each other, guided five evaluators, guided five project partners, and guided the evaluation processes. This arrangement of having a project 'mentor' and an 'evaluator' built a supportive mechanism between the two that provided insights, clarified the steps, reconfirmed the process, and supported discussions about the challenges as the evaluation process progressed. The evaluator was not left alone with full responsibility for managing the evaluation. On the other hand, as a distant mentor, I felt at times as if I wanted more immediacy in terms of my awareness of the process and activities related to the implementation of the evaluation in the projects. Both the mentor and the evaluator felt equally responsible for the total process and the completion of the evaluation.

As I indicated earlier, prior to DECI, I had more experience as an evaluator than as a mentor. That was why, when I was assigned as a mentor in DECI, I had my own fears and anxieties about not knowing what exactly it meant to be a mentor. My initial role was primarily to enable the evaluators to gain confidence and an understanding of UFE. Gradually, I built rapport with the evaluators and entered into on-going discussions about the nuances of each of the 12 steps. I made it easy for the evaluators to get in touch with me so we could build and maintain a close evaluator–mentor relationship throughout the UFE process. The team of mentors and the DECI team leaders from Canada played crucial supportive roles. The beginning UFE steps also required me, as a mentor, and the evaluators to meet with project management to win their confidence in the UFE process. However, in many instances, the process largely overrode the defined responsibilities of my role as mentor, and I just had to give into what the situation demanded, recognizing the collaborative nature of a process that actively engaged primary users, evaluators, project mentors such as myself, and the overall mentors of DECI in Canada. When I first arrived for the introduction or kick-start to the DECI–UFE process with SIRCA in Bangkok, I had a thoroughly prepared set of slides on the 12 steps of UFE and was very tempted to act like a coach, thrusting the prescribed steps on the participants. The temptation was all the greater, as the first evaluator PANACeA had appointed had to leave and they had only an interim evaluator. The sessions with the project stakeholders (about 25 in number) and the subsequent side-line meetings and deliberations with the core stakeholders taught me to become a patient listener and to guide the process and not force it. For example, there was a great deal of discussion about who should be identified as primary users and the size of the group, and it was necessary to play the coaching role at the beginning. However, I subsequently developed a style that relied on dialogue and joint exploration, and my earlier evaluation experience came in handy for this.

Continuing my reflection about the PANACeA project, I facilitated the identification of primary intended users (Step 3) with Patton's 'Power Versus Interest Grid' (Patton, 2008, p. 80), which distinguished stakeholders based on the level of interest and power, identifying the high-interest and high-power stakeholders as having high potential to be primary intended users. I also supported this discussion by focusing on the personalized approach in UFE, the importance of close involvement of primary users and their ownership of the process and findings, and the practicality of managing the process with equal involvement by each of the primary users. There was genuine resistance to considering one of the smaller groups as a 'primary user group' in a network where they nurtured democratic process in the decision-making and functioning. Also, it was felt that it was impossible for a few members in a network to take ownership for the findings and facilitate their use. I was a mentor as part of a research project, and my role was to leave final decisions to the project team. Although I would have ideally preferred a user group with a smaller number (three to five identified primary users), the project decided to go with a larger-sized group constituting 25 primary users.

We completed the evaluation process, and PANACeA did realize the difficulties entailed in getting all the primary users equally involved in the process of deciding on the methodology and tools, the data analysis and interpretation, and the utilization of the evaluation findings. Nevertheless, the network felt that all the network members were involved and owned the findings and their utilization. However, one lesson from the process is just how crucial the size and involvement of the primary users are to UFE.

The series of face-to-face interactions and deeper reflection on the primary users in the PANACeA project helped me gain greater confidence in my interaction with the evaluator of SIRCA, whom I was meeting just two days later in Singapore. The face-to-face mentoring also helped to establish sufficient rapport and to personalize the work relationship.

Although we had the responsibility of playing a particular 'role' (evaluator or mentor), it did not mean that we stuck strictly to those roles. Such an approach would have made the interactions bone dry and without life, and, especially in the South Asian context, it would not have worked. What worked better was being able to see the individual behind the role, which required personal rapport and a sense of equality in terms of power. We respected each other's experience and point of view and neither was seen as a threat to the other. This made the mentor–evaluator relationship a comfortable one; it built mutual trust and support, which helped the process. The follow-up sharing and interactions through e-mail or Skype—between the mentor and the evaluators or the other stakeholders in the project partnership—became livelier.

Mentoring Tips

Now that we have completed the UFE process, it is easy for me to identify the aspects in mentoring that worked the best.

- **Open communication:** the face-to-face meetings, the flexibility to travel for meetings, and the close communication through Skype and e-mail helped me to know what was happening in the project—both the challenges and the accomplishments—and this made me feel more comfortable. I would also emphasize that free-flowing communication about a project was very helpful. One of the evaluators whom I was mentoring had no hesitation in sending a quick e-mail to see whether I was available for a Skype contact; if I wasn't, she would send a detailed e-mail describing the problems and asking for immediate feedback to help provide insight and an appropriate solution.
- **Shared understanding of the mentor role:** in my experience, the mentor role worked better and was more effective when the project staff had a clear understanding of the role of the mentor and where we—the mentor and the evaluator—could support each other in locating problems, formulate a theory for change within the project, or repeatedly explore the key evaluation questions until we identified answers that were deemed good enough to guide the evaluation. In the absence of a clear understanding by the evaluator or the project staff on the role of the mentor, the

relationship tended to be procedural. An example of this positive relationship is when the SIRCA evaluator reviewed the existing documents and found that the project did not have a clear 'theory of change' (which defines all elements—such as the impact, outcome, results, activities, and inputs—required to bring about a given long-term goal). This was necessary for identifying the intended uses of the evaluation and the key evaluation questions, which we were working on for the evaluation. The evaluator developed this idea of developing a theory of change for the project from her participation in the International Program for Development Evaluation Training. The evaluator took the initiative to develop a theory of change for the project, based on the available project proposal, and as a mentor I also felt, 'why not?' In the end, though the discussion about deriving a theory of change for the project was not strictly within the 12 steps, it was helpful in identifying the intended uses and, hence, the key evaluation questions. It is quite common in India or Asia for projects to lack an explicit trajectory of change. Many project plans and designs do not clearly define the impact, outcome, and results, and it is difficult to find all of these elements identified and described in one place. I found that these discussions and interactions were necessary to bring clarity to the UFE and the project; they also provided me, as a mentor, with a very valuable learning experience.

- **Collaborative approach:** the mentor gets excited and more collective energy is generated when the evaluator engages in evaluative thinking about the utilization-focused process. As I moved along in the mentorship role, I realized that it was not a one-way process or relationship where the mentor was elevated on a pedestal as the ultimate expert. Moreover, I was as new to the UFE framework as the evaluator, albeit with a little more insight and experience with the framework. Similarly, I was not claiming that I was familiar with a wide or complete range of tools for data collection/generation. While we were designing the evaluation (Step 7 of UFE) and the projects had to choose appropriate quantitative and qualitative tools for data collection, I, as a mentor, was also involved and had to be a part of the decision-making process with the evaluators. Before this experience, I was under the impression that I had a fair degree of knowledge and skill in collecting and compiling qualitative data, but I realized I had to learn more. This drove me to revise a couple of the qualitative tools available, one of which was the grounded theory,[5] on which I had to spend a substantial amount of time, learning the basics before modifying and then sharing with the evaluator.

- **Opportunity for reflection:** I cherished the opportunity for reflection, which was available to the evaluators, primary users, and other mentors of DECI. DECI provided excellent backup and support, which helped each of the mentors to reflect and sail through challenging times. The greater experience of the mentors from Canada helped to reinforce aspects of the process where necessary—whether this was adapting to a large number of identified primary users or selecting particular data collection tools or in other instances where I felt unsure. It also provided me with the much-needed confidence to continue with my role as mentor.

Discussion

Challenges and Co-learning

Learning and playing mentor was not a cakewalk. Although there were challenges, with the support of the evaluators and the reinforcement from the other co-mentors in DECI I did learn a lot. The regular interactions with the evaluators seeking clarity on the different steps of UFE gave me the opportunity to use my experiences from the non-UF evaluations and to apply my understanding of Patton's work on UFE. Added to that were 'learning by doing' and a strong element of co-learning with the evaluators and other mentors throughout the whole project. The experience of mulling over and deciding on the primary intended users helped those involved with PANACeA to see the importance of having fewer people in the primary user group and provided an opportunity to apply Patton's 'Power Versus Interest' grid. Nothing worked as expected, but ultimately, as I have indicated earlier, we had to experiment with a larger group (25 members) of primary intended users and learn from it. Although he programme managers, key functionaries, and project partner directors always understood the use of evaluation for the organization as a whole, they felt challenged with the implementation of UFE because the 'use' was related to the individual user or group of users.

Another challenge was related to the skills needed by the project evaluator to implement UFE and to play a facilitative and supportive role—especially as I, as the mentor, was not interacting directly with the project. The project evaluator needed UFE *and* facilitative skills. It was a challenge to get the evaluator to understand this, especially as I was not directly involved the project. It became difficult for me when the evaluator had limited evaluation skills and needed constant coaching and support for learning those skills and for engaging in evaluative thinking during the process. In such situations, I often wished I was there in the midst of the project, directing the evaluation process, instead of staying on the sidelines and spending time with the evaluator. This was even more difficult for me as, at the end of it all, I was not sure whether what I had tried to impart was understood and I had to wait until the results were in to see whether the process had worked. There was always the temptation to jump in and work with the primary users to decide on such things as, for instance, the key evaluation questions, which took a long time to finalize.

I read Patton's book thoroughly, and some chapters more than once, but I must confess that I could not understand it completely. However, after the long process of experimenting with and experiencing the process, I can say that I have gained a more thorough understanding and also have some of my own suggestions for enhancing his marvellous work. Although the underlying concept is simple, Patton tries to include every possible element, making his work very comprehensive and allowing the framework to remain wide open for adaptation, depending on the situation. It was overwhelming, and 'more' did not seem 'better'!

Another challenge was that Patton did not link and present all the material for each of the 12 steps together, which necessitated hunting through the 600-page book for more insights on a particular step. The flexibility and openness of the framework was very useful and it mitigated any possibility for paralysis; however, it left me unsure of some aspects—for instance, whether it was appropriate to move back and forth between the steps or to modify them.

In some situations, we did have to move between the steps, such as between organizational readiness (Step 1) and evaluator's readiness

(Step 2). When I began my mentoring, the process started with Step 1 (organizational readiness) and moved through Step 2, Step 3, and so on. However, after progressing through a number of steps, I often had to bring the project evaluators back to Step 1 (organizational readiness) or Step 2 (evaluator's readiness). Similarly, we often had to move between focusing evaluation (Step 6) and identification of primary intended uses (Step 5) and/or identification of primary intended users (Step 3) or between data analysis (Step 10) and identification of primary intended uses (Step 5). While the 12-step process looked linear, at least on paper, the steps were best approached as guidelines, which required the evaluators to revisit or clarify earlier results based on information that became available during a later step. DECI was a research project, so we had the liberty of learning by doing. Patton's (2011) later book on essentials emphasizes the non-linearity that I witnessed through the DECI–UFE process. If I were to be in a non-UF evaluation, I would not have had the flexibility to move or modify steps and would have had to stick to the TOR, key evaluation questions, and the process prescribed at the outset.

As one progressed through the steps, however, a greater sense of urgency to 'get it done' seemed to develop. The PANACeA evaluation, for example, skipped the step on simulation (Step 8), which was to follow immediately after setting the data collection tools to ensure that the tool had the potential to generate the relevant/desired data. It was a challenge to convince the evaluator and the project team to see the importance of the simulation step and to bring them back to it, even though they had already started collecting data. They were hesitant about abandoning whatever data they had collected. However, they listened patiently to the argument about how the simulation would help them check the data collection tool and ascertain whether it would generate data that could match the primary intended uses and decided to try out the simulation. Much to my surprise, the evaluator felt it was one of the most helpful steps of the process, and, in fact, the project team decided to revise some of the items in the set of questionnaires they had prepared.

Evaluators need to have good facilitation skills to become good mentors, but not all of them possess such skills. I felt that I did well, though I was playing the role of a mentor and learning at the same time. It was a constant challenge, as illustrated in the previous sections. I also realized that the mentorship role was something that could be used more often in the future. As well, a mentoring relationship helps to build evaluation skills in any organization, and I feel that there is value in reaching out and continuing with capacity building in this area. I found it worthwhile to reflect, sort out notes and observations, and distil learning from the mentorship experience, which I realized could be turned into a guidebook or guideline for good mentorship and perhaps contribute new knowledge to the existing guidelines on mentorship.[6]

Learning UFE and Enabling Conditions

It is important to understand the conditions that underpin the success of the process and the learning outcomes of each of the different players—the mentor, the evaluators, the project teams, and the whole DECI research project.

- **Willingness:** to begin with, I realized that the success of the project and the knowledge and skills gained by the different stakeholders were rooted first in their willingness to participate and learn, and, second, in the project partners' willingness to learn. The willingness of the partners to take technical assistance, to make plans, and to get involved in rigorous/systematic evaluation also gathered momentum as projects neared their end, and organizations were eager to know the results of their project's performance. The donor partner, IDRC, encouraged the projects to engage in evaluation and offered them the option of using the UFE framework, while maintaining control over the process, including the identification and selection of users and uses.

In another project, I believe that more would have been learned from the UFE process if the project had not been faced with time and financial constraints, which made 'learning' a luxury. This particular project had to rush through the UFE process, since it was completing its project period and the management felt that if they were to put the findings in use they had to complete the process at least few months before the end of the project.

- **Skills and training:** the skills of the evaluators and mentors were the second enabling factor. All players—including the project partner/programme managers, primary users, evaluators, and mentors—had some anxiety about what UFE was all about. This required the mentors and evaluators to provide support and guidance to create conditions that were conducive to the DECI–UFE project. The initial training and awareness development on UFE was hugely important, as was the early face-to-face contact. The initial training, which we had in Penang, was not adequate for that task. The face-to-face meetings between mentor and evaluator were crucial. As one of the two mentees put it, 'Chella's first visit was very important, it set the expectations, cannot be done by e-mail or virtually.' The project partners, PANACeA and SIRCA, included very sophisticated ICT people, and if they felt this way about virtual communication, we can expect an even stronger response from others in other evaluations.

As a mentor, I was interacting continuously with the evaluators, and I found the interactions to be more productive and easier when the evaluator had good insights on either UFE or evaluation in general and had good evaluative skills, which were critical for the success of the evaluation. Although mentoring support was essential and 'handholding' was required at times, this was less important, for instance, where the local capacity was strong and the evaluator was skilled.

- **Cooperation:** the cooperation between the donor partner and the project partners, evaluators, and the DECI mentors was crucial for the research on UFE. Having worked as a full-time monitoring and evaluation manager for a Swiss-based donor during the early 1990s, I could easily gauge the degree of influence the donor exerted on the partners. Yet, even with this knowledge, I found IDRC—the donor partner of PAN—was doing everything consciously possible to provide the right atmosphere of non-interference. It ensured that DECI and the project partners had an independent say in appointing mentors or evaluators or in the decisions concerning evaluation process—like who should be identified as the primary users or determining the uses of the evaluation. The donor went as far as to affirm and re-affirm that the outcome of the evaluation findings would not influence any of the decisions related to funding or funding relations. IDRC provided the necessary environment for the successful implementation of the UFE. However, shedding influence completely was difficult; the project partners I was mentoring kept trying to see the use of the evaluation from the donor's point of view, and in fact, SIRCA used about 30 per cent of the findings in their next proposal to their donor. PANACeA included a component on fundraising during the middle of the evaluation, after the key evaluation questions had already been formulated, because that was when the project partner—PANACeA—was informed about the timeline for funding. This highlights the importance of clarifying fund availability and commitment for the UFE process before it actually begins.

Another crucial aspect was senior management's cooperation and commitment to UFE, even though they were not involved directly in the process. The primary user in the evaluation had a completely independent say in all matters related to the use, key evaluation questions, and tools. Senior management explicitly reaffirmed the primary user's ability to make decisions independently in the UFE process. However, in practice, the primary user still found it comfortable to have the consensus of senior management and such dynamics have to be accepted in the Asian context.

In both of the projects I was mentoring, another enabling factor was the primary intended user's understanding of UFE and their full commitment to the process—the deeper the understanding, the better the commitment and learning as the steps of the evaluation progressed. Some of the primary users felt that 'if I were to do it again, my commitment and learning would be better.'

Conclusion

Like most other people, I belong to the school that follows the rules as much as possible, and here in DECI-UFE, I tried to master Patton's framework and to 'follow the rules'. When one of the projects I was mentoring decided to include a larger number of users or where the other changed the evaluator and the primary user, I began to feel rather frustrated. However, the close interaction I have had with the evaluators or primary users and with my co-mentors—especially the ones from Canada who provided the much-needed support and reassurance behind the scenes—helped tremendously and reminded me that it was a learning experience for us all.

We have now completed the final phase of the DECI process. Looking back, I would have to say that though the whole process was unnerving at times, it was also exciting. We immersed ourselves in UFE in order to understand it better and to document the process so we could share it and ensure the use of the findings. Even before I took on this task, I had always talked about the importance of process in any evaluation—whether facilitating focus group discussions or conducting interviews. Looking back, I wonder whether I had really understood the essence of 'process'. I do understand it now, however, after going through this particular UFE project, where the users were gradually pulled in and both offered and convinced of their ownership, which I realize is critical to the process in any evaluation.

My perception of evaluation changed from it being a task that I could consider 'complete' once the evaluation was done to a process that I considered incomplete until the findings had been used, and I looked forward to seeing just *how* the findings would be used. The process opened up scope for a new culture of evaluation that went beyond the 'project'. It was a departure from the old culture of evaluation, where I would be hired to create a report as a record, a completion procedure, or for fund-focused accountability.

The 'use' value of an evaluation has attained such prominence for me that I have become an ambassador and advocate for a focus on evaluation use. The 'use' factor has become such an integral part of my practice and professional thinking that it has become the lens through which I view my other evaluative experiences. The whole idea of identifying the use beforehand in the UFE was a tremendous help in focusing the evaluation. Since my DECI–UFE experience, whenever I have had to read or discuss the TOR for an evaluation, the first thing that comes to my mind is the 'use' value of the evaluation. I advocate with conviction for keeping the 'use' as a guiding factor. In many instances, this has led to revising and drawing out the process differently in order to affect the use, which has also helped to focus the work for the client.

I realize that learning new ideas, concepts, and skills is not limited to any particular stage in my career. However, transformative ideas and approaches that are both radical and practical heighten the drive to learn and to apply the new knowledge. In fact, as I said at the outset, evaluators should consciously remove their blinkers, and I feel I have been able to do that and to approach evaluation with a degree of openness and curiosity that allows me to learn continually. The experience with UFE was a career opportunity for me; it not only offered me new knowledge and practical skills but also convinced me of the value of focus on use. The skills I gained have enriched the ones I had already acquired over time—whether in simple surveying and sampling, participatory appraisal, focus group discussion, or most significant change and so on.

As a practitioner, UFE has given me a new evaluation framework and skills. It is interesting to note that the recent trend among clients in Asia is to approach an evaluator, stating a preferred methodology for the evaluation. I met a client recently who specifically stated, 'We prefer to go by the utilization-focused evaluation in our different programme divisions and we are also hopeful that our personnel will learn and develop their capacity in evaluation in general and in particular to use this approach. Can you facilitate the process for us?' I was more than willing to take up the offer, since I was confident about the nuanced skills that I had learned through the DECI–UFE experience.

However, there was a concern among the DECI–UFE partners that the UFE process required more resources—in terms of time and money—than other approaches. The concerns were genuine, especially as the present evaluation culture makes the clients think they can have a quick and relatively inexpensive evaluation that produces findings and recommendations that can be left to the clients and/or evaluants to implement. I hope this concern does not negatively influence and alter the UFE approach. A colleague and DECI co-mentor had the experience in Argentina where a client did not use everything from the UFE checklist because it was 'too much'. They cut out Step 11 and Step 12 of UFE, with money being the limiting factor.

It may also be relevant here to say that in recent interviews with evaluation practitioners and senior managers in reputable research and implementation organizations about the evaluation practice and culture in Asia, and more specifically in India, I was truly amazed to realize the extent and degree of misunderstanding that has arisen about evaluation.

The common misperceptions were that evaluation belonged to the thinkers and senior managers, that only intellectuals could become evaluation
practitioners, that evaluation steps/processes were treacherous, and that
evaluation participants had better provide the right answers. UFE helped
to demystify the process and the field by approaching each step systematically with the users of the evaluation, involving project and donor
management, and having the evaluator/mentor operate as a facilitator
(and not from an ivory tower, but on the ground and in the field).

I have already been roped into playing a mentorship role in facilitating a UFE for a national-level research institution in India. We were still
completing Step 9 of the UFE, when the primary users commented that
the process was so systematic and simple that it has made them believe
that 'we too understand evaluation.'

I do hope that in sharing this piece of my experience with DECI-
UFE with my colleagues, other evaluators, project managers, and other
readers who are interested in evaluation, I will help expand the narrow
perception of evaluation and affirm qualitative, process-oriented, utilization-focused, and constructive evaluation for effective development that
has an impact on the people.

Notes

1. DECI is a research and capacity development project funded by the International Development Research Centre (IDRC). For more information about
   this project, see http://web.idrc.ca/en/ev-148541-201_104932-1-IDRC_
   ADM_INFO.html
2. The five projects were Development Research to Empower All Mongolians
   through Information Communications Technology in Mongolia (DREAM-
   IT); the Information Society Innovation Fund (ISIF) small grants programme;
   Learning Initiatives on Reforms for Network Economies Asia (LIRNEAsia),
   which focuses on policy and telecom research; the Pan-Asian Collaboration
   for Evidence-based eHealth Adoption and Application (PANACeA); and the
   Strengthening ICT4D Research Capacity in Asia (SIRCA) project.
3. See http://www.panacea-evaluation.tk
4. See http://idl-bnc.idrc.ca/dspace/bitstream/10625/46288/1/132777.pdf
5. Grounded theory is a method used for qualitative research (see Strauss and
   Corbin, 1997).
6. DECI is in the process of producing a 'primer' as a meta-evaluation of the
   DECI–UFE process.

References

Patton, M.Q. (2008). *Utilization-focused evaluation* (4th ed.). Thousand Oaks, CA: SAGE Publications.

———. (2011). *Developmental evaluation: Applying complexity concepts to enhance innovation and use.* New York: Guilford.

Strauss, A. and Corbin, J.M. (1997). *Grounded theory in practice.* Thousand Oaks, CA: SAGE Publications.

7

Enhancing the Use of Evaluation: Experiences from the Field

Manas Bhattacharyya and
Khilesh Chaturvedi

Background

Michael Quinn Patton (2008, p. 37) comments in his book on utilization-focused evaluation (UFE) that 'Evaluations should be judged by their utility and actual use . . . therefore, evaluators should facilitate the evaluation process and design any evaluation with careful consideration of how everything is done, from beginning to end, which will affect use'.

Evaluation is considered a major component of any kind of development programme today. Evaluation serves the purpose of learning from past experiences and making appropriate changes in the strategy and approach of any development programme or project. This helps to increase the effectiveness and efficiency of the programme targeted to benefit and empower poor, vulnerable, and marginalized communities. All organizations involved in implementing development programmes and committed to the cause of socio-economic improvement, particularly of the marginalized sections of the society, have laid substantial emphasis on the need for conducting evaluations. Evaluation exercises help assess the results achieved, the development process undertaken, the use of resources, and the levels of capacity in order to generate knowledge and enhance efficiency and effectiveness. More and more projects have evaluations built right into the project design itself.

However, the most crucial question of any evaluation is whether its findings and recommendations will be used to make improvements to the intervention being evaluated. Nowadays, use is considered a very important aspect of any evaluation because necessary changes in a project, programme, or organization will come about only if the recommendations of the evaluation are accepted and implemented properly and in a timely manner. Thus, apart from evaluating the programme, another important focus of evaluation is to ensure that the findings and recommendations are utilized to the maximum extent possible for increasing the relevance, effectiveness, and efficiency of the programme being evaluated or to improve the quality of implementation. Evaluation introduces questions about what can be learned from the evaluation and how this knowledge can be applied to all relevant contexts. The factors that drive UFE include enabling organizations to grow from reflecting on and analysing their interventions and functioning, facilitating efficiency and accountability in the development sector, and building knowledge for wider application.

In this chapter, we examine the factors in the evaluation process that influence use, based on our own experiences in the field. First, we explore the meaning and purpose of evaluation and look at the focus on the use of evaluation findings and recommendations. Then we present a number of case studies where evaluation has been used to create change and examine the factors that inhibited or promoted utilization at each of the different stages of the evaluation cycle.

What Is Evaluation All About?

To begin with, the literal meaning of the term 'evaluation' is assessment, appraisal, or estimation. It is a methodological and systemic area of study differentiated from social research. Better theorizing about evaluation's role has cleaned out some earlier weaknesses where the evaluations were perceived both by the evaluators and the organizations as fault-finding exercises or policing or inspection, and the facilitative and learning sides of evaluations were ignored. Evaluation has a learning function, which is now more clearly understood, and its negative connotation as a type of audit or inspection is fading. One very positive consequence of this development is the respect accorded to formative evaluations for mid-course learning. International organizations such as the International Monetary Fund and the World Bank have independent evaluation functions, and the various funds, programmes, and agencies of the United Nations have a mix of independent, semi-independent, and self-evaluation functions, which have organized themselves as a system-wide UN Evaluation Group (UNEG). The UNEG works to strengthen the function and to establish UN norms and standards for evaluation.

The generic goal of most evaluations is to provide 'useful feedback' to a variety of audiences, including sponsors, donors, client groups, administrators, staff, and other relevant constituencies. Most often, feedback is perceived as 'useful' if it aids in decision-making. There is broad consensus that the major goal of evaluation should be to influence decision-making or policy formulation through the provision of empirically driven feedback.

Evaluation is a rigorous and independent assessment of either completed or on-going activities to determine the extent to which they are achieving stated objectives and contributing to decision-making. Evaluations can be conducted on many things, including an activity, project, programme, strategy, policy, topic, theme, sector, or organization. Evaluation helps assess results achieved, process of development undertaken, utilization of resources, and levels of capacity with a view to facilitate and support learning and enhance efficiency and effectiveness. Evaluation facilitates reflection and learning by identifying the strengths, as well as the limitations, in on-going development interventions. It helps to strengthen development programmes and initiatives by identifying best practices and providing evidence to support decision-making about effective strategies for achieving objectives and future goals. At the organizational level, evaluation plays a key role in identifying the 'right approach to development'. It helps in taking stock and measuring results and sets the ground for capacity building. In today's context, evaluations are carried out to provide feedback to inform decision-making at all levels—community, regional, and national—for internal and external accountability, for providing feedback to stakeholders, for credibility and further motivation if measurable results are achieved, and for building knowledge for generalization and wider application.

Utilization-focused Evaluation

Evaluation is a process that helps to reveal the different dimensions and crucial components of programmes and institutions; assessment is important to enable the development institutions/organizations to mature and sustain themselves, provided the recommendations of the evaluations are used. If used, evaluation helps to identify strengths and limitations, which can be addressed to foster structural and functional capacity improvements. UFE leads to a greater degree of awareness of results, constant improvement through efficient and effective use of resources, and, ultimately, to a sense of responsibility among the people in the organizations and institutions where the evaluations were carried out.

Thus, the main concern is how the stakeholders apply evaluation findings and experience the evaluation process. Therefore, the focus of UFE is on 'intended use by intended users' (Patton, 2002, p. 1). Patton also says that the evaluators also need to be prepared to have their effectiveness judged by the use of the evaluation by the intended users of the evaluation.

Focus on utilization of evaluation findings developed after 1990, in the third generation of evaluation practices (see Table 7.1); the first- and second-generation evaluations focused on measuring and comparing the results or establishing transparency and accountability from the assessment of the result achievements (Segone, 2006).

Table 7.1
Stages in Evaluation Thinking and Practices

Stage	Objective	Focus
First generation (1950s–1970s)	Measurement/comparison	Results
Second generation (1980–1990	Transparency/accountability	Results
Third generation (1990+)	Understanding/learning/decision-making/positive accountability	Results/process/utilization

Source: Segone (2006), p. 9.

Traditionally, in the context of international development assistance, the objective of evaluation has been to measure project and programme outputs and outcomes. According to Cracknel (1988), in the 1950s, evaluation began to be implemented in organizations such as the World Bank, United Nations, and USAID, focusing on appraisal rather than evaluation. Agencies were trying to design projects according to a logical model and to establish mechanisms and indicators to measure project outputs. In the 1970s, the Logical Framework Approach (LFA) was developed as a tool for planning, implementing, monitoring, and evaluating projects according to criteria that permitted measurement of successful outputs. Clearly, during this stage, evaluation was results focused and was seen as a product and not as a process. In the second phase, during the 1980s, there was an expansion of interest in evaluation. International agencies began institutionalizing evaluation and evaluation units were set up, not only in the USA but also in Europe, mainly as an accountability tool to satisfy public opinion and the government's need to know how public aid funds were used. At this stage, international organizations became more professional in carrying out evaluations focused on the long-term impact of aid assistance. In the third and current phase, agencies have internalized the importance of the use of the evaluation findings and recommendations.

Evaluation methods and approaches are rapidly advancing in all programmatic frontier areas. There is no thematic area you can name—trafficking, violence, environmental preservation, governance, and so on—that is not undergoing interesting conceptual and methodological experimentation. Likewise, evaluation is reaching deeper into social spaces by better analysing exclusion and by incorporating stakeholder consultation as a professional norm. This does not mean that all technical and conceptual problems are being solved, but few are being ignored. In today's context, evaluations are being used for problem solving and decision-making, positive accountability and excellence, and knowledge construction and capacity building.

Facilitating the Use of Evaluation Findings—What Experience Teaches

The Association for Stimulating Know How (ASK) has been involved in facilitating and conducting evaluations at international, national, regional, and grassroots levels for the past 19 years. We have been involved in a number of evaluations that have led to effective and long-term changes within organizations and their programmes. In many cases, the process led to strategic planning and organization development. During the past few years, ASK has designed and perfected a unique style of 'participatory evaluation' that creates the appropriate environment of trust (through verbal and non-verbal communication) and fully engages the implementing organization, community participants, and other stakeholders in a process of analysis. We want to share what we have learned from our experience with this approach to evaluation about what facilitates and enhances of the use of evaluation findings and recommendations, that is, what we have found to be the facilitative and the inhibitive factors in making evaluation utilization focused.

Case Studies: Evaluations Used to Promote Change

While ASK has been involved in numerous evaluations, we have selected six case studies from India—St. Joseph's Development Trust (SJDT), Tamil Nadu; Diocesan Social Service Society (DSSS), Manipur; Bihar Voluntary Health Association (BVHA), Bihar; Voluntary Health Association of Sikkim (VHAS), Sikkim; Navajeevan Bala Bhavan Society (NBBS), Andhra Pradesh; and Shimoga Multipurpose Social Service Society (SMSSS), Karnataka—to illustrate how the evaluation process and findings led to concrete changes. As ASK maintains a long-term relationship with the majority of the organizations where it has conducted evaluations, it was possible for us to observe whether these organizations did or did not use our evaluation findings and recommendations and to identify and analyse the underlying factors that led to their use or non-use.

St. Joseph Development Trust (SJDT), Tamil Nadu

SJDT is a non-profit and non-governmental grassroots-level organization established in 1992. The organization is working for the integrated development of the poor and most neglected groups in their target area in the districts of Theni, Dindigul, Puthukottai, Nagapattinam, Cuddalore, and Kanyakumari. They are working with women through self-help groups (SHGs), children through daycare centres and complementary schools, disabled persons through community-based rehabilitation programmes, and destitute/orphan/HIV-affected children through an orphanage and street and working children's programme. SJDT widened its area of operation in 2005, after the unprecedented effect of the Tsunami, responding to the needs of the people affected. It took various measures to reconstruct and help rebuild the lives of the people in the Tsunami-affected areas of Nagapattinam, Cuddalore, and Kanyakumari districts.

SJDT decided to change its intervention focus from being activity based to results based and invited ASK to orient and train staff on results-based management. It was clear during the evaluation that the focus of the projects at that time was on accomplishing specific tasks and carrying out related activities but not on achieving results. Although the organization's different programme and project plans clearly described target activities, they did not describe intended results in a specific and measurable manner. Similarly, there was a need to improve the system or mechanism to measure the changes (results) that occurred due to the interventions. The reporting system also did not fully capture the concrete results. A system was needed to measure or capture the results for different projects—including schools and daycares, SHGs, and institutional loans—at the time of evaluation.

Post-evaluation follow-up training helped the organization move from a target-oriented to a process-oriented focus. It also helped the organization develop a plan to build staff and community capacities around community-based programmes for people with disabilities, entrepreneurship development, facilitation skills, and sustainable community organizations. As well, the follow-up training dealt with issues related to project-level flexibility, innovation, and proactiveness.

As a result of the training, SJDT decided to move from a service delivery approach to a self-help approach and to integrate the principles of results-based management in their planning, implementation, monitoring, and reporting systems. A series of training workshops were organized to help the organization to

- develop its programmes and monitoring and evaluation system in a results-based manner,
- establish an effective internal monitoring and evaluation mechanism,
- develop a detailed plan and strategy for building the capacity of the overall organization, and

- develop systems and policies for sustainability, networking, linkage, and advocacy.

Diocesan Social Service Society (DSSS), Manipur

DSSS is a registered voluntary non-governmental organization (NGO) and the developmental wing of the Archdiocese of Imphal, Manipur. DSSS initiates, plans, formulates, implements, monitors, and evaluates projects and programmes. Major interventions made by the organization in different districts of Manipur include capacity building, empowerment of women, women and child development, self-help organizations, social welfare, income generation activities, natural resource management, organic farming, sustainable rural development, and emergency relief. The services are offered by the organization to individuals in need, irrespective of caste, colour, or religious belief or faith.

ASK evaluated two of their major programmes: SHGs (for the empowerment of women) and Organic Farmer's Groups (OFG), supported by Caritas Denmark. Both Caritas Denmark (the donor agency) and DSSS, Manipur (the implementing agency), took ASK's evaluation findings and recommendations seriously and planned to develop new and appropriate interventions in the areas of socio-economic empowerment of women through SHGs and development of organic farmers' groups. Representatives from Caritas Denmark attended the follow-up workshops, which focused on finalizing programme designs and building the organization and staff capacity in the areas of programme planning, monitoring and evaluation, and reporting and documentation. Concrete strategies were developed to address the core issues and concerns raised during the programme evaluation, such as

- sustainable use of the natural resources and sustainable agricultural practices,
- building the farmer's capacity for cost-benefit analysis and record keeping,
- handling the food security issue effectively,
- introducing the market study and market linkages,
- making the farmer's cooperative society functional,
- strengthening the internal management and operational issues at the women's groups and the farmers' groups, and
- strengthening lobbying and advocacy skills and activities.

Working together, DSSS and Caritas Denmark made serious efforts to address the concerns that came out of the programme evaluations and developed a detailed strategy and plan to address the concerns.

Bihar Voluntary Health Association (BVHA) and Voluntary Health Association of Sikkim (VHAS)

Both organizations are implementing health-related programmes with financial support from Simavi, a Dutch public health organization. BVHA is working against female feticide and building public awareness on related laws in the state of Bihar. VHAS is a state-level capacity-building organization involved in promoting small grassroots NGOs throughout the state of Sikkim by building their capacity in organizational management and involving them in health care improvement for the poor people in the state. ASK conducted evaluations of their programmes and both the implementing organizations and the donor organization, Simavi, were seriously interested in using and implementing the evaluation recommendations.

Both BVHA and VHAS decided to focus on strengthening and improving their programmes by integrating results-based management in their planning, monitoring, evaluation, reporting, and documentation activities. ASK supported both BVHA and VHAS in the transition by providing a series of training workshops. For BVHA, ASK also developed detailed strategies for sensitizing various community stakeholders so that they would support saving female foetuses and giving girls the same opportunities as boys in an attempt to address the imbalance created by the existing gender ratio (the gender ratio in Bihar was 916 women to 1,000 men). BVHA redesigned its programme interventions to be specific, measurable, attainable, reasonable, and time-bound. Simavi and BVHA developed strategies to address concerns about including the people who are actually involved in female feticide, the need for the community to effectively advocate and put pressure on the government to take concrete action on female feticide, building mass awareness, and strengthening networking, linkage, advocacy, and campaigning activities. Simavi and BVHA jointly decided on the strategies that would be used to address evaluation findings, concerns, and recommendations.

In the case of VHAS, the funding and implementing agencies also jointly decided to conduct a strategic planning and visioning exercise to develop the organization's vision, mission, and goal statements and to make several important strategic decisions about their work in Sikkim and in North East India. The process of strategic planning and visioning exercise was followed by several other exercises, such as the development of monitoring systems and tools and needs-based policies. Thus, the evaluation findings and recommendations were taken seriously by both the organizations and their donor agency, and a process of implementation was begun with the assistance of ASK.

Navajeevan Bala Bhavan Society (NJBB), Andhra Pradesh, and Shimoga Multipurpose Social Service Society (SMSSS), Karnataka

NJBB is a voluntary, non-profit organization with the vision of working towards creating a child-friendly society where all children, and particularly those in challenging and vulnerable situations, are ensured of their rights—such as the right to life, survival, development, and participation—as enshrined in United Nations Convention on the Rights of the Child. The organization presently operates 34 different types of programmes related to children in difficult circumstances, particularly street and working children.

SMSSS is the 'development' arm of the Diocese of Shimoga, Karnataka, India. It is committed to influencing positive change in the lives of the people of the Diocese. It has been engaged in various developmental programmes in the Diocese since it was started in 1989. SMSSS caters to the needs of the poor and marginalized of the Diocese irrespective of caste, creed, or race, through various kinds of services in more than 605 villages in three districts of Karnataka—Shimoga, Davangere, and Chitradurga.

Both NJBB and SMSSS engaged ASK to conduct an overall organizational assessment. The organizational assessment for both organizations was comprehensive and focused on organizational performance, motivation, and capacity, and the external environment.

Both organizations took the findings and recommendations very seriously and mapped out detailed strategies to address the issues and concerns that arose from their assessment. Both developed strategic plans, an activity that was followed by developing systems, policies, and mechanisms—such as a human resource management system, a planning-monitoring-evaluation system, and a reporting and documentation system. All these systems helped the organizations streamline their internal organization systems and mechanisms and strengthened their capacities and policies to address different issues and concerns in the areas of administration, finance, human resources management, governance, and programmes. SMSSS also engaged ASK to conduct a detailed evaluation of two specific programmes, based on recommendations provided during their organization assessment. This focused evaluation began less than six months after the completion of the organizational assessment.

Factors Facilitating and Inhibiting Evaluation Use—the ASK Experience

ASK found that by following certain principles and integrating certain factors into the evaluation process—from conceptualization to submission of the evaluation report—it was able to ensure that many of the organizations used the findings and recommendations of the evaluations. This section details and explores these factors, which can also be generalized to the evaluation process undertaken by any professional evaluator or evaluation agency involved in conducting evaluations.

The factors that facilitate and/or inhibit the use of evaluations are identified and examined here by each of the key phases, which include

- planning,
- implementation, and
- documentation.

The Planning Phase

The planning phase involves understanding the issues and nature of the projects, delineating the objectives, identifying the stakeholders, and preparing the tools and methods to be used. There are factors during the planning stage that have an impact on the use of evaluation findings and recommendations, particularly as they relate to developing the terms of reference (TOR), selecting the evaluation team, and ensuring commitment to the evaluation among all key stakeholders.

Preparing the TOR

In preparing the TOR, there are a number of factors that can have a positive impact on use of findings. These include

- engaging and involving all relevant stakeholders in preparing and finalizing the TOR,
- scheduling a pre-evaluation visit,
- seeking feedback and comments on the draft TOR before beginning the evaluation,
- ensuring complete clarity among all stakeholders about the provisions of the TOR before beginning the evaluation, and
- including and planning for a debriefing session at the end.

Preparation of the TOR is the first important step where **active involvement and engagement of all relevant stakeholders** is crucial to ensure that all stakeholders understand and consent to the evaluation. This is a good opportunity to **create genuine interest in the donor and the implementing agency for the need for an evaluation with a focus on the utilization of the findings**. If the TOR is prepared only by the donor agency or the agency commissioning the evaluator or sponsoring the evaluation, the chance of internalization and acceptance of the terms of the evaluation—including the objectives, scope, and methodologies—among other stakeholders will be reduced, leading to lack of ownership. Lack of a sense of ownership of the TOR or the evaluation proposal or agreement may then lead to a lower level of acceptance of the evaluation scope, processes, and methodology, which in turn would lead to resistance towards the evaluation findings and recommendations. This makes it difficult for an organization to implement any of the recommendations.

In four of the six organizations profiled in this chapter—SJDT, DSSS-Manipur, NBBS, and SMSSS, the TOR was made in consultation with the relevant agencies (both funding and implementing agencies,) and the authors clearly observed that these organizations showed more seriousness, interest, and sense of ownership towards the evaluation process and findings than did organizations where the TOR was prepared mainly by the donor agencies. The TOR was not prepared in consultation with either the BVHA or the VHAS, but there were other factors that ensured that the organizations used the evaluation findings.

A reconnaissance visit to the NGO and the communities where they are working before starting the actual evaluation is always helpful for seeking feedback and comments on the draft TOR from the NGO and the beneficiaries, especially about the scope and methodologies. The community's perspective and specific expectations for the evaluation can be integrated in the TOR if such visit is organized. This will also provide an opportunity for the evaluation team to disseminate information about the evaluation and to explain the concept, purpose/objectives, process, overall strategy, scope, and methodology of the evaluation to the NGO staff and target beneficiaries.

This process is helpful in understanding the viewpoints of the organization and the community, gathering ideas and suggestions to strengthen the process, and above all, creating a sense of ownership among the stakeholders right from the beginning. ASK has conducted such initial pre-evaluation visits in a few organizations like SJDT, and these visits were always helpful in **integrating community feedback** and creating the sense of involvement, leading to a sense of ownership among the key stakeholders of the process, findings, and recommendations. During the pre-evaluation visits, evaluators need to communicate their open-mindedness and willingness to learn; this will help create a non-threatening environment and encourage organizations and communities to share their perspectives, expectations, and feedback. Maintaining cultural sensitivity during these visits also heightens beneficiary acceptance of the process.

When ASK conducted such pre-evaluation reconnaissance visits, ASK evaluators remained attentive listeners and observers throughout the process. They solicited the thoughts and ideas of the stakeholders, maintained the necessary level of flexibility, and showed respect to the NGOs, staff, and community members. They did not start evaluating during such visits and did not provoke or intimidate community members or project staff at any point. However, reconnaissance visits were not possible for some of the ASK evaluations, because of time and resource constraints, though ASK made effort to include this step in the evaluation process wherever possible.

Reconnaissance visits also give evaluators a chance to examine context, prior experience with evaluation, or other factors that might affect use of findings. Evaluation use is dependent on people and context. Use is likely to be enhanced when the evaluation takes into account and is adapted to crucial situational factors—like the organization's prior experience with evaluation, possible barriers or resistance to use, factors that may support and facilitate use, resources available, upcoming decisions/deadlines/timelines that may influence the use of the evaluation, the intended users' level of evaluation knowledge and experience, and political context. Reconnaissance visits allow evaluators to engage in what Patton (2002) calls a 'situational analysis', an important part of any UFE.

Pre-evaluation or reconnaissance visits help **ensure consultation with all stakeholders (to the extent possible) before preparing and finalizing the TOR** for the evaluation, which helps increase the possibility of the findings being used at a later stage. ASK experience indicates that evaluators need to gather input from all stakeholders (where possible), including the community, on the TOR before finalizing it. At this stage, the evaluators need to ensure that all relevant aspects—such as the objectives, scope, process, methods and tools, and respondents—are described clearly in the TOR, and to establish clarity on the roles of different stakeholders, especially in cases of participatory evaluations. It is also necessary to **develop complete clarity among all** concerned (donor agency, evaluation agency, implementing agency) about different components of the TOR—such as the objectives and scope of the evaluation, the process and methodologies to be adopted/applied, the tools to be used, the steps and stages, the expected outputs and deliverables from the evaluation, the timeline to implement different stages, and role of the participants—before starting the actual evaluation.

Including a debriefing session in the TOR ensures that it is seen as a key element of the evaluation and won't be overlooked or left out. The debriefing is important because it helps make the whole evaluation process transparent and contributes to ensuring that the organization is accountable to the community. It also helps the community understand the strengths, the areas of concern, and the factors that contribute to both success and failure. Sharing this knowledge helps stakeholders understand how the findings can be used and promotes their actual use.

Selecting the Evaluation Team

In the case of multi-stakeholder participatory evaluation, where organization staff and community beneficiaries are also part of the evaluation team and process, ASK has found that **selecting and training the**

right staff and community members increases the possibility of acceptance and sense of ownership of the evaluation findings. The neutrality, objectivity, transparency, and analytical skills of an individual need to be the basic criteria for the selection of the organization representatives, whereas for the community members, interest, maturity, a basic understanding of the organization's interventions, and a positive outlook need to be the main criteria for becoming the member in the team. ASK is able to build involvement and a sense of ownership (leading to better acceptance and use of the findings) through training and facilitation, such as it did with organizations like SJDT in Tamil Nadu, India, and the DSSS in Manipur, India, where both project staff and representatives from the beneficiary communities were part of the evaluation team. ASK began the process by organizing specialized training for the selected staff and community members. This training led to an understanding of the purpose of the evaluation and its process, methods, and tools, as well as the expected behaviours of the evaluators. Most important, the training led to the identification of the role to be played by the different stakeholders, including the community representatives, in the evaluation.

Ensuring Commitment to the Evaluation among All Stakeholders

Michael Quinn Patton (2002), in his checklist for UFE, has stressed that the key people who want the evaluation conducted need to understand and be interested in and committed to the utilization of the evaluation findings, and the programme needs to be ready to spend time and resources on evaluation. As well, the evaluator is responsible for explaining the evaluation, enhancing readiness among the key stakeholders, communicating the value and requirements of the evaluation, and assessing the commitments and building commitments as needed. ASK has found that the **awareness, readiness, and commitment of the key stakeholders** for conducting the evaluation is critical in determining whether the findings will be used. Demonstrating commitment to full participation should involve **finalizing the evaluation framework and tools in consultation with the stakeholders**.

The Implementation Phase

The implementation phase is where the evaluation is conducted and findings emerge. There are factors during this phase that have an impact on the use of the findings and recommendations, particularly as they relate to the processes used to conduct the evaluation and the role and skills of the evaluators.

Processes Used to Conduct the Evaluation

At this stage, how involved the implementers and programme participants are in measuring, recording, collecting, processing, and analysing information is important. Evaluation processes that are participatory, iterative, and focus on capacity building are more likely to promote utilization of findings and recommendations.

A **participatory process** at the implementation phase that ensures actual and meaningful participation of all stakeholders in the process of evaluation helps in building a sense of ownership towards the findings. The focus of the evaluation team should not be merely on 'compliance aspects' but also on the 'change aspects' of the project.

Through its past evaluation work, ASK has observed that a multi-stakeholder, participatory evaluation that creates the appropriate environment of trust (through verbal and non-verbal communication) and fully 'engages' the implementing organization, community participants, and other stakeholders in a process of analysis, increases the chance of utilization of the findings. The process moves forward with **open communication and analysis, fully engaging the respondents in on-the-spot discussion,** leading to logical analysis and the drawing of inferences.

ASK has successfully practised participatory evaluation in its work with SJDT, DSSS, and NJBB. We found that involving project staff and beneficiaries made the process of accepting, internalizing, and owning the evaluation findings smoother and easier than it was for those evaluations that were done without involvement of the project staff and beneficiary. The two biggest post-Tsunami evaluations conducted by ASK for the Catholic Organization for Relief and Development Aid (Cordaid) and ICCO-Kerk in Actie (all Netherlands-based donor agencies) also involved participatory processes, but ASK could not follow up with these organizations to check on whether evaluation findings were used; therefore, these cases are not being cited as proof of participatory evaluations leading to better utilization of the recommendations.

ASK has also found that including project holders (representatives from the implementing organizations or the project staff) in the team makes it easier to continually discuss and build consensus on issues.

This iterative approach ensures that the findings of the evaluations never come as a surprise to the implementing organizations and their management/staff. At the institutional and target-community levels, ASK has found that one of the important factors in determining the ownership and use of the evaluation findings is whether findings are shared with the concerned agency for cross-verification throughout the process, so as to build consensual agreement about findings instead of just passing a 'verdict' at the end. The perceptions of all stakeholders are important in ascertaining the accomplishments, the gaps, and the overall impact of the development interventions.

Apart from carrying out the evaluation, it is important for the evaluation team to **work with the participants to develop realistic and feasible corrective strategies for inducing necessary changes and improvements in the development programme.** If, during the implementation phase, the evaluation team develops a needs-based and simple strategy for effective programme implementation, keeping in view the ability of the programme participants to use it, it will lead to increased utilization.

One of the most crucial tasks of the evaluator is to make the organization realize that the evaluation process is not a fault-finding exercise but one that **focuses on building capacity** and on enabling the organization to overcome those constraints that act as hurdles in achieving the desired development results. Therefore, a problem-solving and solution-oriented approach to the evaluation leads to creating ownership towards the findings and the implementation of the recommendations.

The major findings, both in terms of areas of strength and areas for further improvement, should be **shared with major stakeholders immediately after conducting the evaluations**, and before leaving the organization/field, so that there is a shared understanding and agreement about the findings and the required corrective measures.

The Role and Skills of the Evaluators

The evaluators play an important role in contributing to a number of factors that influence use, from the development of the TOR, through conducting the evaluation, to writing the final report and conducting debriefing sessions. Evaluators need to have the **knowledge, skills, and experience that will allow them to assess impact and make robust conclusions about the strengths and gaps**. They also need to **follow**

standard guiding principles (see Box 7.1) while carrying out the data collection, compilation, and analysis process.

Box 7.1: Standards and Guiding Principles for Evaluators

In ASK's experience, the quality of evaluation and the principles followed by the evaluators have a direct impact on the acceptance, internalization, and implementation of the findings and recommendations by the stakeholders.

The American Evaluation Association (2004) has published *Guiding Principles for Evaluators*, which details five overriding principles:

- **Systematic inquiry:** Evaluators conduct systematic, database inquiries about whatever is being evaluated.
- **Competence:** Evaluators provide competent performance to stakeholders.
- **Integrity/honesty:** Evaluators ensure the honesty and integrity of the entire evaluation process.
- **Respect for people:** Evaluators respect the security, dignity, and self-worth of the respondents, programme participants, clients, and other stakeholders with whom they interact.
- **Responsibilities for general and public welfare:** Evaluators articulate and take into account the diversity of interests and values that may be related to the general and public welfare.

The Joint Committee on Standards for Education Evaluation (1994)—a coalition of major professional associations interested in evaluation quality, and to which the Canadian Evaluation Society belongs—has prescribed standards for conducting evaluations in terms of utility, feasibility, propriety, and accuracy.

ASK has also developed its own Code of Conduct and Guiding Principles for conducting evaluations and follows them diligently. If the evaluators follow and practise a set of guiding principles and adhere to the highest technical standards appropriate to the methods being used, it will contribute positively to promoting the utilization of the evaluation findings.

The effort made by the evaluation team to understand the context and the perspectives of the stakeholders communicates their genuine interest in the growth of the work. At the same time, the critical assessment, a focus on the best interest of the target group, and the professional conduct of the team also convey a strong commitment to objectivity. In addition to the skill of analysing and conveying the findings, evaluators need to be able to **listen, dialogue, and communicate** with the stakeholders.

As evaluation is also a part of capacity building, the process needs to be non-threatening if we want to ensure use of the findings. It is the evaluators' job to **create a non-threatening environment** for conducting the evaluation with the organization as well as with the community. It is only under these circumstances that the actual concerns of the community are revealed. A non-threatening environment also means being culturally sensitive, especially when dealing with different and diverse communities. However, there should be no compromise on objectivity, and if required, the evaluators may 'challenge' certain of the organization's perceptions, opinions, views, or decisions to ensure independent, unbiased, and high-quality evaluations. Creating and demonstrating a balance between sensitivity and rigour may also enhance the use of the evaluation.

The evaluator needs to be **empathetic** towards the implementing organization and its staff and should be able to understand their situations, problems, and constraints without compromising objectivity. This includes giving due weight to the organization for all the good work it has done. The evaluation process offers insight to the organizations about its inputs and outcomes. Hence, it is important to recognize the strengths of the organization and the project to be able to replicate them in different circumstances in the future.

Box 7.2: Learning from an ASK Participatory Evaluation

In 2006, ASK conducted and facilitated a large participatory evaluation where a major focus was on creating a sense of ownership about the findings of an evaluation among all relevant stakeholders. This was a mid-term evaluation of the Tsunami relief, rehabilitation, and reconstruction projects implemented by several NGOs in India and supported by two Netherlands-based donor agencies (ICCO and Kerk in Actie) where project/organization staff and beneficiary representatives were engaged in the process as 'evaluators'. ASK learned much from this exercise and was able to apply the lessons and strategies learned to a large evaluation of a similar nature, involving 10 organizations and supported by Cordaid in the Netherlands. Key factors that ASK was able to leverage were

- **Opportunity to use evaluation findings:** Some participants had concerns about the utility of the evaluation, as they considered the intervention

---

Box 7.2 continued

Box 7.2 continued

finished and could see no further use for any findings. Thus, they had to be convinced that the lessons learned from this evaluation could be utilized for other similar programmes. In the case of donor-supported programmes of a specific duration, applying the findings and recommendations is problematic because the programmes are finished. However, there are often other opportunities to use and apply the findings and the evaluators may need to explore these with the participants.

- **Pre-evaluation meetings:** A pre-evaluation meeting with the NGO heads in the first evaluation would have provided an opportunity to discuss and address any issues *before* the evaluation started. In the subsequent evaluation, a pre-evaluation meeting allowed ASK to explain the evaluation design and ensure that the organization was on board with the process, and hence, the findings. Involving NGO participants in developing the evaluation questions assured the organization that the process was transparent and truly participatory. This led to better understanding, acceptance, and implementation of the evaluation findings and recommendations.
- **Active community participation:** The participation of the community members was extremely important to the process. One advantage was that they were able to provide first-hand experience with the projects being evaluated; another was that they related well to the beneficiaries participating in the evaluation. On the basis of their own experience, they probed into issues and raised specific concerns and queries that were eventually beneficial in gaining an insight into the people's perceptions. Active community participation helps to create ownership of the evaluation findings within the beneficiary communities and makes it easier for the implementing agency to make appropriate changes at the community level based on the evaluation recommendations.

The Documentation Phase

The documentation phase involves the preparation, presentation, discussion, and finalization of the report, which brings into focus the findings and recommendations. There are factors during the documentation stage that have an impact on the use of evaluation findings and recommendations, particularly as they relate to debriefing, how and when the report is shared, and the kind of support provided to an organization or community for making decisions about the use of the findings and recommendations.

As previously noted, ASK has emphasized including a **debriefing session with the community** in the TOR, in addition to their participation in the entire evaluation process as respondents and, in some cases, as participants. It is important to take some care in creating the groups that come for debriefing to make them **sufficiently representative of the community** as a whole. In one instance, ASK conducted debriefings in different villages covered by the project to provide information to as many beneficiaries as possible, although, due to time and money constraints, this is not always possible. The debriefing is important because it helps make the whole evaluation process transparent and contributes to ensuring that the organization is accountable to the community. It also helps the community understand the strengths, the areas of concern, and the factors that contribute to both success and failure. Sharing this knowledge helps stakeholders understand how the findings can be used and promotes their actual use.

ASK always **shares the draft report** with the NGO and/or donor agency to receive their input, feedback, and comments on the report before it is finalized. This gives the implementing and funding organizations another opportunity to look at the findings and recommendations and provide feedback to the evaluator. It also promotes utilization. The report is usually first shared with the implementing organizations before being shared with the donors to give the implementers a chance to comment on the report, which is important, especially if there are any major factual errors.

Sharing the draft report gives a clear message to the agencies that even though the debriefing has been done and the findings are accepted, their opinion and comments on what is written in the official document matter. The agency has a chance to ensure that the final report is consistent with the agreed upon findings and that there are no new surprises or interpretations included in the report.

Utilization of findings is helped significantly if the documentation and sharing phase includes **organizing decision-making workshops at the end of the evaluation**. Decision-making and strategy-formulating workshops were organized by ASK in all the profiled evaluations. First, the evaluation team debriefed the stakeholders on the evaluation findings. Second, they facilitated a discussion among stakeholders to consider the findings and then accept or reject them, and, if necessary, prioritize those about which decisions had to be made. Thereafter, the stakeholders discussed and took decisions, with or without the facilitation of ASK.

team members (the role of ASK team members in this situation changed from that of evaluator to that of facilitator, with a clear understanding of the boundaries that come along with being the facilitator). Decision-making workshops help the participating organization to develop appropriate strategies and action plans based on the findings of the evaluation.

ASK conducts its evaluations in a way that allows the organizations involved to internalize and own the findings and further utilize them to improve their programmes and projects. Thus, there is adequate focus on the utilization of the findings in future programme planning, implementation, and monitoring. The process does not end with the evaluation itself; rather it encourages optimum utilization of the findings and knowledge gained from the evaluation process.

For the evaluation process to be 'objective', it needs to achieve a **balanced analysis**, recognizing bias and reconciling the perspectives of different stakeholders (including primary stakeholders) through the use of different sources and methods. Evaluation **findings must be sufficiently credible to influence decision-making** by programme partners on the basis of lessons learned.

Conclusion

Improving the usage of evaluation findings and recommendations depends on a large number of factors (see Box 7.3). These range from the design of evaluation itself to the composition of the team to the level of engagement of the implementing agency throughout the process of evaluation. ASK has particularly found that facilitative evaluators—those who can discuss issues related to implementation in the field and make the implementing agency staff think about and analyse their own practice—help to ensure that the stakeholders internalize the evaluation process and findings. Another very important part of the evaluation, from the point of view of its use, is how the evaluators handle the concluding stages. The evaluation process should not end abruptly with the submission of the report with a set of findings and recommendations but should allow space and time for discussion. Multiple stakeholders need to be engaged in these discussions, and the evaluators need to have the patience to not rush the recommendations and findings into a final document. Open discussions are very important and need to be facilitated in an effective manner. There also needs to be some room to look more deeply into some of the issues that arise from the discussion, if the goal is to improve uptake of findings and recommendations. Decision-making workshops and follow-up meetings can and should be built right into the TOR at the beginning of the evaluation process.

Box 7.3: Factors That Enhance the Use of Evaluation Findings and Recommendations

In the Planning Phase

- Engage and involve all relevant stakeholders in preparing and finalizing the TOR.
- Create interest in the need for an evaluation with a focus on the utilization of the findings.
- Schedule a pre-evaluation visit to the organization and the communities involved.
- Seek feedback and comments on the draft TOR before beginning the evaluation and integrate this feedback into the evaluation plan.
- Ensure complete clarity among all stakeholders about the provisions of the TOR before beginning the evaluation.
- Include a debriefing session in the TOR.
- Select and train the right staff and community members to be a part of the evaluation team.
- Ensure the awareness, readiness, and commitment of the key stakeholders.
- Finalize the evaluation framework and tools in consultation with the stakeholder.

In the Implementation Phase

- Use a participatory process that ensures actual and meaningful participation of all stakeholders.
- Encourage open communication and analysis, fully engaging respondents in on-the-spot discussion and analysis.
- Engage in an iterative approach, which ensures that the findings of the evaluations never come as a surprise to the project holders.
- Work with the participants to develop realistic and feasible strategies for improvement and change.
- Focus on building capacity.
- Share major findings with all major stakeholders before leaving the field.

Box 7.3 continued

Box 7.3 *continued*

- Ensure the evaluators have the knowledge, skills, and experience that will allow them to assess impact and make robust conclusions about the strengths and gaps in a programme.
- Ensure that evaluators follow standard guiding principles while carrying out the data collection, compilation, and analysis process.
- Ensure that members of the evaluation team also have good people skills, including being able to listen, dialogue, and communicate with the stakeholders; create a non-threatening environment; and be empathetic.

In the Documentation and Final Phase

- Hold a debriefing session with the community; include individuals and groups that are sufficiently representative of the community.
- Share the draft report with the NGO and/or donor agency.
- Organize decision-making workshops at the end of the evaluation.
- The evaluation process needs to be seen as objective, offering a balanced analysis.
- Evaluation findings must be sufficiently credible to be able to influence decision-making and the process

The ability to properly assess impact and offer robust conclusions about the gaps is also very important in enhancing the acceptance and use of the evaluation findings, and this is where the knowledge and skills of the evaluators are so important. As mentioned in the report of the Evaluation Gap Working Group (2006, p.2),

> [E]ven when impact evaluations are commissioned, they frequently fail to yield useful information because they do not use rigorous methods or data. . . . A systematic review of the United Nations Children's Fund estimated that 15 percent of all its reports included impact assessments but noted that many evaluations were unable to properly assess impacts because of methodological shortcomings.

The report describes that utilization of the evaluations was not possible because of lack of concrete and robust conclusions and improper assessment of the impacts.

ASK acknowledges and agrees that the appropriate methodologies for an evaluation that stresses the utilization of the findings is not fixed or rigid, but flexible, and needs to be decided upon by the intended users of the evaluation. ASK has experimented with different approaches and has direct experience that a flexible and user-responsive approach works. This is similar to the International Development Research Centre's (n.d.) approach, which is

> [f]ramed in utility: evaluations must have a clear use and respond to the needs of the user(s), whether management, a program, a donor, or research team. We equally value the use of rigorous methods. We do not promote or expect any particular evaluation design or focus. Our approach helps users select the most appropriate content, model, methods, theory, and applications for their evaluation needs. The quality of the evaluation is judged on its accuracy, ethics, feasibility, and use.

References

American Evaluation Association. (2004). *Guiding principles for evaluators.* Fairhaven, MA: AEA.

Cracknel, B. E. (1988). Evaluating development assistance: A review of the literature. In *Public administration and development,* 8: 75-83.

Evaluation Gap Working Group. (2006). *When will we ever learn? Improving lives through impact evaluation.* Washington, D.C.: Center for Global Development. Retrieved from http://www.cgdev.org/files/7973_file_WillWeEverLearn.pdf Accessed on June 19, 2014.

International Development Research Centre. (n.d.). *Evaluation at IDRC.* Retrieved from   http://www.idrc.ca/EN/Programs/Evaluation/Pages/Approach.aspx. Accessed on June 19, 2014.

Joint Committee on Standards for Education Evaluation. (1994). *Program evaluation standards.* Thousand Oaks, CA: SAGE Publications.

McNamara, Carter C. (n.d). *Basic guide to program evaluation (including outcomes evaluation).* Free Management Library. Retrieved from http://www.managementhelp.org/evaluatn/fnl_eval.htm#anchor1578833. Accessed on June 19, 2014.

Patton, M. Q. (2002). *Qualitative research and evaluation methods (3rd ed).* Thousand Oaks, CA: SAGE Publications.

———. (2008). *Utilization-focused evaluation.* Thousand Oaks, CA: SAGE Publications. (UFE Checklist also retrieved from http://www.wmich.edu/evalctr/archive_checklists/ufe.pdf). Accessed on June 19, 2014.

Segone, M. (2006). Why evaluate? The evolution of the evaluation function. In M. Segone (ed.), *Evaluation working papers: New trends in development evaluation* (No. 5, pp. 9–30). New York: International Program Evaluation Network and UNICEF. Retrieved from http://www.unicef.org/ceecis/New_trends_Dev_EValuation.pdf. Accessed on June 19, 2014.

8

The Importance of Understanding Context and Structures in Programme Evaluation: A Case Study from India

Suneeta Singh, Sangita Dasgupta, and Y. Dayanand Singh

Evaluation and Knowledge Translation: Ideas for Uptake

In 1999, Rossi, Lipsey, and Freeman described evaluation as 'the systematic application of social research procedures for assessing the conceptualization, design, implementation, and utility of . . . programs'. However, definitions of evaluation have continued to be debated (Hurteau et al., 2009) and over the past three decades, there has been tremendous theoretical and methodological development within the field of evaluation. Evaluation has progressed from a focus on the mechanics of doing evaluation, that is, methodology, to one on the effect of evaluation, that is, use. A 2004 World Bank report highlights this saying:

> When conducted at the right time, and when they focus on key issues of concern to policy-makers and managers, and when the results are presented in a user-friendly format, evaluations can provide a highly cost effective way to improve the performance and impact of development policies, programmes, and projects. But evaluations that fail these criteria may produce no results—even when they are methodologically sound.

It has been generally recognized by the international development community that evaluation should be an important input into decision-making. In March 2005, the Paris Declaration, signed by more than 100 heads of agencies and ministers to improve the quality and impact of aid, added momentum to evaluation of programmes. Underpinning the declaration was the attention that donor nations were beginning to give to the impact and effectiveness of aid (Organisation for Economic Co-operation and Development, 2008).

Evaluation in South Asia has undergone a similar evolution. A chapter from the United Nations Children's Emergency Fund (UNICEF) report on 'Evaluation South Asia' by the Community of Evaluators (Jayakaran, 2008) found that South Asia is grappling with issues of effectiveness, impact, and use. It suggests that two main categories of evaluation are seen in the region:

- *Donor-mandated outcome evaluation*: Most of the evaluations in the region currently fall in this category. These are undertaken to meet reporting requirements of donors and generally focus on programme performance.
- *Impact/evidence-based evaluation*: There is an increase in the number of impact studies being conducted in South Asia, primarily because of the growing interest in evidence-based policy-making.

Programme evaluation is of particular interest to knowledge translation since development programmes apply knowledge to meet the needs of people. A development programme usually applies a promising technical approach to an identified problem, using institutional arrangements to deliver the solution efficiently, and allocates financial outlays to cover the costs of both. Thus, programme evaluation has typically focused on these three aspects: the technical solution, the institutional arrangements, and the financial outlays. This chapter argues that such a focus is perfectly logical, but while these aspects are *necessary*, they are *not sufficient* for the solution to be actualized and development change to take place.

Various researchers (Contandriopoulos and Brouselle, 2012; Green et al., 2009; McDonald and Viehbeck, 2007; Saunders, 2012; Sudsawad, 2007) have found that other characteristics affect the uptake of programmes. These can be grouped into two broad categories: the way that societies and communities are structured, and the overall environment or context in which the programme plays out. Often, social structures and context are ignored in programme evaluation, leaving implementers doomed to repeatedly seek reasons for why their programmes do not work. In our opinion, evaluation must address structures and context to understand why some programmes work and others do not. This chapter therefore asks: can a framework that explores both *necessary* and *sufficient* conditions help to capture the reasons why programmes work or not?

Necessary and Sufficient Conditions for Uptake: A Logic Model

Our model—the Necessary and Sufficient Conditions (N&S) Logic Model—is simple (see Figure 8.1). The model proposes that while the technical approaches, institutional arrangements, and financial outlays represent the *necessary* conditions for development programmes to be put into play, structural and contextual factors represent the *sufficient* conditions for the uptake of development programmes (Singh et al., 2010).

Necessary Conditions

Necessary conditions consist of the building blocks of a programme: what to do, how to do it, and with what to do it.

- **Technical approaches** are promising or known technical solutions that, when applied, could create the outcome that is being sought. An example of a technical approach is a medicated bed net to prevent malaria.

Figure 8.1
Necessary and Sufficient Conditions (N&S) Logic Model

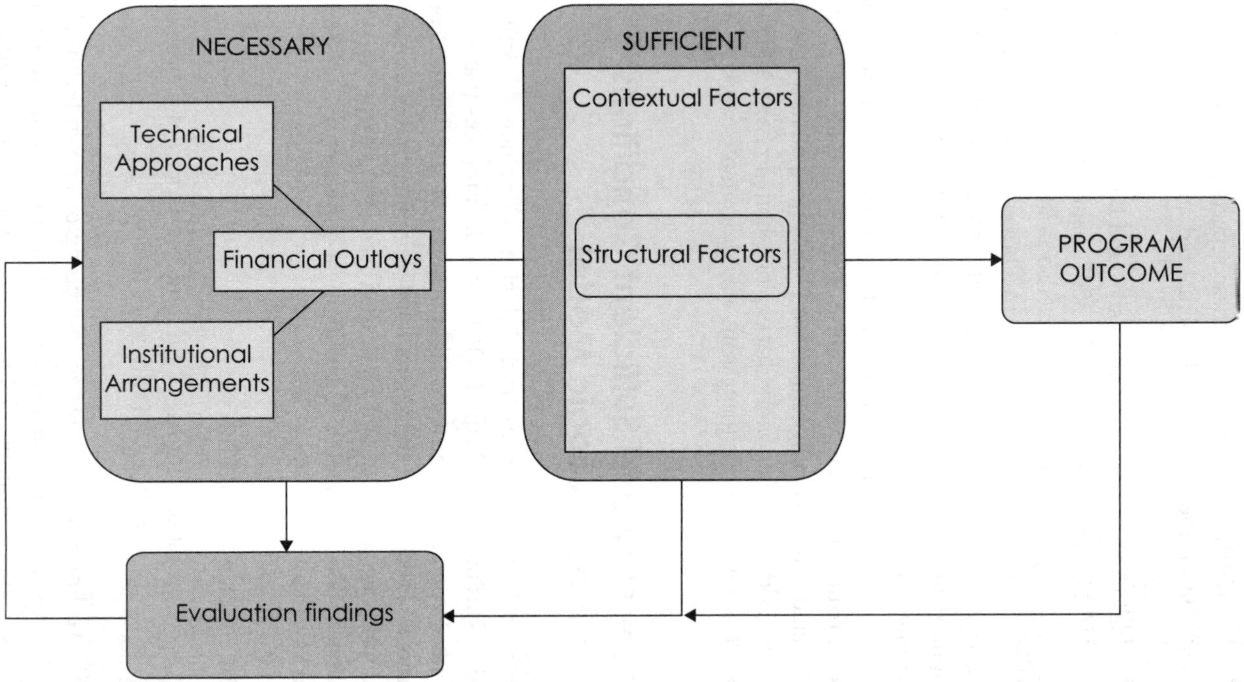

Source: Singh, Dasgupta and Singh (2010).

- **Institutional arrangements** are the mechanisms created or used to apply technical solutions to achieve the outcome. An example is a system to distribute and re-medicate bed nets.
- **Financial outlays** are the funds to carry out all the activities necessary to run the programme effectively.

Sufficient Conditions

These represent the fabric of the society in which the development programme is being undertaken. These factors may directly or indirectly affect the programme.

- **Structural factors** include social norms that have a direct bearing on outcomes. An example related to HIV programmes is attitudes to homosexuality.
- **Contextual factors** are all those factors of the socio-economic landscape that may affect outcomes in an indirect or unexpected way. An example of a contextual factor could be poverty or a particular law.

Applying the Model: Understanding the Status and Uptake of Evaluation

In this chapter, we present a preliminary study to indicate whether a systematic use of such an analytic framework could assist in programme evaluation. We use the N&S logic model to examine programming for men having sex with men (MSM) interventions within the National AIDS Control Programme (NACP) of India. There are several reasons why we chose the NACP and its interventions with regard to the MSM community. First, NACP is a flagship programme and is counted among the Government of India's most successful health programmes. It has extensive documentation and data are easily available in the public domain. Because the programme targets high-risk groups that face considerable marginalization, the discussion is very rich. Finally, owing to their professional engagements, the authors have had a close-up view of NACP events, personal knowledge of the field, and access to information not otherwise commonly available.

Through a detailed review of published and grey literature, we sought to identify the 'domain of the known' leading to significant change in the effectiveness of MSM programming in the NACP at various points in its trajectory. We arrived at a set of milestones in the roadmap of uptake of evidence. Donor-sponsored evaluation and other studies have been undertaken by non-government bodies and academic institutions. Over time, the programme has established increasingly sophisticated and extensive data collection for monitoring and evaluation (Singh et al., 2009). We asked ourselves whether such evidence was applied to the programme and whether it resulted in uptake of the programme.

A Brief History of the National AIDS Control Programme (NACP)

India established a national response to HIV and AIDS in 1986. Since then, the burden has grown with an estimated 2.27 million people living with HIV in India in 2009 (National AIDS Control Organization [NACO], 2010). The NACP has seen several phases, the two most recent being Phase II (1999–2007) and Phase III (2007–2013). NACP has in these phases concentrated on establishing focused HIV prevention interventions, that is, targeted interventions (TI) consisting of specific technical approaches to address most at-risk populations, such as female sex workers, MSM, and injecting drug users.

MSM has been identified as a high-risk group in the context of the HIV epidemic. MSM is an umbrella term used in India to denote a heterogeneous group, variously categorized on the basis of their gender identity and sexual preference encompassing, among others, kothi, hijra, gay, and transgendered individuals. In terms of the prevention of HIV, all face a similar set of vulnerabilities and require a similar set of interventions. Many MSM practise unprotected anal sex, have multiple partners, are unable to access good-quality services for sexually transmitted infections, suffer from lack of negotiation power and skills, and have poor knowledge of how to prevent HIV infection. In India, there is evidence to suggest that many MSM are in fact bisexual (Khan, 2004) and could act as jump points for HIV to the wider heterosexual community. However, only recently have interventions for the prevention of HIV among

MSM been offered systematically, with the provision of a clear technical approach, institutional arrangements, and financial outlays.

It is this MSM programme within the NACP that is being used as a case study to apply the N&S logic model to examine why it has taken so long for knowledge, that is, what has been known as good preventive practice among MSM for some time, to reach the vulnerable through the delivery of appropriate and well-resourced programme.

Key Knowledge and MSM Interventions: What Evidence Was Available and When

In this section, we present the technical and institutional knowledge that was available for the NACP. We also point out that adequate funding has been available to put the technical solutions and institutional arrangements in place since Phase II of the NACP. Yet it was not until five to seven years after Phase II began that the programme began to achieve results in this area. What changed? Why was the programme now able to achieve what it had planned to do five years previously?

Necessary Conditions
Technical Approach
There has been fairly good knowledge regarding technical approaches to prevent HIV infection among MSM. Yet interventions have been slow to be established and once in place, to 'take'.

- **Knowledge of the epidemiology of HIV in MSM communities:** In 2000, surveillance studies were conducted among known MSM communities for the first time in order to get better data on HIV prevalence among MSM. Although widely varying figures have emerged from studies carried out by government and non-government organizations (Chakrapani et al., 2002, p. 48; Khan, 2004, p. 2), the community has always been taken to be a high-risk population. In 2010, the government's UN General Assembly Special Session (UNGASS) Country Progress Report presented a trend analysis that showed that prevalence among MSM has continued to be high (NACO, 2010).

- **Understanding the distribution of the community:** Previous attempts to gather mapping information on MSM had been poor. However, in 2008, NACO took up a mapping of MSM communities in 17 states of the country. The study concluded that there were about 2.35 million MSM and provided specific details on hotspots of MSM traffic and activity (Singh et al., 2013). This information helped to clarify where MSM TIs ought to be located. These data were used to develop MSM-directed TIs, but the programme was able to achieve only limited coverage until recently.
- **Special considerations in use of condoms for prevention:** Condoms are advocated as a means to prevent the transmission of HIV. In 2005, the Working Group for NACP III on condoms had reviewed available studies to suggest that special thicker condoms be advocated for anal sex and that these be provided along with additional lubricants. Despite these recommendations, these interventions were not put into place.

Institutional Factors

Important institutional innovations to respond to the epidemic among the MSM have been special configurations of the TI model to address vulnerability, introduction of condom vending machines, and support to establish community-based organizations and networks.

- **Tweaking the targeted intervention model:** The TI model was a crucial strategic choice made by NACP in 1998. Specific methodologies to access MSM tested by various partners were available to encourage uptake among the MSM populations. Yet the coverage of MSM population with TIs remained low during Phase II of the NACP (NACO, 2006).
- **Support to establish community-based organizations and networks:** During Phase II, the Department for International Development (DFID) supported the setting up of a national platform to increase the visibility of marginalized MSM and transgender groups. The Programme Management Office of DFID supported seven projects addressing the information, service, networking, and research needs of these communities.

- **Introduction of condom vending machines:** Another institutional response recognized the poor uptake of condoms distributed through TIs or sold through special depots. NACP made recommendations to install condom vending machines to improve condom uptake. In 2007, a technical support group responsible for condom social marketing suggested that lubricant pouches also need to be made available through these machines. However, action was slow to take place.

Financial Factors

A key feature of the NACP has been the large number of donors available to support the programme. The availability of funds either directly through the donors themselves, or indirectly through their funding of government and non-government programmes, permitted a greater scope for research and pilot testing of approaches than is usual in health programmes. These important financial factors included funding for programme activities, funding for programme research and pilot testing of various approaches, and parallel funding at scale.

- **Funding for programme activities:** The second phase of NACP considerably expanded the scope of work carried out with vulnerable communities. Three-quarters of the resources have been devoted to preventive interventions (NACO, 2007). Significant investments were made by development partners that were at that time experimenting with institutional arrangements such as State AIDS Control Societies, TIs, community care centres, and drop-in centres and a surge in formative research with high-risk groups to understand the drivers of risk. It was also during this phase that a number of new donors entered India, notably the Global Fund against AIDS, TB, and Malaria, and the Bill and Melinda Gates Foundation. Both brought new funding and new funding paradigms, which also changed the financial landscape in India considerably (NACO, 2010).
- **Parallel funding at scale:** Phase III of the NACP has seen a massive increase; the government outlay is about US$1,100 million within an overall allocation of US$2,000 million. Thus, more than US$900 million was budgeted out of donor funding.

Sufficient Conditions

Structural Factors

Structural factors that played a key role and affected the uptake of the programme were the

- attitude of wider society towards MSM issues,
- attitude of individuals within the MSM community itself, and
- ability to coalesce and form organizations and networks.

- **Attitude of wider society towards MSM issues:** When Phase II of the NACP began, the MSM community in India was viewed with suspicion. Societal attitudes were often derogatory, with reports of routine harassment by the police and degradations such as sexual favours and even rape. MSM cruising sites were raided and individuals locked up without recourse to legal aid. There was little attention to their plight by the wider community, and connections and communication between the 'straight' and the MSM community remained limited to sexual encounters.

- **Attitude of individuals within the MSM community itself:** The community itself was deeply fragmented, and several research and operational reports produced at the time documented the various subgroups within the community. However, it was also at this time that the community began to change from within. This was a great period marked by consolidation among groups, development of group identities, and hope for both social acceptance as individuals and as a community. DFID-supported networks such as the Integrated Network for Sexual Minorities, the Indian Network of People Living with HIV/AIDS, and those supported by Naz Foundation International provided impetus for individuals and community-based groups to come together.

- **Ability to coalesce and form organizations and networks:** By 1999, several community-based organizations had emerged, such as the Humsafar Trust, Lakshya Trust, and Sahodaran and Social Welfare Association for Men (SWAM). It was also at the close of the decade that the first Pride March was held in Kolkata. By 2008, the Pride had been held in several cities of India and had become an annual feature. Several initiatives were undertaken as part of NACP II to enforce the rights of people living with HIV and AIDS and people vulnerable to infection (Lawyers Collective, 2010). These too helped to change the attitudes of people at risk of HIV.

Contextual Factors

Aspects of the socio-economic landscape that had a bearing on the attainment of the outcome included: growing globalization, repeal of Section 377 of Indian Penal Code, concerted interest of development partners in MSM issues, and a sympathetic media.

- **Growing globalization:** Growing globalization changed the equation around the MSM community. It led to a strengthening of the lesbian-gay-bisexual-transgender (LGBT) movement as news about the LGBT movement worldwide reached India. There was greater exchange of ideas within India, and it facilitated the 'coming out' of LGBT leaders. Globalization also contributed to the formation of stable community-based organizations advocating for the rights and services of LGBT people.
- **Section 377 of the Indian Penal Code:** This little known provision of the Indian Penal Code criminalizes homosexual behaviour and has been responsible for the denial of various fundamental rights—such as life, liberty, health, privacy, speech, movement, and so on—to sexual minorities. This led to the enhanced vulnerability of MSM to HIV and AIDS by driving them underground and making it difficult to provide them with sexual health-related services and HIV prevention education. The repeal of Section 377 became the locus of initiatives by the community to reinstate its members in the broader Indian polity since the mid-1990s. The movement helped strengthen the acceptability of homosexuality among the NACP programme implementers, as well as those in other parts of government concerned with policy development.
- **Interest of development partners in MSM issues:** The vulnerability of MSM to HIV had been established by Phase II of NACP. Between 2001 and 2009, a discourse towards acceptability and mainstreaming of homosexuality had built up in the country, changing the landscape inhabited by those of the community forever. A key indicator of this was the development of an HIV Bill. The consultative process undertaken to draft the legislation resulted in greater visibility of the issues in society at large.

- **Sympathetic media:** Globalization and growing discourse on Section 377 has also been successful in creating a media sympathetic to the cause of the LGBT community in the country. After 2006, the media has been helpful in providing visibility to LGBT issues and thereby helping to create an attitudinal change of the mainstream society.

Discussion

The history of the NACP shows that the programme's ability to provide effective interventions to the MSM community took much longer than anticipated. TI implementation, long held to be the key to prevention among most at-risk groups, remained poor through Phase II of the NACP. Despite a wealth of information on where the community was located, their attitudes and behaviours, the best approaches to preventing HIV among them, and the extent of the epidemic, the programme was unable to institute an effective response to the epidemic.

The N&S logic model helps to explain why the available information could not be used effectively by the programme earlier. On the basis of the review, we were able to identify a series of milestones (see Figure 8.2) in the roadmap of uptake of evidence. The roadmap helped to identify certain inflection points in the knowledge map of the programme, which resulted in better service provision. Turning points were associated with change in the attitude of people or changes in the social and legislative framework of society.

In the early period, the emphasis of evidence gathering was on developing an understanding of the extent of the problem, distribution of those at risk, and institutional configurations that might work best. Thus, much was known or becoming known about how to set up the *necessary conditions* of the programme. Nevertheless, the place of MSM within society remained tenuous.

The *sufficient conditions* began to change only later, as the programme became established. Structural factors had played a contrarian role, with widespread indifference to the situation of MSM, stigma, and discrimination. The wider heterosexual population and policy-makers remained in denial, attributing HIV to those 'with loose morals'. This may help to explain why despite high prevalence of HIV among the MSM population

Figure 8.2
Time Spiral for Developing Robust MSM Interventions in NACP

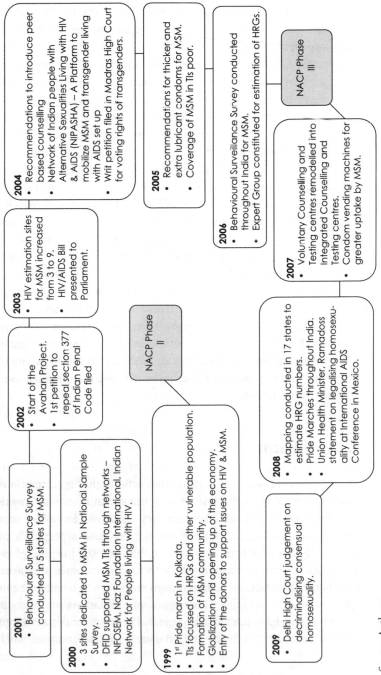

2001
• Behavioural Surveillance Survey conducted in 5 states for MSM.

2000
• 3 sites dedicated to MSM in National Sample Survey.
• DFID supported MSM TIs through networks – INFOSEM, Naz Foundation International, Indian Network for People living with HIV.

1999
• 1st Pride march in Kolkata.
• TIs focussed on HRGs and other vulnerable population.
• Formation of MSM community.
• Globlization and opening up of the economy.
• Entry of the donors to support issues on HIV & MSM.

NACP Phase II

2002
• Start of the Avahan Project.
• 1st petition to repeal section 377 of Indian Penal Code filed

2003
• HIV estimation sites for MSM increased from 3 to 9.
• HIV/AIDS Bill presented to Parliament.

2004
• Recommendations to introduce peer based counselling
• Network of Indian people with Alternative Sexualities Living with HIV & AIDS (NIPASHA) – A Platform to mobilize MSM and transgender living with AIDS set up
• Writ petition filed in Madras High Court for voting rights of transgenders.

2005
• Recommendations for thicker and extra lubricant condoms for MSM.
• Coverage of MSM in TIs poor.

2006
• Behavioural Surveillance Survey conducted throughout India for MSM.
• Expert Group constituted for estimation of HRGs.

NACP Phase III

2007
• Voluntary Counselling and Testing centres remodelled into Integrated Counselling and Testing centres.
• Condom vending machines for greater uptake by MSM.

2008
• Mapping conducted in 17 states to estimate HRG numbers.
• Pride Marches throughout India.
• Union Health Minister, Ramadoss statement on legalising homosexuality at International AIDS Conference in Mexico.

2009
• Delhi High Court judgement on decriminalising consensual homosexuality.

Source: Authors.

there were few exclusive interventions for them during Phase II. On the contextual front, many unexpected developments were taking place. A long-forgotten section of the Indian Penal Code had become a significant barrier to meaningful interventions with the MSM community. The dramatic challenge to Section 377 of the Indian Penal Code resulted in what might be termed a 'social movement'. On the one hand, it helped to organize and mobilize the community to come forward and seek their rights as citizens of the country, and on the other, to garner support from the general population. Growing globalization and the interest of development partners had changed the situation of MSM who were now coalescing into stable community groups.

Only a short three years into NACP Phase III, the picture had changed dramatically. By 2009, the joint midterm review of the programme showed that coverage of MSM had gone up to 78 per cent, the highest among the three high-risk groups identified by the NACP. What led to such an extraordinary change?

Using the N&S logic model, we postulate that remarkable changes in the structural and contextual factors led to better uptake of the evaluation findings in the third phase of the NACP. Public discourse had changed the situation of MSM within society forever, auguring a new reality. A new attitude surfaced among MSM and in society at large, gaining vigour just in time to result in more effective interventions for MSM in Phase III of the NACP.

Conclusion

Programmes are suites of constructive actions that accelerate a development trajectory. Technical approaches, institutional arrangements, and financial outlays are the *necessary conditions* for a development programme. Evaluation typically focuses on these aspects. This focus is perfectly logical when, as is usually the case, the purpose of evaluation is limited to understanding what technical outcomes were achieved, whether the institutional configurations worked, and whether the money given was spent usefully. These types of evaluations are often driven by those who have funded the project. However, understanding these aspects alone is not sufficient to understand *why* programmes work.

Understanding the *sufficient conditions* (comprising structural and contextual factors) is necessary to understand why some programmes 'take' and others do not. These are more difficult to discover and can usually be done by carefully collecting qualitative data regarding social, economic, and political conditions of the society in which development change is sought to be delivered.

Thus, evaluation of the *necessary conditions* can be used to assess project implementation and progress on how far the technical approach, institutional arrangements, and resource allocations achieved the objectives of the programme. However, in order to explain why the programme worked or failed and draw learning from programme outcomes, it must enter the realm of the *sufficient conditions* in exploring the circumstances, perspectives, experiences, and expectations of the stakeholders involved.

References

Chakrapani, V., Row-Kavi, A., Ramakrishnan, L.R., Gupta, R., Rappoport, C., and Raghavan, S.S. (2002). *HIV prevention among men who have sex with men (MSM) in India: Review of current scenario and recommendations* (Background paper prepared for SAATHII [Solidarity and Action against the HIV Infection in India]). Retrieved 12 October 2012 from http://www.indianlgbthealth.info/Authors/Downloads/MSM_HIV_IndiaFin.pdf

Contandriopoulos, D. and Brouselle, S. (2012). Evaluation models and evaluation use. *Evaluation*, 18(1), 61–7.

Green, L.W., Ottoson, J.M., Garcia, C., and Hiatt, R.A. (2009). Diffusion theory, knowledge dissemination, utilization, and integration into public health. *Annual Review of Public Health*, 30, 151–74.

Hurteau, M., Houle, S., and Mongiat, S. (2009). How legitimate and justified are judgments in programme evaluation? *Evaluation*, 15(3), 307–19.

Jayakaran, R. (2008). New participatory tools for measuring attitude, behaviour, perception, and change. In I.B. Williams and M. Shankar (eds), *Evaluation South Asia* (pp. 47–60). Kathmandu, Nepal: UNICEF.

Khan, S. (2004). *MSM and HIV/AIDS in India*. Lucknow, Uttar Pradesh, India: Naz Foundation International. Retrieved 10 October 2012 from http://www.nfi.net/NFI%20Publications/Essays/2004/MSM,%20HIV%20and%20India.pdf

Lawyers Collective. (2010). *HIV/AIDS Bill 2007*. Retrieved 11 October 2012 from http://www.lawyerscollective.org/hiv-and-law/draft-law.html

McDonald, P. and Viehbeck, S. (2007). From evidence-based practice making to practice based evidence making: Creating communities of (research) and practice. *Health Promotion Practice*, 8(2), 140–4.

National AIDS Control Organization. (2006). *Strategy and implementation plan.* New Delhi, India: NACO.

———. (2007). *UNGASS Country Progress Report India 2006.* New Delhi, India: NACO.

———. (2010). *UNGASS Country Progress Report India 2010.* New Delhi, India: NACO.

Organisation for Economic Co-operation and Development. (2008). *The Paris Declaration on aid effectiveness and the Accra agenda for action.* Paris: OECD. Retrieved 12 October 2012 from http://www.oecd.org/development/aideffectiveness/34428351.pdf

Rossi, P.H., Freeman, H.E., and Lipsey, P.W. (1999). *Evaluation: A Systematic Approach.* 6th edition. SAGE: Thousand Oaks, CA.

Saunders, M. (2012). The use and usability of evaluation outputs: A social practice approach. *Evaluation*, 18(4), 421–36.

Singh, S., Dasgupta, S., and Barua, N. (2009). *Recognizing and tackling vulnerabilities responding to HIV-AIDS in India* (Working Paper 4). New Delhi: The Research Group, Amaltas Consulting Pvt. Ltd.

Singh, S., Dasgupta, S., and Singh, Y.D. (2010). *Necessary and sufficient conditions— Evaluation, evidence, and knowledge translation* (Working Paper 6). New Delhi: The Research Group, Amaltas Consulting Pvt. Ltd.

Singh, S., Dasgupta, S., Patankar, P., and Sinha, M. (2013). *A People Stronger: The Collectivization of MSM and TG groups in India.* New Delhi: SAGE Publications.

Sudsawad, P. (2007). *Knowledge translation: Introduction to models, strategies, and measures.* Austin, TX: National Center for the Dissemination of Disability Research.

World Bank. (2004). *Evaluations that improved the performance and impacts of the development programs: Case studies and lessons learned in influential evaluations.* Washington, D.C.: World Bank. Retrieved 11 October 2012 from http://www.oecd.org/derec/worldbank/36483282.pdf

9

The Need for Methodological Diversity in Evaluating Complex Health Interventions

Anuska Kalita

Background

Health systems have to evaluate a wide array of existing and newly proposed complex interventions to learn what is effective about any given intervention so that it can be more widely applied throughout the system. Compared with drug trials, for instance, the design of a health service intervention, especially one involving communities and systems, is highly complex. In practice, such interventions are often defined pragmatically, according to local circumstance, rather than building on any specific theoretical approach (Shepperd et al., 1995). Even if an approach or model can be grounded clearly in theory and evidence, it must still be operationalized and evaluated among specific practitioners and communities.

Thus, the evaluation of complex interventions is a continuous challenge in health systems research, and increasingly we are seeing that quantitative methods alone cannot tell us why an intervention was or was not successful or whether the theory and evidence informing the intervention were appropriate or needed revision. While quantitative experimental research designs—comparing outcomes in intervention groups with those of control and comparison groups—are optimal for minimizing bias and provide the most accurate estimate of a complex intervention's efficacies and effectiveness, they do not adequately explain the multifaceted causal pathways of these interventions and their interactions with contextual sociopolitical factors (Bradley et al., 1999). To gain a comprehensive understanding about the reasons behind acceptance and rejection of hypotheses related to complex health interventions, qualitative methods are often essential (Bradley et al., 1999).

To clarify the challenge and the need, this chapter examines a complex health intervention—the Reduction of Low Birth Weight Project—focusing on one of its secondary health outcomes—iron deficiency anaemia. It looks at the limits and potential of different methodologies in terms of understanding the causal factors contributing to project outcomes and of evaluating the project's impact.

Complex Health Intervention—A Definition

A complex intervention comprises a number of components, which may act both independently and interdependently (Medical Research Council [MRC], 2000). It is not easy to define the 'active ingredients' of a complex intervention precisely, as they encompass several dimensions of complexity—the evidence and theory that inform the intervention, the tasks and processes involved in applying the theoretical principles, the range of possible outcomes and/or their variability in the target population, and the people with whom and the context within which the intervention is operationalized.

Complex interventions are widely used in public health practice and in areas of social policy that have important health consequences. Conventionally defined as interventions with several interacting components, they present a number of special problems for evaluators, in addition to the practical and methodological difficulties that any successful evaluation must overcome (MRC, 2008). Many of the additional problems relate to

- the difficulty of standardizing the design and delivery of the interventions (Hawe et al., 2004; Rifkin, 2007),
- their sensitivity to features of the local context (Rychetnik et al., 2002),
- the organizational and logistical difficulty of applying experimental methods to service or policy change (Ogilvie et al., 2006; Wolff, 2001), and
- the length and complexity of the causal chains linking intervention with outcome (Petticrew et al., 2005).

An Example of a Complex Health Intervention: The Reduction of Low Birth Weight Project

The state of Jharkhand, formed in Eastern India in 2000, is predominantly rural with a large tribal population, a hilly terrain, and scattered settlements. The maternal and child health scenario in Jharkhand is dismal. Health indicators include

- an infant mortality rate of 70 (Office of the Registrar General and Census Commissioner of India, 2001),
- 54.6 per cent of children underweight (International Institute for Population Science [IIPS], 2009),
- 41.7 per cent babies born with low birth weight (LBW),[1]
- more than 80 per cent home deliveries (IIPS, 2009),
- almost 4 of every 10 women undernourished (IIPS, 2009), and
- about two-thirds of women in the childbearing ages anaemic (IIPS, 2009).

There is also an acute shortage of health care facilities (with low utilization of and poor access to those that do exist) and significant shortfalls in health infrastructure in Jharkhand—with 38 per cent of sub-centres,

64 per cent of primary health centres (PHCs), and 82 per cent of planned community health centres (CHCs) having never been built (Department of Health, Medical Education and Family Welfare, Government of Jharkhand, 2004). The state's health infrastructure has significant challenges that need to be addressed.

The Reduction of Low Birth Weight Project was established in 2003 as a partnership of the ICICI Centre for Child Health and Nutrition (ICCHN), the Krishi Gram Vikas Kendra (KGVK), the Child in Need Institute (CINI), and the Government of Jharkhand. The project's specific research objective was to evaluate the effectiveness of life-cycle-based community-level interventions with mandated health services in reducing the incidence of LBW and improving maternal, infant, and adolescent health in two blocks—Angara and Sili—of Ranchi district in Jharkhand, covering a population of around 200,000. The project had two complementary sets of interventions: community-level behavioural interventions and interventions to ensure the provision of mandated public health services (see Table 9.1).

Table 9.1
Specific Interventions Delivered at Different Levels

Household Level
• Promoting positive health practices for pregnant women (diet, reduced workload, timely rest)
• Improving access to mandated services and promoting timely referrals (antenatal check-ups, institutional deliveries, referral for danger signs and sudden emergencies, suspected reproductive tract and sexually transmitted infections (RTI/STI)
• Promoting involvement of and sharing among family members in the responsibilities related to pregnancy and parenthood
• Case management with individualized inputs to pregnant women and their families on maternal and infant health
Hamlet Level
• Increasing health awareness, identifying and acting on local health concerns
• Work closely with grassroots health functionaries and enhancing the communities' linkages with them

Table 9.1 continued

Table 9.1 continued

- VHCs collect funds to form the village health kosh to be used by the villagers to facilitate access to health care and to address community health issues
- Encouraging the formation of and guiding adolescent groups in raising and addressing community health concerns
- Conducting nutrition demonstration camps

Cluster Level

- Sharing information drawn from the cohorts with the ANMs and AWWs
- Provide convergence between communities and health delivery systems to ensure enhanced coverage of mandated services and address local priorities
- Strengthening services at the sub-centre
- Placing medical van in remote areas

Public Health System Level

- Improving access to sub-centres by conducting participatory rural appraisals (health resource mapping in villages) for the demarcation of health facilities
- Renovating sub-centres (by VHCs and community groups)
- Training of AWWs, ANMs, and MOs in 46 sub-centres
- Regularizing supplies of drugs and equipment at two public health centres and 46 sub-centres
- Involving the state government through the project's steering and implementation committees

Source: Authors.

Community-level Behavioural Interventions

The community-based interventions included hamlet-level female community health volunteers (Sahiyyas) selected and supported by Village Health Committees (VHCs) comprising community representatives. The project also created a supportive structure for the Sahiyyas at different levels, comprising master trainers and VHCs at the village level, supervisors at the cluster level, and coordinators at the block level. These cadres of personnel support the training of the Sahiyya, provide on-going support, and supervise her work. Equipped with this training, a support structure, and the cohort register (a pictorial tool that records details about each woman and child), the Sahiyya plays a role in prevention and health promotion. She focuses on changing dietary practices, reducing workload during pregnancy, procuring antenatal care (ANC) from health facilities, promoting appropriate child feeding and caring practices, and building awareness about health and nutrition issues in her hamlet. Together, the VHCs and the Sahiyyas act as agents of community mobilization by facilitating behaviour change for better maternal and child health practices, providing prevention and health promotion case management in the area of maternal and infant health, building ownership and initiating action on community health issues, and helping communities link to health services. Peer groups were created for adolescents at the village level, facilitated by the Sahiyyas and the VHCs and led by a peer leader, to address knowledge, attitudes, behaviours, and practices related to nutrition and reproductive health.

Interventions to Ensure Provision of Mandated Public Health Services

At the service-delivery level, the focus was on

- bridging existing gaps in mandated public health care delivery by ensuring regular supplies of essential drugs,
- building provider capacity building through the orientation and training of public health functionaries,
- building and renovating sub-centre facilities,
- ensuring the availability of emergency obstetric care through equipped health facilities, and
- ensuring the provision of medical services in remote and inaccessible areas.

As one of the central roles of the Sahiyya is to act as a link between the public health system and the community, the project included various training, sensitization, and orientation initiatives for public health personnel, such as auxiliary nurse midwives (ANMs), medical officers (MOs,) and Anganwadi workers (AWWs) to support the Sahiyyas and their work. The monthly cluster meetings with Sahiyyas, master trainers, supervisors, VHC members, ANMs, and AWWs illustrate the principles of supportive supervision, the use of a problem-solving approach to training, collective community participation, linkages with the public health system, and synergies between the health and nutrition systems at hamlet, village, cluster, and block levels.

Evaluation Methods

Diverse methodologies were used to assess the Reduction of Low Birth Weight Project. A quantitative study was used for hypotheses testing, which involved a baseline–end line comparison with cluster randomization, and a qualitative study—involving in-depth interviews and focus group discussions—was used to understand the changes in the community during the project period.

Quantitative Study Design

Four administrative blocks of Ranchi district—Angara, Mandar, Sili, and Sonahatu—were selected based on presence of local civil society partners (as shown in Figure 9.2). Each block has an average population of 10,000 (based on the 2001 census) and is usually served by one primary health centre.

The project had three arms:

- T2 (a combination of community-level behavioural interventions and interventions to ensure provision of mandated public health services),
- T1 (only interventions to ensure provision of mandated public health services), and
- T0 (comparison of areas without any intervention).

Sili and Angara blocks were assigned to the intervention arms (T2 and T1) while Mandar and Sonahatu were assigned to the control arm (T0). Random sampling was then used to allocate 50 per cent of the sub-centres in Angara and Sili to T1, the other 50 per cent to T2, and 50 per cent of the sub-centres in Mandar and Sonahatu to the comparison arm—T0 (see Figure 9.1).

The three research hypotheses tested by the study and their related outcome indicators are described in Table 9.2.

Figure 9.1
Map of Ranchi Showing Intervention and Comparison Blocks

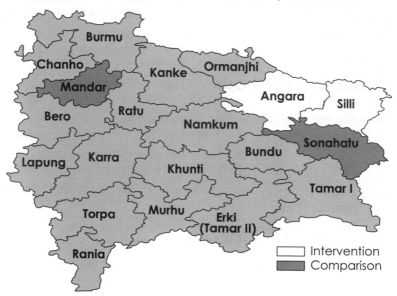

Source: Study Protocol—Reduction of Low Birth Weight Project and www.map-sofindia.com

Figure 9.2
Study Design

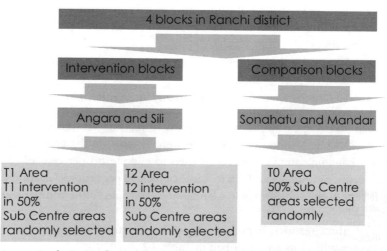

Source: Study Protocol—Reduction of Low Birth Weight Project.

Table 9.2
Research Hypotheses with Outcome Indicators

Research Hypothesis	Outcome Indicators
Hypothesis 1: The proportion of LBW infants in areas with community-level intervention along with mandated primary health care delivery system (T2 areas) will be significantly lower than that in areas with mandated primary health care facilities alone without community-level interventions (T1 areas) at the end of the project period.	• LBW (<2500 grams) measured within 48 hours of birth using a Salter Scale (primary outcome indicator)
Hypothesis 2: Maternal, child, and adolescent health outcomes will be significantly better in T2 areas than that in T1 areas.	Maternal nutrition and care during pregnancy/lactation: • Body Mass Index (BMI) (kg/m^2)[i] • Anaemia measured with HaemoQ[ii] • Food practices during pregnancy/lactation • Workload and rest during pregnancy Child feeding and caring practices: • Breastfeeding (initiation, colostrums, and exclusive) • Complementary feeding (initiation at 6 months) • Immunization (any and full immunization)[iii] • Newborn care • Health seeking Adolescent (15–24 years) nutrition and awareness: • Anaemia among adolescent girls measured with HaemoQ • BMI of adolescents • Knowledge and attitudes about nutrition and reproductive health among adolescents
Hypothesis 3: Antenatal and child health care service utilization in T2 areas will be significantly greater than utilization in T1 areas.	ANC: • Access and uptake of ANC • Full ANC check-up[iv] • Number of ANC visits[v]

Table 9.2 continued

Table 9.2 continued

Research Hypothesis	Outcome Indicators
	Institutional delivery: • Place of delivery for last pregnancy Postnatal care (PNC): • Access and uptake of PNC • Number of PNC visits[vi] • Full PNC check-up[vii]

Source: Authors.
Notes:
i. A BMI of 18.5kg/m² is considered normal.
ii. A haemoglobin (Hb) level of 11 g/dl is considered normal. An Hb level between 10.0 and 10.9 g/dl is mild anaemia, Hb level between 7.0 and 9.9 g/dl is moderate anaemia, and Hb level of less than 7.0 g/dl is severe anaemia.
iii. The full immunization schedule includes BCG vaccine, three doses of DPT vaccine, and three doses of Oral Polio Vaccine and measles vaccine.
iv. Full ANC check-up includes measurements of weight, height, and blood pressure; blood test; urine test; abdominal and internal examination; ultrasound; two tetanus toxoid vaccines; 90 iron folic acid (IFA) tablets; and ANC advice about diet, danger signs, delivery care, newborn care, and family planning.
v. Recommended minimum of three visits, one in each trimester.
vi. Recommended minimum of three visits—after two days, one week, and two months of delivery.
vii. Full PNC check-up includes abdominal examination, newborn and infant feeding/caring advice, and family planning advice.

Data Collection

For the purpose of the evaluation, baseline data were collected[2] through four population-based surveys—the household (HH) survey, the ANC survey, the PNC survey, and the adolescent health survey—conducted concurrently. The data measured maternal and child health status, awareness levels, health and nutritional status of adolescents, and demographic factors, along with the status of provisions for health services. Trained surveyors at the community level measured birth weights within 48 hours after birth using a Salter Scale and anaemia for pregnant women and adolescent girls using the HaemoQ.

At the end of the intervention period (2003–07), an end-line evaluation was conducted to study the impact of the intervention in 2008.

Sampling Frame

The sampling frame comprised the four administrative blocks selected for the study—Angara, Mandar, Sili, and Sonahatu. Random sampling was used to allocate sub-centres from within each of the four blocks to each of the three study arms: T1, T2, and T0.

Villages from each of the study sub-centres were randomly selected for the baseline survey, and included 58 T1 villages, 72 villages where T2 was implemented, and 61 villages that would remain in the comparison arm (T0). Households within the selected villages were enumerated, and four different survey questionnaires were used to collect data (see Figure 9.3 and description below).

At the end of the study period, villages were again randomly selected from each sub-centre service delivery area and included 63 T1 villages, 73 villages where T2 had been implemented, and 59 T0 villages. End-line and baseline data were collected using the same survey questionnaires.

Data Collected

Household (HH) survey: The data for the HH survey were obtained from 3,536 (at baseline) and 3,509 (at end line) women having at least one live birth in the last five years from the date of the survey. In the case of two or more pregnancies in the five-year period, details were taken for the last pregnancy. The sample was generated by randomly selecting two or three villages in the catchment areas of each of the 72 sub-centres serving the study area. In each survey village, all households were listed and 22 women per village were randomly selected. Thus, a total of 195 villages were covered in the surveys. The sample covered one respondent from each household.

ANC survey: For the ANC survey, all pregnant women in the third trimester of pregnancy from the 195 villages were included in this survey. This represented 996 women at baseline and 1,349 women at end line. Information on nutrition, workload, and rest during pregnancy was analysed from the ANC survey.

Figure 9.3
Multistage Sampling and Data Collection Tools

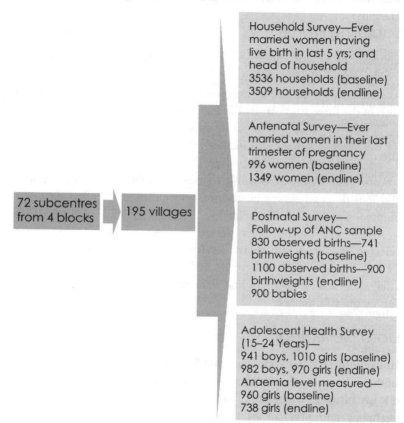

Source: Study Protocol—Reduction of Low Birth Weight Project.

PNC survey: For the PNC survey, out of the 996 and 1,349 women of the ANC survey at baseline and end line, 830 women and 1,100 women, respectively, were followed up after birth. Information on infant and child-feeding/caring practices, PNC for the mother, immunization, and health care-seeking behaviour was analysed. Out of these observed births, birth weights were obtained for 741 babies at baseline and 900 babies at end line within 48 hours of delivery.

Adolescent health survey: For the adolescent health survey, 941 boys and 1,010 girls were randomly selected at baseline and 982 boys and 970 girls at end line. Out of the total sampled adolescent girls, informed consent was obtained and anaemia levels were measured with HaemoQ for 960 girls at baseline and 738 girls at end line.

Although the project started with a quantitative experimental design with cluster randomization, the interventions and the research design itself were impacted significantly by political factors and implementation realities in Jharkhand. For instance, the civil violence in certain areas of Jharkhand affected the project by reducing the reach and intensity of some of its community-based and systemic interventions because of safety concerns for project personnel. Given that one of the main aims of the project was to strengthen the mandated health services through the government system, liaising with an unstable state government with frequent changes in political and bureaucratic leadership was particularly challenging.

While the project was able to inform state policies through the scale-up of the Sahiyya Programme across Jharkhand (2004) and the Accredited Social Health Activist (ASHA) programme (2005) within the National Rural Health Mission (NRHM), the result was a 'contamination' of the study design (from the point of view of a conventional experimental paradigm), with project interventions being implemented across all areas, including comparison blocks. Although in an underresourced and vulnerable context like Jharkhand this was a welcome policy decision, this universalization would be expected to reduce the statistical significance of the difference in outcomes between the original 'intervention' (T2 and T1) and 'comparison' blocks (T0). The resulting, and hence confusing, preliminary findings from the study led to the design of a qualitative study of the project to conduct stakeholder mapping and to understand the project's life cycle, the evolution of the intervention processes and interrelationships among them, the intended and unintended outcomes, and the impact of external factors.

Qualitative Study Design

The study design for the qualitative evaluation comprised theoretical sampling of villages on the predetermined criteria of the predominance of tribal/non-tribal population and distance from the nearest sub-centre to maximize divergence. Through discussions with community organizers and project implementers, it was felt that these two categories represented unique characteristics that added to maximum divergence among villages across the study area. This sampling was done across the three arms: T1, T2, and T0. Table 9.3 shows the categories of villages included in the sample, based on these criteria.

Six villages were selected from each of the T2, T1, and T0 areas, leading to a total of 18 villages in the final sample (see Table 9.4).

Table 9.3
Sampling Criteria for Maximizing Divergence

Population of village	Distance from the nearest health sub-centre			Across all three arms (T2, T1, T0) and all four blocks (Angara, Sili, Sonahatu, and Mandar)
Tribal	Far	Medium	Close	
Non-tribal	Far	Medium	Close	

Source: Authors.

Table 9.4
Stakeholders and Data Collection

Stakeholders for In-depth Interviews	Numbers in Each Village	Total Interviews
Villages from the T2 area		
VHC member	2	12
Sahiyya	1	6
Woman above reproductive age (>40 years of age)	1	6
Woman in reproductive age (<40 years of age)	1	6
Government functionaries (ANM, AWW)	1 each	12
Key informants from village (identified on field visits with community organizers)	2	12
Villages from the T1 and T0 areas		
Woman above reproductive age (>40 years of age)	1	12
Woman in reproductive age (<40 years of age)	1	12
Government functionaries (ANM, AWW)	1 each	24
Key informants from village (identified on field visits with community organizers)	2	24

Source: Authors.

Data were validated by conducting two focused group discussions (FGDs) with the project supervisors and master trainers. In an iterative manner, which is a specific characteristic of qualitative methods, one-third of the data were analysed for identification of gaps. Some of these data gaps were filled through FGDs with key informants in two villages.

Semi-structured interview guides were prepared—based on the main areas of enquiry (identified through consultative workshops with the project team) and the main objectives of the study, and—to explain some of the findings of the quantitative evaluation. A group of six trained researchers collected the data; the tools were piloted in two villages chosen specifically for this purpose and all interviews were audio taped.

The qualitative study collected and analysed data about the village (population, main occupations, food practices, sources of water, social groups, and agricultural practices); general health problems in the village; changes in health practices over time; facilities available for health problems and changes in services over time; specific health issues related to pregnancy and child birth; and the performance of various health functionaries (Sahiyyas, project VHCs, and ANMs, MOs, and AWWs of the public health system). It also sought information from project functionaries (supervisors and master trainers) about implementation realities during the entire project period in terms of the impact of the changing political economy and the sociocultural context of the state.

The Case Study: Using Diverse Methodologies to Understand the Causes of Rising Anaemia

To illustrate the need for diverse methodologies in evaluating complex public health interventions, such as the Reduction of Low Birth Weight Project, we will focus on one set of indicators—the prevalence of anaemia among pregnant women (using data from the ANC surveys) and adolescent girls (using data from the Adolescent Health surveys).

Iron deficiency anaemia is the most pervasive of all nutritional deficiencies among women and adolescent girls in India. Anaemia during pregnancy can increase the risk of LBW, premature births, poor foetal growth, and maternal morbidity and mortality (Black et al., 2008).

Maternal haemorrhage is one of the top 10 leading causes of death among adolescent girls, especially in cases of low age at marriage and at first pregnancy. The major cause of iron deficiency anaemia is low consumption of meat, fish, or poultry, especially in poor people (Bhargava et al., 2001; Black et al., 2008). Women of childbearing age are at high risk for negative iron balance because of blood loss during menstruation and the substantial iron demands of pregnancy (Black et al., 2008).

Due to its implications for birth weight and maternal health, the prevalence of anaemia was one of the secondary outcome indicators of the Reduction of Low Birth Weight Project. It was related to the second hypothesis of the project: *at the end of the project period, maternal, child, and adolescent health outcomes will be significantly better in areas with community-level interventions along with a mandated primary health-care delivery system (T2 areas) than that in areas with mandated primary health care facilities alone, without community-level interventions (T1 areas).*

Anaemia was measured for pregnant women and adolescent girls (15–24 years of age) with the HaemoQ, after obtaining informed consent from the participants and ethical approval from the concerned Institutional Review Board.[3] Anaemia levels were classified as 'mild' (Hb levels between 10.0 and 10.9 g/dl), 'moderate' (Hb levels between 7.0 and 9.9 g/dl), and 'severe' (Hb levels below 7.0 g/dl).

Table 9.5 describes the project interventions that aimed to address iron deficiency anaemia.

Table 9.5
Interventions to Address Iron Deficiency Anaemia

Household Level
• Counselling pregnant women and their families about the prevalence, symptoms, effects, and cure for iron deficiency anaemia
• Promoting iron-rich foods for pregnant women and adolescent girls through dissemination of knowledge about green leafy vegetables (GLVs), meat, fish, and eggs by the Sahiyya
• Improving access to antenatal check-ups through referrals and health behaviour by the Sahiyya for detection of anaemia during pregnancy and receiving IFA tablets distributed free of cost at government health facilities to pregnant women

Table 9.5 continued

Table 9.5 continued

- Motivating pregnant women to consume IFA tablets
- Providing case management with individualized advice and support to pregnant women and their families on nutrition and care during pregnancy

Hamlet Level

- Building awareness about the prevalence, symptoms, effects, and cure for iron-deficiency anaemia among pregnant women and their families by the Sahiyya and the VHC
- Facilitating the formation of and guiding adolescent groups and building awareness about the prevalence, symptoms, effects, and cure for iron-deficiency anaemia among adolescent girls by the peer leader, the Sahiyya, and the VHC
- Conducting nutrition demonstration camps in collaboration with the Anganwadi Centre and the ANM to promote recipes with locally available iron-rich foods

Cluster Level

- Convening cluster meetings with participation from community members, VHCs, Sahiyyas, AWWs, and ANMs to create convergence between communities and public health delivery system to ensure enhanced coverage of mandated services and address the issue of anaemia

Public Health System Level

- Training of AWWs, ANMs, and MOs in 46 sub-centres focusing on causes and prevention of LBW and undernutrition among women, adolescent girls, and children (including iron deficiency anaemia)
- Regularizing supplies of IFA tablets at 46 sub-centres and 2 PHCs

Source: Authors.

Findings from the Quantitative Evaluation

The baseline survey found a very high prevalence (88.2 per cent) of anaemia among pregnant women in the study area, with the proportion of women suffering from 'severe' anaemia being 6.5 per cent. The moderate form of anaemia was more widespread among the surveyed pregnant women (58.3 per cent) than was mild anaemia (23.3 per cent). Among adolescent girls (15–24 years), the prevalence rate was 66.4 per cent, with 39.6 per cent mildly anaemic, 56.7 per cent moderately anaemic, and 3.7 per cent severely anaemic.

During the four-year intervention period in the T1 and T2 areas, the T2 areas received all the specific intervention components as listed in Table 9.5, and the T1 areas received only the health system-level intervention components. At the end of the intervention period, the end-line survey was conducted between January and July 2008, with the same study design and data collection tools.

The results of the end-line survey found that the total prevalence of anaemia among pregnant women had increased across the study area from 88.2 per cent at baseline to 93.7 per cent, as had prevalence for severe (8.6 per cent) and moderate (71.7 per cent) levels; there was a decrease in mild anaemia, from 23.3 to 13.4 per cent. The end-line data for adolescent girls also showed a similar increase in anaemia levels in total prevalence (from 66.4 to 74.7 per cent) and for moderate (from 56.7 to 61.5 per cent) and severe levels (from 3.7 to 5.9 per cent); the prevalence of mild levels of anaemia decreased from 39.6 to 32.6 per cent. Table 9.6 presents the comparison in anaemia levels between baseline and endline.

These prevalence rates across the study area are comparable to the trend observed in data from the last two National Family Health surveys (NFHS 2 conducted in 1998–99 and NFHS 3 conducted in 2004–05), with 64 per cent prevalence of anaemia among pregnant women in the 15- to 49-year age group in NFHS 2 (IIPS, 2004), which increased to 68.4 per cent in NFHS 3 (IIPS, 2009).

Table 9.6
Comparison between Baseline and End-line Prevalence of Different Levels of Anaemia

Prevalence of Anaemia	Levels of Anaemia	Mild (%)	Moderate (%)	Severe (%)	Total (%)
Anaemia among pregnant women	**Baseline**	23.3	58.3	6.5	88.2
	End line	13.4	71.7	8.6	93.7
Anaemia among adolescent girls	**Baseline**	39.6	56.7	3.7	66.4
	End line	32.6	61.5	5.9	74.7

Source: Authors.

Table 9.7
Comparison between Baseline and End-line Prevalence of
Anaemia across T0, T1, and T2 Areas

Prevalence of Anaemia	T0		T1		T2	
	Baseline (%)	End Line (%)	Baseline (%)	End Line (%)	Baseline (%)	End Line (%)
Anaemia among pregnant women	82.5	91.8	92.3	95.6	88.2	93.7
Anaemia among adolescent girls	62.0	71.7	74.9	81.0	64.5	72.2

Source: Authors.

Table 9.7 shows the baseline and end-line data disaggregated into the treatment areas: T0, T1, and T2.

A regression analysis was conducted to detect any significant differences between the treatment groups.

In the case of data on **anaemia among pregnant women**, the Chi-Square analysis for comparison between baseline and end-line data in T0, T1, and T2 areas showed no significant difference among the three treatment areas (at 0.05 confidence interval [CI], degree of freedom = 2, with χ^2 = 5.036). Therefore, the inference is that, despite the interventions directed towards reducing anaemia prevalence among pregnant women in the intervention areas, there was no difference in the prevalence rates as compared with the rates for the other areas.

With regard to the data on **anaemia prevalence amongst adolescent girls**, from a regression analysis using Chi-Square at 0.05 CI and degree of freedom f = 2, a comparison between baseline and end-line data showed that the prevalence of anaemia significantly increased across all the three treatment areas, irrespective of interventions in T1 and T2 to address the issue. Furthermore, the regression coefficients for both T2 and T1 were positive for the baseline data, though only the latter was statistically significant. In other words, the level of anaemia prevalence was significantly higher in T1 areas compared with the level in T0 areas, whereas the prevalence level in T2 was similar to that in T0. However, in the end-line data, the level of anaemia among the adolescent girls did not differ between the three areas, meaning the differences seen were not statistically significant.

Another noticeable observation was a significant difference in the level of anaemia by caste/tribe and education of the parents in the base-line data. The percentage of girls having any level of anaemia was signifi-cantly smaller among the general caste and among girls whose parents were both educated, compared with the percentages for adolescent girls from the tribal communities and from non-literate households. Such dif-ferentials seem to have disappeared in the end-line data, as anaemia lev-els increased across the population.

The lack of significant difference in anaemia prevalence between T1 and T2 areas indicates that the research hypothesis mentioned above— that the prevalence rates in T2 will be lower than in T1 areas—is rejected.

A rejected hypothesis may indicate a failure of implementation and not necessarily a failure of the intervention. To rule out failure of imple-mentation, we analysed the data on the intervention sets aimed to reduce anaemia. The results are shown in Tables 9.8, 9.9, and 9.10.

A test of significance among the three arms for baseline and end-line data showed that for ANC for pregnant women, there were significant differences (at CI = 0.001) for the changes between baseline and end-line uptake rates in T2 areas, whereas the difference in T1 areas was significant at CI = 0.005, and in T0 areas the uptake decreased between baseline and end line. Thus, the improvements in ANC uptake among

Table 9.8

Comparison of Baseline and End-line ANC across T0, T1, and T2 Areas

ANC Components for Pregnant Women	T0		T1		T2	
	Baseline (%)	End Line (%)	Baseline (%)	End Line (%)	Baseline (%)	End Line (%)
Received ANC check-up	82.5	75.9	70.7	73.1	75.5	78.9
Advice on diet received during ANC	67.2	71.6	62.6	64.3	63.7	73.6

Source: Authors.

Table 9.9
Comparison of Baseline and End-line IFA Supplementation across T0, T1, and T2 Areas

IFA Supplementation for Pregnant Women	T0		T1		T2	
	Baseline (%)	End Line (%)	Baseline (%)	End Line (%)	Baseline (%)	End Line (%)
IFA tablets/syrup received during last pregnancy	58.3	80.0	63.4	82.7	64.1	88.1
Received enough iron tablets to last for about three months	74.6	85.6	70.9	90.0	69.6	89.4
All IFA tablets consumed	60.8	63.9	70.3	76.0	69.9	71.4

Source: Authors.

Table 9.10
Comparison of Baseline and End-line Awareness Levels across T0, T1, and T2 Areas

Indicators of Increased Awareness among Adolescent Girls about Possible Cures for Anaemia	T0		T1		T2	
	Baseline (%)	End Line (%)	Baseline (%)	End Line (%)	Baseline (%)	End Line (%)
Those who believe anaemia is curable if they take IFA tablets daily	83.9	90.7	86.9	88.4	84.5	90.3
Those who believe anaemia is curable if they take plenty of GLVs	93.0	92.6	93.9	94.1	92.4	94.7
Those who believe anaemia is curable if they take plenty of fish, poultry, and meat in diet	33.2	46.3	29.9	39.2	25.2	46.9

Source: Authors.

pregnant women in T2 areas were better than in T1 areas. Similarly, for advice on diet during pregnancy received at the ANC visit, the differences among the three arms were significant at CI = 0.001. From these results, we can infer that pregnant women in the intervention areas received significantly more ANC for possible detection of anaemia and also received advice about appropriate iron-rich diets to address the issue.

Chi-square analysis for IFA supplementation for pregnant women showed that there were significant increases in the number of women receiving IFA tablets during their last pregnancy, the number receiving IFA doses for 3 months, and the number consuming all their IFA tablets between baseline and end line in the intervention areas compared with the respective numbers for women in T0 areas.

Regression for the indicators of increased awareness among adolescent girls about possible cures for anaemia showed that there were significant improvements in awareness levels between baseline and end line for the intervention areas compared with the improvements in awareness among adolescent girls in the T0 areas.

The above tables show that the interventions aimed at reducing anaemia among pregnant women and adolescent girls were implemented as intended, with positive expected outputs. Hence, the increase in anaemia cannot be attributed to gaps in implementation. This takes us back to questions about the reasons behind the increases in the prevalence of anaemia—what are the barriers that inhibit the translation of knowledge into practice or of any such complex intervention into intended outcomes?

Findings from the Qualitative Evaluation

In this section, on the basis of an analysis of the data, we explore all the themes that help us better understand the results of the quantitative evaluation of rising anaemia levels. The qualitative data were collected through in-depth interviews and FGDs with people from the communities in the study area. The data provided researchers with insight and information about established and changing food practices and the reasons for such changes: occupations and livelihoods among the community members, differentials among caste and tribe groups, and the larger macro-systemic context in which smaller political economies operate.

Using Atlas-ti software, all the data were coded as per the lines of inquiry of the study. A preliminary code list was developed, interviews were coded by multiple coders, and the code list was revised based on discussions. A final code list was formed by consensus. The data were analysed based on content and themes identified in the interviews.

The qualitative data showed a complex relationship between traditional knowledge of food practices and the changing context in which such knowledge is applied. The erosion of traditional knowledge about, and use of, local foods among tribal groups in Jharkhand as a result of deforestation, urbanization, modernization, and 'co-option into the mainstream' has contributed to an actual change in food behaviours as well as to a decrease in the availability of food items high in iron.

For example, the decrease in the availability of meat (because of a decline in game and changes in lifestyles) is not compensated by increases in other sources of iron-rich foods, such as GLVs or lentils. As well, because of the substitution of subsistence and forest-based tribal economies with a market economy, community dependence on government food programmes has increased. In a context of poverty, landlessness, and lack of purchasing power, the availability of rice and wheat through the public distribution system (PDS; replacing coarse grains such as millets—mahua, jowar, maize, and so on, which are richer in iron and were part of local diets earlier) has led to a change of dietary patterns and a loss of variety, which in turn could have led to the high rates of anaemia.

The main themes that emerged from the data on food practices in the project area are discussed below. The findings showed that changing food patterns were influenced significantly by

- the erosion of forest produce and the emergence of markets,
- urbanization and aspirations of 'modernity',
- hunger and poor quality diets, and
- the PDS.

The Erosion of Forest Produce and the Emergence of Markets

Rampant deforestation and the usurpation of tribal rights over forests have adversely affected the consumption of forest produce—fruits, nutritious roots, mushrooms—by the dependent tribal communities.

The emergence of markets and market-based economies has also shifted agricultural patterns and food consumption behaviours.

As a Sahiyya in Cherudi village (T2) of Sili said,

> Earlier we would usually eat makkai (maize) and mahua (millets). Now we have started eating rice, roti (bread made of wheat,) and sabji (vegetables). We eat twice a day, once in the morning we eat rice and at dinner we eat chapatti. Earlier people would eat whatever was grown in the bari (kitchen garden, forest land), but now we have to buy food from the market.

A key informant from Asri village (T1) in Angara reiterated:

> We used to get food from the forest, but now the forest is decreasing day by day. So we get very few things from the forest. . . . In the past fruits, vegetables, wood everything was available but now it has got very limited or literally unavailable.

A respondent in Asri village (T1) in Angara reported the changes in food patterns and the emergence of markets:

> Now we do not eat mahua (millets), but when I came to this village after marriage we used to eat mahua. People have stopped growing (mahua), now they grow only paddy. . . . Because cultivation of mahua is input- and resource-intensive and the food grown is also traditional and not of much economic value. . . . These changes have come in the last 5 to 10 years. The younger generation does not like it (to work in fields and eat traditional foods). They would rather go to work in Ranchi to earn money and eat food from the market.

Urbanization and Aspirations of 'Modernity'

Due to migration to urban centres for work, tribal communities are more exposed to urban ways of life and notions of modernity. Food is one of the most significant symbols of any culture, including what may be called 'modern culture'. As tribal communities start identifying with these symbols and aspirations for 'modernity' increase, food patterns change. Vegetarianism may be considered as an 'improvement'. This is closely linked with aspirations of people and the *Sanskritization* (or mainstreaming into dominant cultures) of tribal groups. This, combined with emergence of market-based economies and the erosion of forest-based/subsistence agricultural economies, results in significant changes in food consumption behaviour. The quantitative and qualitative data about food consumption (two or less meals per day) clearly indicate the prevailing hunger in the communities. The quantitative data also show that daily meat/fish/egg consumption has declined over the past five years, with the biggest decreases in T2 areas (from 7.2 per cent in the baseline survey to 2.6 per cent in the end-line survey) and in the consumption frequency category 'a few days of a week' across all three areas. In fact, there was a small increase in the number of people who did not consume meat/fish/eggs at all in the T2 area.

A key informant from Dulmi village (T0) in Sonahatu summarized:

> They (young people) go out and learn from there (cities). They want to change the culture of the village. They earn money and eat different foods. This is the reason that earlier the people were 'nirog' (without diseases), now many diseases are prevalent in the village.

A respondent from Suwarmara village (T1) said:

> People eat rice, dal (pulses), and vegetables, muri (puffed rice), and basi bhat (rice with starch). People now eat chapatti (wheat bread) as well— those who can afford it! But yes, earlier people used to eat jowar, gunduli, and mahuwa (millets). Now people are richer and more educated. So they eat rice and wheat . . . Rural ignorant/illiterate people used to eat millets. People from the cities eat rice.

A VHC member from Kasidih village (T2) in Sili spoke about this, '. . . that time people used to eat rice, green vegetables, meat and fish, though not daily. Jowar, gundli, mahuwa was popular earlier. Now things are improving. Now they prefer to eat rice, wheat.'

Poverty, Hunger, and Poor Quality Diets

Lack of livelihood options for tribal groups in the modern market-based economy has led to extreme poverty and hunger, as their dependence on market produce has increased without any commensurate increase in their ability to procure this produce. Lack of land ownership and rights over forests has limited their ability to either grow food for subsistence or gather food from forests. There is landlessness among the households across all the project area villages. Data from the quantitative study also showed that agriculture is the main occupation for an average of 80 per cent of the households across T0, T1, and T2 areas. A comparison between baseline and end-line data showed that ownership of land has declined across all three areas during the five-year project period. Thus, landlessness has increased among the communities in the project area.

This is compounded by the seasonal and temporary nature of most occupations and work for tribal groups—daily wages in construction, agricultural farms, and mines, and contract labour in factories. As with most tribal land-ownership patterns, forests are considered common property and agricultural land ownership is not considered a priority. While conventional tribal identities and statuses were not based on land ownership, this is becoming the primary criterion for determining inter-tribe hierarchy in today's market economy and modern society.

Subsistence agriculture is the main occupation in the project areas. Due to very low levels of land ownership and complete dependence on rainfall for irrigation, households do not have surplus produce and most only manage to produce enough for consumption for about six months a year.

Vegetable farming occurs only in the monsoons and in very small landholdings, mostly in kitchen gardens. The farmland is dedicated to paddy cultivation; wheat and pulses are not grown in these areas.

This has had a significantly negative impact on the quality of diets—a shift from consumption of multiple grains and vegetables high on nutritive value to consumption of only rice or wheat has decreased diet diversity. Rising anaemia in the region may be attributed to these changes in food consumption. Across T2 and T0 villages, people reported eating only twice a day. The quantitative data also supported this, with a mean of around 70 per cent of the people reporting the consumption of only two or fewer meals in a day. As well, the number of people consuming GLVs more than once per day decreased significantly between baseline and end line across all three arms of the study. This was also the case with consumption of vegetables more than once per day. Only approximately 10 per cent across the three arms consumed more than the usual amount of food during pregnancy.

A Sahiyya in Khutam village (T2) in Sili said, 'We eat rice, pulses, and vegetables, if we can afford it. We take rice, as we prefer rice over wheat. Initially, some six years ago, we used to eat rice and starch, mahua, corn, vegetables, gundli, kaduwa, jowar, and makai (millets).'

A key informant from Asri (T1) in Angara summarized the food consumption behaviours as follows:

> We eat very simple food. We eat mar-bhat (rice with starch)—that's all!
> . . . We do not have the concept of breakfast in the village. We directly eat
> around eleven in the morning. Very few families eat breakfast. We eat whatever we get. When we get saag (leafy vegetables) or other vegetables, we eat
> that. We can eat very less dal (pulses). You know the present high price of
> the dal! We have to buy dal and vegetables from the haat [weekly market]
> in the block, at a distance of five kilometres. We do not eat non-vegetarian
> food . . . very less, might be once a month. We do not get meat nowadays in
> the forests, and buying meat is not for poor people like us.

A Sahiyya shared her frustration about the futility of her advice because of the widespread poverty in the community:

> Only rice and dal are eaten by villagers, both in the afternoon and in the
> night. The only vegetable they can eat is potato. Those who are well-off buy
> fruits and other vegetables. Non-vegetarian foods are not possible . . . as
> there is limited money. So I ask them to eat chana with gur [grams and jaggery] in the morning, as this is good for anaemia. But they don't even have
> the money to buy these things.

Only people from a few villages, where fishing is one of the main occupations (T1 villages in Angara), reported daily consumption of fish:

- 'People eat rice and water only. They also eat fish at least once a week' (a respondent from Asri village, Angara).
- 'Dal (pulses) is very expensive, we cannot afford it. We don't produce dal much. So we eat fish with rice' (key informant from Suwarmara village, Angara).
- 'Not much has changed in food. We usually eat rice and fish, sometimes meat if we can get it' (a woman from Childag village, Angara).

The PDS
Another reason for changing food patterns in these tribal communities—from millets to rice—is the PDS. As a central government programme, it is centralized and lacks any flexibility to take into account unique contextual realities, locally available foods, and/or local food practices.

The PDS distributes primarily rice, and sometimes wheat. In the absence of purchasing power—because of extreme poverty, lack of land ownership among most tribal groups for sustainable agriculture throughout the year, and an erosion of forest rights—the communities are left with little choice but to depend on the PDS for their food. This dependence gives them little choice in deciding the grains that they would like to consume. Given widespread hunger, rice and wheat have replaced millets as staple grains in these regions:

- 'We eat rice, which we get from the PDS. People having red and yellow card get wheat. Otherwise, where do we get food from? Change has taken place with time' (a woman from Cherudi village [T2], Sili).
- 'Earlier there was poverty everywhere. Now there has been a positive change. We used to eat roots and fruits, which we would bring from the forests. Now we don't do that. We don't go to the forest anymore. We get rice from the Antyodaya card since the last two to three years. So we have started eating rice' (key informant from Kantatoli [T2]).

Income and Food Practices

One important observation from the data is that communities reported improvements in food practices and health-seeking behaviour due to community-based interventions and nutrition counselling *only* in areas where the income levels improved. This has not been seen in many of the T2 villages, which have reported widespread hunger and lack of employment opportunities. On the other hand, in T1 and T0 villages with better-performing public programmes (such as those implemented under the Mahatma Gandhi National Rural Employment Guarantee Act), better irrigation, a wider range of occupations, and relatively better incomes, respondents were more likely to have reported that the Sahiyyas, ANMs, and AWWs had an impact on their knowledge and behaviour. This clearly indicates that although knowledge and awareness about appropriate diets (through project interventions) increased significantly in the T2 areas, other factors—such as land ownership, irrigation, lack of market linkages for agricultural and forest produce, deforestation, and erosion of forest rights of tribal communities, widespread hunger, and shifting identities of tribal groups—have impeded the translation of knowledge into practice.

Conclusion and Implications for Evaluations

In evaluating a complex intervention, such as the Reduction of Low Birth Weight Project, how complexity is dealt with will depend on the aims of the evaluation. A key question in evaluating a complex intervention is about practical effectiveness—whether the intervention works in everyday practice (Haynes, 1999). To assess its practical effectiveness, it is important to understand the whole range of effects—how they vary among recipients of the intervention, between sites, over time, and so on, and the causes of that variation. A second key question in evaluating complex interventions is *how* the intervention works; in other words, what are the active ingredients within the intervention and how are they exerting their effect (Michie and Abraham, 2004)? Only by addressing this question, can we build a cumulative understanding of causal mechanisms, design more effective interventions, and apply them appropriately across different groups and settings.

Many different study designs are available to address the above questions in evaluation; different designs suit different questions and different circumstances (Victora, Habicht, and Bryce, 2004; McKee, Britton, Black, McPherson, Sanderson, and Bain, 1999). Awareness of and openness towards the whole range of experimental and non-experimental approaches and quantitative and qualitative designs should lead to more appropriate and diverse methodological choices contributing to better evaluations (MRC, 2008).

Increasingly, it is recognized that qualitative research methods can 'reach the parts other methods cannot reach' (Pope and Mays, 1995, p. 42). Qualitative methods can be used to explain findings after quantitative research has been completed, especially in cases where confusing findings cannot be explained by statistical analysis alone. Based on our experiences of integrating quantitative and qualitative methods in the evaluation of the Reduction of Low Birth Weight Project and the specific focus on the prevalence of anaemia in the study area, we argue here that the use of diverse methods in the evaluation of complex interventions can contribute significantly and efficiently to both assessing and understanding the impact of new health services.

Another inference that we draw from the assessment of this complex health intervention is that rigorous formative research is critical to the design of an intervention. This is especially true in contexts such as Jharkhand, which are completely underrepresented in public health research and, hence, whose realities are perhaps excluded from any indexed published literature in the topic areas. Therefore, taking a step back from evaluating the *outcome* of a complex public health intervention, it would be important to also analyse and rethink the intervention design and formulate it to respond to contextual realities. Perhaps behaviour-change communication would not have been selected as an effective intervention to address maternal and child health issues in an area where basic access to food, health care, and employment were critical problems. While the baseline survey presented the demographic and epidemiological realities of the region, the needs, practices, and challenges that the communities face in achieving better health would only have been authentically and fully described, documented, and understood through qualitative research and mixed methodologies.

At the deeper level of analysis of emergent themes, qualitative research methods can help researchers and evaluators develop an understanding of the processes whereby particular outcomes come about. They can thus enable a more sophisticated definition of what needs doing—such as identifying the reasons for rising anaemia trends in the case study examined in this chapter. They can also examine and test the theoretical basis of an intervention and question or affirm the principles on which the tasks and processes have been based. In this case, the qualitative analysis explained the rising anaemia trends in the community and the lack of significant difference produced by the interventions (which were derived from rigorous theory and evidence). Rather than simply rejecting the concerned hypothesis, the application of both quantitative and qualitative methodologies allowed researchers to further explore the reasons for a rejection, expanding the scope of the evaluation to include the complex social, economic, political, and environmental factors that interacted to produce the observed (and quantified) outcomes. These resulting theoretical ideas and explanations are open to future hypothesis testing.

Conclusions and inferences drawn from rejected hypotheses in complex interventions may have far-reaching, and sometimes adverse, implications for policy and programme design. For instance, in the Reduction of Low Birth Weight Project evaluation study, the inference (based on the quantitative statistical analyses) that the interventions addressing anaemia—such as counselling of pregnant women, promotion of iron-rich foods, consumption of IFA, community health workers engaged in prevention and health promotion roles, strengthening primary care, and enhancing knowledge of adolescent girls—are ineffective, or worse still, lead to negative outcomes, is incorrect.

To guard against such incorrect conclusions, it is imperative to understand what led to the increase in anaemia levels in the project area, despite all the interventions. A quantitative analysis was not useful in explaining the increase, but the data from the qualitative evaluation yielded possible explanations. Health behaviours are extremely complex, with multi-level determinants. While health behaviours may be manifested or evaluated at an individual level, the causal pathways range from proximate factors in the immediate environment, to macro-level factors in the sociopolitical and economic realm.

In summary, an approach that integrates quantitative and qualitative methods for evaluating complex interventions in health service research is both efficient and generalizable. It allows for a better assessment of the transferability of potentially effective programmes to other settings, helps interpret quantitative findings, and questions underlying theory and assumptions to better inform future hypotheses and intervention designs.

Notes

1. This data is taken from the baseline survey (2004) of the Reduction of Low Birth Weight Project.
2. Both baseline and end-line data collection was undertaken by a third party in order to maintain objectivity.
3. Ethical approval was obtained for the study from the Institutional Review Board (IRB) at Johns Hopkins Bloomberg School of Public Health. In addition, members of the community were informed about the study design at the time of obtaining consent to participation. This was done at the community level, in a Gram Sabha meeting. Individual consent was obtained at the time of both baseline and end-line data collection.

References

Bhargava, A., Bouis, H.E., and Scrimshaw, N.S. (2001). Dietary intakes and socioeconomic factors are associated with the haemoglobin concentration of Bangladeshi women. *The Journal of Nutrition*, 131(3), 758–64.

Black, R.E., Allen, L.H., Bhutta, Z.A., Caulfield, L.E., De Onis, M., Ezzati, M., and Rivera, J. (2008). Maternal and child undernutrition: Global and regional exposures and health consequences. *The Lancet*, 371(9608), 243–60.

Bradley, F., Wiles, R., Kinmonth, A.L., Mant, D., and Gantley, M. (1999). Development and evaluation of complex interventions in health services research: Case study of the Southampton Heart Integrated Care Project (SHIP). *BMJ*, 318(7185), 711– 15.

Department of Health, Medical Education and Family Welfare, Government of Jharkhand. (2004). *Jharkhand health report 2003–04*. Ranchi, Jharkhand, India: Government of Jharkhand.

Hawe, P., Shiell, A., Riley, T., and Gold, L. (2004). Methods for exploring intervention variation and local context within a cluster randomised community intervention trial. *Journal of Epidemiology and Community Health*, 58(9), 788–93.

Haynes, B. (1999). Can it work? Does it work? Is it worth it? The testing of healthcare interventions is evolving. *BMJ*, 319(7211), 652–3.

International Institute for Population Science. (2004). *National Family Health Survey 2 (1998–99)*. New Delhi, India: Government of India.

———. (2009). *National Family Health Survey 3 (2005–06)*. New Delhi, India: Government of India.

McKee, M., Britton, A., Black, N., McPherson, K., Sanderson, C., and Bain, C. (1999). Interpreting the evidence: Choosing between randomised and non-randomised studies. *BMJ*, 319(7205), 312–15.

Medical Research Council. (2000). *Developing and evaluating complex interventions*. London: MRC.

———. (2008). *Developing and evaluating complex interventions: New guidance*. London: MRC.

Michie, S. and Abraham, C. (2004). Interventions to change health behaviours: Evidence-based or evidence-inspired? *Psychology and Health*, 19(1), 29–49.

Office of the Registrar General and Census Commissioner of India. (2001). *Sample Registration Survey Statistical Report 2001*. New Delhi, India: Government of India.

Ogilvie, D., Mitchell, R., Mutrie, N., Petticrew, M., and Platt, S. (2006). Evaluating health effects of transport interventions: Methodologic case study. *American Journal of Preventive Medicine*, 31(2), 118–26.

Petticrew, M., Cummins, S., Ferrell, C., Findlay, A., Higgins, C., Hoy, C., et al. (2005). Natural experiments: An under-used tool for public health. *Public Health*, 119(9), 751–7.

Pope, C and Mays, N. (1995). Reaching the parts other methods cannot reach: An introduction to qualitative methods in health and health services research. *BMJ*, 311(6996), 42–5.

Rifkin, A. (2007). Randomised controlled trials and psychotherapy research. *American Journal of Psychiatry*, 164(1), 7–8.

Rychetnik, L., Frommer, M., Hawe, P., and Shiell, A. (2002). Criteria for evaluating evidence on public health interventions. *Journal of Epidemiology and Community Health*, 56, 119–27.

Shepperd, S., Jenkinson, C., and Morgan, P. (1995). Randomised controlled trials and health services research (letter). *BMJ*, 310(6972), 125–6.

Victora, C.G., Habicht, J.-P., and Bryce, J. (2004). Evidence-based public health: Moving beyond randomised trials. *American Journal of Public Health*, 94(3), 400–5.

Wolff, N. (2001). Randomised trials of socially complex interventions: Promise or peril? *Journal of Health Services Research and Policy*, 6(2), 123–6.

10

Operationalizing the Capability Approach (CA) for Evaluating Small Projects

Ram Chandra Khanal

Background

As a normative proposition, a capability approach (CA) has been proposed by development scholars as an alternative development concept. Amartya Sen (1999, p.3), one of the main exponents of the approach, stated that development is 'a process of expanding the real freedoms that people enjoy' and poverty is a capability deprivation. Sen's ideas differ from prevalent development thinking, which focuses on maximizing utility, income, or primary goods to increase well-being (Sen, 1999). He convincingly argues for a more human-centered, pluralistic, and open-ended conception of well-being. This line of argument is a fundamental departure from the conventional understanding of well-being.

Main Concepts of the CA

According to Alkire and Deneulin (2009), the CA contains three central concepts: *functionings*, *capabilities*, and *agency*. The Human Development and Capability Association (HDCA) defined these three concepts in a briefing note (HDCA, 2010, pp.1–3).[1]

Functionings are the valuable activities and states that make up people's wellbeing—such as a healthy body, being safe, being calm, having a warm friendship, an educated mind, a good job. Functionings are related to goods and income. They describe what a person is able to do or be as a result. When people's basic need for food (a commodity) is met, they enjoy the functioning of being well nourished. . . . Functionings can relate to different dimensions of well-being, from survival to relationships to self-direction to arts and culture.

Capabilities are 'the alternative combinations of functionings that are feasible [for a person] to achieve'. Put differently, they are 'the substantive freedoms he or she enjoys to lead the kind of life he or she has reason to value'. Capabilities are a kind of opportunity freedom. Just like a person with much money in her pocket can buy different things, a person with many capabilities could enjoy many different activities, pursue different life paths. For this reason, the capability set has been compared to a budget set. So capabilities describe the real and actual possibilities open to a person.

Agency refers to a person's ability to pursue and realize goals that he or she values and has reason to value. An agent is 'someone who acts and brings about change'. The opposite of a person with agency is someone who is forced, oppressed, or passive. . . . Agency expands the horizons of concerned person beyond a person's own well-being, to include concerns such as saving the spotted owl or helping others. In this perspective, people are viewed to be active, creative, and able to act on behalf of their aspirations. Agency is related to other approaches that stress self-determination, authentic self-direction, autonomy and so on. The concern for agency means that participation, public debate, democratic practice, and empowerment are to be fostered alongside well-being.

Existential and Axiological Stands

Existential and axiological aspects of being human and engaging in activities play an important role in CA. According to Max-Neef (1991), human needs can be divided into two categories: existential and axiological. The existential needs include *being* (attributes of person, group, village, etc.), *having* (non-material tools, norms, institution), *doing* (various individual and collective activities), and *interacting* (social and political context). The axiological needs deal with values (focusing on ethics and aesthetics) and relate to those things that human beings consider an important part of their life and livelihood—subsistence, protection, affection, understanding, participation, leisure, creation, identity, and freedom.

Alkire (2002, p. 186) analysed various dimensions of human development, building on the categories of basic reasons for action noted by John Finnis, including life itself; knowledge and aesthetic experience; some degree of excellence in work and play; friendship; self-integration; self-expression, or practical reasonableness; and religion. Mathai (2003) then adapted these dimensions using the CA and arrived at nine dimensions of human development:

- **life**—its maintenance and transmission—health and safety;
- **knowledge**—knowing reality;
- **aesthetic experiences**—appreciating beauty and whatever intensely engages our capacities to know and feel;
- **some level of excellence in work**—the transformation of (or partnership with) the natural world to create value and meaning;
- **recreation/play**—relaxation, resting, entertainment, and so on;
- **friendship**—various forms of harmony between and among individuals and groups of persons—living at peace with others, neighborliness;
- **self-integration**—the harmony of one's inner feelings with one's judgments and choices;
- **self-expression** or practical reasonableness—the harmony between one's judgments, choices and behavior, or the consistency between one's self and its expression; and
- **religion**—attempts to gain or improve harmony with some more-than-human source of meaning and value, and can take many forms.

CA and Evaluation of Development Initiatives

Development is about people not about objects (Max-Neef, 1991). However, traditional development paradigms focus more on the quantitative growth of objects—such as household income or gross domestic product (GDP)—and most conventional development initiatives were based on this premise. Recently, the concept of development has shifted towards enhancing people's quality of life, and the global development trend has been towards human development based on CA. Nevertheless, how to determine which development process is best in terms of enhancing quality of life has been a challenging task for development planners across the globe.

There are a plethora of evaluation paradigms, tools, and methods. Each has its own strengths and weaknesses. Among them all, empowerment evaluation, participatory evaluation, and evaluation based on the CA share a common underlying set of values. All move beyond traditional approaches to evaluation to focus more on empowering people.

Changes in development thinking and management necessitate a change in evaluation frameworks and criteria for development intervention. The CA, as described by its exponents, such as Amartya Sen, Martha Nussbaum, Sabina Alkire, focuses not only on what a person does or acquires but also on what a person has as a freedom and is able to do to enhance his or her well-being. Hence, two shifts can be noticed from earlier approaches to evaluation. First, the analysis shifts from focusing on the economy to the person and his or her preferences. Second, the unit or criteria of assessment shifts from money, such as dollars earned per year or GDP growth rate, to non-financial aspects, including preferences and values.

Hence, in order to evaluate development projects/initiatives based on the CA, new perspectives and knowledge are needed to conceptualize and devise an evaluation framework and evaluation tools. This would not only contribute to the epistemology of evaluation but would also broaden the interface of development theories and practices. In the changing development paradigm, it is also important to have evaluation tools and systems that can answer questions about how people differentiate being from doing, what people value and how their freedom of choice is shaped, how they prioritize, and the implications at personal, household, and societal levels. Although there are some examples of the CA being used in development project evaluation (see, for example, Legido-Quigley, 2004; Mathai, 2003), specific evaluation tools and methods applicable in the rural development context are still at very nascent stage.

Relevancy of the CA Approach for Evaluation

The main purpose of this study was to test some evaluation tools and techniques to assess the relevancy of the CA for evaluating community-level development interventions. Based on the CA, the study explored different hierarchies of contributions, that is, the functionings, capabilities, and agency of a group of women, and proposed an evaluation framework. The study also attempted to use existential and axiological aspects in assessing and prioritizing people's normative perspectives in specific development interventions.

Methods

The case study used was a women's group with two on-going development projects—non-formal education (NFE) classes for women and a multipurpose irrigation canal—located in a particular village that was selected on the basis of researcher's prior knowledge of that area. The site was visited two times—the first in November 2009 and the second in May 2010. Two focus group discussions (FGDs) were carried out that included all members of the women's group. Later on, two key informant (knowledgeable persons in the community) discussions were carried out and a site observation was conducted to verify and consolidate the findings.

All qualitative data drawn from these different methods were categorized according to theme. These themes were then analysed based on the frequency and emphasis given by the participants on specific issues or questions within each theme.

Conceptual Framework

Unlike conventional evaluation processes, CA evaluation processes follow human-centric approaches and evaluation criteria are determined by people's values. In this study, an evaluation framework has been devised that includes functionings, capabilities, agency, and other evaluation-related issues (see Figure 10.1). A human need matrix—an assessment of the value of an activity/project, based on the degree to which it meets the existential and axiological needs of human beings—was also used

Figure 10.1
Conceptual Framework of the Study

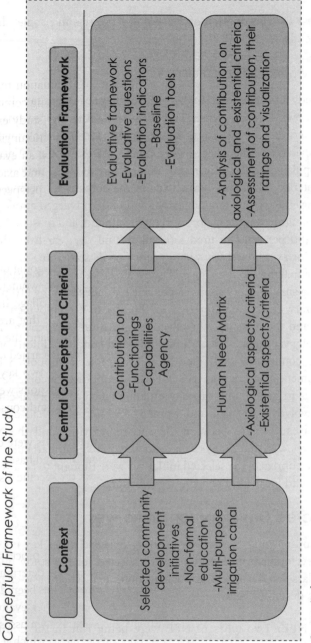

Context

Selected community development initiatives
-Non-formal education
-Multi-purpose irrigation canal

Central Concepts and Criteria

Contribution on
-Functionings
-Capabilities
Agency

Human Need Matrix
-Axiological aspects/criteria
-Existential aspects/criteria

Evaluation Framework

Evaluative framework
-Evaluative questions
-Evaluation indicators
-Baseline
-Evaluation tools

-Analysis of contribution on axiological and existential criteria
-Assessment of contribution, their ratings and visualization

Source: Author.

to assess the contribution of the selected projects in people's lives and livelihoods.

Study Site Description

The study was undertaken in the Pinthali village of Mangaltar VDC, Kavrepalanchowk District, Nepal. The village is situated approximately 150 kilometers east of Kathmandu and comprises 125 households with about 625 inhabitants. The village-level data showed that about 60 per cent of the population in the village were women and about 30 per cent of them were literate. Almost all households in the community belonged to the Tamang ethnic group (an indigenous and underprivileged ethnic group).

Agriculture was the major source of livelihood, and most of the households (80 per cent) secured food all around the year from their own land. However, in last few years, young people started to search for new ways of making a living. The FGDs revealed that people were engaged in running small grocery shops (5 per cent), poultry farming (10 per cent), temporary emigration (for two to three years), employment (15 per cent), and the remainder involved in agriculture. The community was culturally very rich, with both Buddhist and Hindu traditions present.

The community had some local-level projects supported by non-government organizations (NGOs). These supported income generation (such as irrigation) and capacity building (such as informal education) and involved both men and women. The initiatives had also clearly defined causal links between the various activities and the intended objectives. As the CA goes beyond the purely utilitarian/individual-income approach, the selected initiatives were thought to be a good testing ground for the use of a CA to evaluation.

Selected Development Initiatives

Based on meetings with the women's group and other key informants, two development interventions were selected for the study purpose— NFE classes and a multipurpose irrigation canal. Their basic characteristics are described below.

- **NFE:** Two types of NFE were being run in the community. One was supported by the government through the District

Education Office (DEO) and the other was supported by an NGO. The NFE classes were run either in the evening after dinner or in the afternoon. For the past two to three years women in the village had been participating in these kinds of NFE classes, where they learned to read and write as well as about agricultural works, health issues (such as reproductive health), and legal literacy (including women's rights, property rights, and equality rights).

- **Multipurpose irrigation canal—irrigation, electric power, and grinding machine:** While water resources are very scarce in many villages in the region, this community enjoys a year-round water supply from a nearby stream for irrigating crops, generating electric power, and running a grinding machine. The canal is about 2 kilometers long, and at the time of the study it had a water discharge rate of about 300 litres per second supporting the irrigation of 500 hectares of land and generating 12 kilowatts of electricity. The community also used the water for household, livestock, and sanitation purposes. The canal was called 'a real blessing' for the community.

Development Initiatives and Their Contributions

After selecting the two community-level development initiatives, the central concepts of the CA—functionings, capabilities, and agency— were used to analyse the initiatives and their contribution to people's lives and livelihoods.

Analysis of Functionings

NFE Class

The NFE class served most of the women in village, who were illiterate or minimally literate. Women in the community generally understood Nepali, but most of them could not speak it. The class provided an excellent opportunity to learn Nepali, which enabled women to sign their name and to recognize and count money. These classes were helpful to the women, especially in selling vegetables and other farm products or when they bought goods at nearby market. As well, those with children just starting school were able to help and guide them. Some members revealed that they were proud of these new achievements. One woman said, 'I can now read the [health-related] poster that was pasted on my house.' The discussions clearly demonstrated that women in the community put more emphasis on basic skills and knowledge that 'empowered' them and enhanced their ability to manage their livelihoods than on securing income alone. The pride they gained when they were able to manage their transactions and read posters cannot be measured in monetary terms alone and is difficult to compare with what they might gain from the income resulting from a different kind of intervention.

The NFE was not only about reading and writing; it was also about understanding and learning about other issues such as conserving water, maintaining sanitation, and engaging in community work. The NFE participants also learned about other relevant topics, such as the basics of agriculture, community health, education, and the legal rights of women. The focus group participants said that they particularly appreciated the courses related to reproductive health, nutrition, and sanitation. The content of some of the NFE topics was very practical and addressed problems and challenges they had been dealing with for a long time—such as family planning issues and the proper use of different contraceptive devices. Legal literacy was another important part of the NFE offerings—women in the village came to understand some of their fundamental legal entitlements, such as the right to parents' property, the right to citizenship (in the mother's name), female trafficking, and laws related to domestic violence against women.

There were some secondary-level benefits of attending NFE classes. Women who participated in the NFE classes also voluntarily contributed 5 rupees per month into a group savings plan. Although the savings were not large, they were used to provide credit to its members for different purposes. Some got a loan for goat keeping and others for vegetable farming. The group also provided an interest-free loan (6,000 rupees) to a woman whose husband died in an accident. When they formed a group—Ama Samuha (meaning 'mother group')—and worked together, they began to address violence against women and were able to raise this issue both within and outside the community. The chairperson of Ama Samuha brought rural women's issues to the members of the

Constituent Assembly when the Constitution Assembly team visited the village to solicit local views on Nepal's constitution, which was in the process of being developed. The group seemed capable of raising issues related to violence against women, and in some cases, they decided to punish offenders at local level. One member reported that they had imposed a fine and requested an apology (both of which were received) when someone was found guilty of being involved in domestic violence against women in the community

The group members also felt that their ability to contribute to and make decisions at the household level was strengthened after attending the NFE classes, as they had more knowledge about their legal rights and about other important issues such as public health and small-scale income generating activities. Traditionally, Tamang women had the power to make decisions about household issues and were a stronghold within their own households. However, financial transactions, which were controlled by men, became an important part of their livelihoods and women's decision-making power had been gradually slipping away. The NFE class, however, helped to enhance women's capability on a number of issues, and hence, their position in the household decision-making process was improved.

Local women also highly valued learning the Nepali language and being able to communicate in Nepali with outsiders. Some class participants developed enough confidence in their vocabulary and ability to speak the language to be able to visit district headquarters and deal with their own problems without having to bring someone else (usually a male) to accompany them or speak for them. One participant said, 'I am very happy that I can visit Dhulikhel (district headquarters) and Banepa (another town) alone and can buy goods myself.'

Multipurpose Irrigation Canal

All households in the community were dependent on agriculture, and their farming system was invariably dependent on water. Hence, the irrigation canal was critical to the success of their crops and their livelihood. All households in the community had access to water for their household and agricultural needs. From the main canal, small sub-canals were constructed to increase outreach, and a community-level irrigation committee provided regular monitoring and management.

Compared with other villages, Mangaltar community members had better access to water so that they could sow and plant their crops on time. During the study visit (April 2010), farmers were busy irrigating maize. The community had year-round access to irrigation facilities, which allowed them to grow three crops a year, which was rare for their region. They also grew vegetables for their own consumption and for sale. Garlic, for example, was grown on a commercial scale and was sold in Banepa and Dhulikhel. Some farmers also managed to sell garlic in Kathmandu.

The water used for irrigation had a triple use: it was used first for a grain-grinding machine during the day, then for generating electric power through the evening and night, before being used to irrigate the crops. This multiple use of water reduced women's workload—they did not need to travel far for grinding grain or need to collect firewood for cooking. They had a good source of electricity (this was important, as during the study period, Nepal was facing about 10 to 12 hours load shedding daily) so that they could read and write with their children in the evening.

Women did most of the work at their homes. They were responsible for feeding livestock, cleaning house, and keeping their children clean. All this work was possible only because they had access to water at their home or nearby. Without this easy access to water, they would have had to travel far to fetch water, which would have consumed a lot of time.

The multipurpose irrigation canal also brought additional benefits to the community, such as food security. The chairperson of Ama Samuha said,

> We are always busy working at our farm, as we can grow three crops in a year and do not need to buy food from outside. Instead, we sell vegetables and some cash crops in the local market. Most of our houses are with tin [corrugated zinc plate] roof, which shows the prosperity of the village. Other people from the nearby communities often say our village is a small city.

After achieving a degree of economic stability from their farming and being aware of basic health and hygiene principles from their literacy classes, the village women started to go to the health centre in the nearby village for health and family planning services. Some of the women and households were able to send their children to the private school, where English is taught.

The canal also served as a thread that bound the community together. While different groups of people were responsible for the irrigation schemes, the micro-hydro plants, the grinding machine, community forestry, and the mother and other groups, the initiative was the central point of contact and management. This initiative was also successful in bringing some additional resources into the community, such as cement for the canal from the Singhalama project and assistance for the hydropower project from the Rural Energy Development Programme.

The canal also helped to increase employment at the local level. Besides decreasing underemployment in the agriculture sector, as farmers increased their cropping intensity (three crops in a year), some local workers got jobs running the grinding machine and maintaining the micro-hydro systems. Recently, about 10 households also started poultry farming, which helps provide regular employment for approximately 20 people.

Analysis of Capabilities

A capability is a person's *freedom* to enjoy various functionings—to be or do things that contribute to their well-being (Alkire and Deneulin, 2009, p. 22). Freedoms are not only the primary ends of development; they are also among its principle means. According to Amartya Sen, both instrumental freedoms (political freedoms, economic facilities, social opportunities, transparency guarantees, and protective security) and substantive freedoms (to choose a life one has reason to value) help to enhance the general capability of a person (Sen, 1999, pp. 10, 38). It is also important to note that one type of freedom contributes to the achievement of another type of freedom.

In the given case study, the scope of the study was limited to the two interventions and their associated issues in that particular community. Both the instrumental and substantive freedoms were governed mainly by the social, economic, and political context and their respective determinants. Although in general these contexts would remain unchanged in the short term, these interventions had some level of contribution to both the instrumental and the substantive freedoms of women in the community.

In both cases (the NFE classes and the multipurpose irrigation canal), women gained in terms of their functionings but did not have adequate freedoms (both instrumental and substantive) that would allow them to fully achieve the different combinations of functionings. For example, maintaining security (body, household, and community) was not only determined by money and/or household income but also by public policy, social/political conflicts, economic/monetary policy, governance issues, and social accountability processes.

Both the NFE and the multipurpose irrigation canal initiatives provided awareness about the rights and responsibilities of women and enabled them to participate in local-level advocacy and awareness. That also helped them to participate actively in economic activities in their households and community. As they participated in community-level social work—such as a public health campaign, saving and credit activities, and public awareness on women's legal rights—the self-esteem and some aspects of the instrumental freedoms of other women in the community also increased. Although all women did not benefit equally from the initiatives, some members were able to translate the skills they acquired into actions. Most were able to communicate in Nepali language, manage their businesses, and speak out against discrimination and domestic violence against women. However, any contribution towards substantive freedoms was yet to be realized. The analysis showed that the community has enjoyed an increased level of functionings through the expansion of valuable freedoms (freedom to be educated, speak without fear, and work in group) to enhance capability. However, a close review showed that there was a disproportionate achievement among the members.

Analysis of Agency

Women's agency refers to a woman's ability to pursue and realize goals that she values and has reason to value. According to Sen (1999, p. 189), 'agency aspects are beginning to receive some attention [at last], in contrast to the earlier exclusive concentration on well-being aspects'. The FGDs, key informant surveys, and site observations revealed that there was some increase in women's agency—both individually and in a group—over the past five years. Given that the women in the group were now literate in a number of different areas and had the ability to speak Nepali, their short-term goal of being independent or free (a least in some areas) had been met. Another gain was that Ama Samuha was entrusted, even by men in the village, to make decisions about issues related to domestic violence against women and other women-related issues. Thus, the group had reached beyond their individual and group interests and tried to serve the interests of women as a whole.

Based on the discussions with the group, the contributions of the two initiatives were categorized according to the central concepts of capability—functionings, capabilities, and agency. Figure 10.2 shows several activities the women in the community value—such as being literate, starting group saving, working on women's right issues, increased community-based work, increased income from selling vegetables, using irrigation facility—in terms of enhancing their well-being. These activities are classified as functionings. However, undertaking such functionings is not sufficient for achieving the goal of improved quality of life. To achieve this longer-term development goal, it is important to have freedoms (both instrumental and substantive). These freedoms allow people to combine their functionings—such as increased social action, food security, education, mental health, income security, and ability to negotiate—and make the best use of possible alternative combinations to enhance their capabilities. Capabilities enable people to attain what they value.

One of the central goals of human development is enabling people to become agents in their lives and in their communities (Alkire and Deneulin, 2009, p. 27). Once people's freedom to choose and to maximize functionings is expanded, they move to shape their destiny (Sen, 1999, p. 53) and decide upon the types of development they would like to pursue. In some cases, some groups or people transform themselves into agents of change for society. The assessment of the two initiatives in the study site shows enhanced capabilities in the majority of group members but the development of 'agency' in only a few members.

Evaluative Framework

The capability-based evaluative perspective is an emerging paradigm (Legido-Quigley, 2004; Mathai, 2003). The evaluation of development projects is challenging because of the complex interaction of activities

Figure 10.2
Relation of Functionings, Capabilities, and Agency

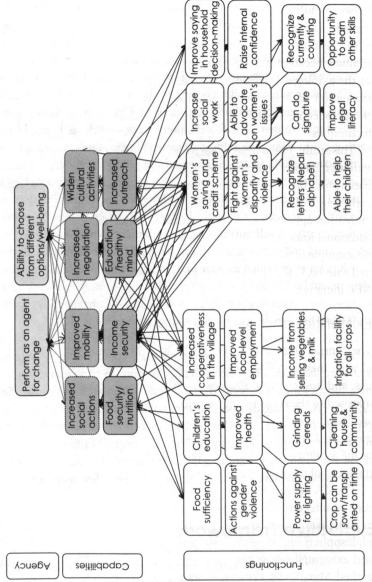
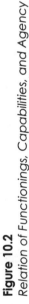

Source: Study findings (2010).

and their outputs, outcomes, and impacts. The CA further complicates the challenge by adding another dimension of complex interactions between multiple functionings, capabilities, and agency, in addition to embracing the 'value' aspect in development projects. The value aspect is intrinsic to both activities and outputs but difficult to dissect and evaluate because of its complexity. Incorporating the concept of value, or the axiological perspective, in development further complicates the evaluation of development activities using the CA, as it is based on the perspective of the individual and requires qualitative assessment techniques.

This study, based on the literature review and interactions with community members, proposes a simple CA evaluative framework. CA evaluation for this kind of small community-level initiative is still in the early stages of development; more work needs to done to apply the CA evaluation approach to different situations and initiatives and to gather additional knowledge and insight to make the framework more robust. An example of what a CA evaluation framework would look like is given in Table 10.1, which shows the proposed evaluation framework for the NFE initiative.

Existential and Axiological Stands

The central idea of the CA is to discover what people value (in terms of what they would like to do), how they select their unique set of values, and how to integrate them in enhancing people's quality of life. As opposed to the conventional development paradigm/approaches, which are based on a predetermined set of 'valued' actions, outcomes, and goals, the CA is based on the metaphysical and ideological world view—or the activities and outcomes defined as valuable by the people who are the focus of the initiative or project.

The CA approach has tried to address some evaluation challenges, such as integrating value and ethics perspectives that expert-led as well as participatory development practices were unable to address. Different philosophers and thinkers have proposed different kinds of axiological and existential stands that are compatible with the CA. Mathai (2003) grafted Max-Neef's existential categories onto Finnis's axiological categories, to arrive at what is called the Finnis–Max-Neef–Alkire (FMNA)

Table 10.1

Proposed Evaluation Framework for the NFE Initiative

Evaluative Area	Focus of Main Evaluative Questions	Indicators	Baseline	Methods of Assessment	Assessment/ Rating
Functionings	Area or level of skill(s) achieved	Percentage of women able to sign	Baseline for indicators	Survey	
	Area or level of knowledge achieved	Percentage of women able to converse in Nepali		Survey	
	Types and level of activities performed	Percentage of women visiting district headquarters independently		Survey	
		Percentage of women adopting contraception		Survey	
		Percentage of women constructing family toilets			
Freedoms	Contribution to political freedoms	Women's level of participation in local group decision-making	Baseline for indicators	Qualitative assessment (FGD and spider net method)	
	Contribution to economic facilities	Percentage of women progressively participating and sustaining selves in economic activities			
	Contribution to social opportunities				
	Contribution to transparency guarantees	Women's level of participation in social actions/activities			
	Contribution to protective security	Women's indication of their confidence when travelling outside village			
	Contribution to substantive freedoms	Women's indication of their ability to share their views at village-level meeting			

Capabilities	Access to decision-making process	Ability of women's group to deal with women-related issues	Baseline for indicators	FGD survey
	Choice in rights-based options for livelihoods	Women's perception of available options for making a living		
	Increased role of women in social development	Women's contribution to wider social community		
Agency	Women as agents of change	Number of cases dealt with by women's group on violence-against-women issues	Baseline for indicators	FGD/survey
	Women's empowerment	Women's use of knowledge and power to influence and contribute to decision-making at the wider community level		

Source: Study findings (2010).

Matrix. This was adapted and converted into an evaluation tool (called the Human Need Matrix) that would reflect the CA to evaluation by creating a space for participants to indicate their preferences/priorities in terms of the existential/axiological categories, which included a discussion and a detailed ranking based on the category's contribution to people's capability and agency. Details about how this was applied to the case study are discussed below.

Prioritizing Matrix Categories and Initiative Contribution to Capabilities

First, both axiological and existential criteria were discussed with a women's group involved in both the NFE and the multipurpose irrigation canal initiatives. Participants were asked to order the main axiological and existential contributions of each initiative in terms of enhancing their capabilities.

The discussion revealed that from the axiological perspective, the NFE classes contributed the most to knowledge, self-expression, self-integration, and friendship; the multipurpose irrigation canal contributed the most to life, some level of excellence in work, and friendship.

From the existential perspective, the main contributions of both the NFE and multipurpose irrigation canal initiatives were on 'being' and 'doing'.

Next, the contributions toward the various axiological and existential categories were further discussed and verified with a group of more knowledgeable persons in the community (i.e., those who knew more about development and the local context and who could define and parse some of the complex issues and interactions), which included school teachers, community-level development workers, and elites. In examining the NFE classes, the combined contribution of both categories to improving human capabilities and enhancing human agency was assessed. At the beginning of the meeting, the group of knowledgeable persons were asked to provide their individual thoughts; later on, the group was tasked with developing a consensual rating of contribution. The group was instructed to give a higher number of Xs for higher contribution and a lower rating for a lower contribution. (See Tables 10.2 and 10.3 for the participant [here participants included individuals in the women's groups and the knowledgeable persons in the community] ratings for each initiative.)

Table 10.2
Human Need Matrix: Participant* Rating of NFE Initiative

	Existential Categories				
Axiological Categories	Being (Attributes of Person, Group, Village, and so on)	Having (non-material Tools, Norms, Institution)	Doing (Various Individual or Collective Activities)	Interacting (Social and Political Context)	Total
Life	X	XXX	XXX	XX	9
Knowledge	XXXX	XXX	XXXX	XX	13
Aesthetic experience	X	X	XX	X	5
Some level of excellence in work	X	XX	XX	XX	7
Recreation/play	XX	X	XX	X	6
Friendship	XXX	X	XX	XX	8
Self integration	XXX	X	XX	XX	8
Self-expression or practical reasonableness	XXX	XX	XX	XX	9
Religion	X	X	X	X	4
Total	19	15	20	15	**69**

Source: Study findings (2010).
Note: *Participants include individuals from the women's group and the knowledgeable persons from the community.

The tables show that the total contribution of the NFE initiative along the combined axiological and existential strands towards achieving capability was higher (69) than the contribution of the multipurpose irrigation canal (49). This reveals that the NFE initiative played a greater role for women in enhancing their capabilities and agency. This result is different from what one might expect, as the multipurpose irrigation canal provided for many basic needs such as food, reducing women's workload, and contributing to generating household farm income. However, in this study, the participants noted that before the NFE initiative they

Table 10.3
Human Need Matrix: Participant* Rating of Multipurpose Irrigation Canal

	Existential Categories				
Axiological Categories	Being (Attributes of Person, Group, Village, and so on)	Having (non-Material Tools, Norms, Institution)	Doing (Various Individual or Collective Activities)	Interacting (Social and Political Context)	Total
Life	XX	XXX	XXX	XX	10
Knowledge	XX	X	XX	X	6
Aesthetic experience	X	XX	XX	X	6
Some level of excellence in work	X	X	XX	X	5
Recreation/play	X	–	–	X	2
Friendship	X	XX	XX	XX	7
Self integration	XX	X	X	X	5
Self-expression or practical reason-ableness	XX	X	X	X	5
Religion	X	X	X	X	4
Total	13	12	14	11	**49**

Source: Study findings (2010).
Note: *Participants include individuals from the women's group and the knowledgeable persons from the community.

lacked basic health and financial knowledge; did not know how to read, write, or speak in Nepali; and could not manage even small economic transactions. Nevertheless, they realized that the NFE initiative provided opportunities for them to learn to read, write, and speak Nepali and to do some basic financial calculations and transactions. This opened up their world and presented them with many new opportunities, which was a great benefit for them and they valued these achievements very much.

Challenges Encountered during Assessment

The study faced several conceptual and operational challenges. Some of the concepts in the CA were not clearly defined and were difficult to operationalize or describe to others. This meant that the development workers, researchers, and community members involved in the evaluation may not have shared the same understanding and view about the CA. Second, in the context of a small project/initiative, it was difficult to demarcate the scope of functionings, capabilities, and agency, as they are interconnected. As well, a local-level project is generally limited in its scope and, hence, its ability to create an enabling environment for instrumental and substantive freedoms and agency. It was also difficult to identify a causal link between agency and the impact of activities or outputs of the projects, as there were several other factors contributing to the impacts.

During the exercise, it took considerable time to explain existential and axiological aspects to the people involved in the study. It was even more difficult to identify the types and extent of contribution made by the selected initiatives in people's lives and livelihoods. Ranking specific issues in relation to axiological and existential aspects added further complexity to the analysis. From engaging in the pilot study, it became apparent that additional discussions and trials are needed to further adapt and/or develop tools to support a capability approach to the evaluation of small projects.

Conclusion

The pilot study tested two tools—a CA evaluation framework and a human need matrix—to assess the contribution of local-level projects to people's lives and livelihoods. In the process, some conceptual and operational challenges were encountered, and further assessment and probing are needed to verify the reliability of the tools, especially the Human Need Matrix. The study, however, revealed the potential of developing a CA-based evaluation framework that could be applied to small local-level projects.

Note

1. While the definitions are taken from the HDCA briefing note, which can be found at http://www.capabilityapproach.com/pubs/HDCA_Briefing_Concepts.pdf, HDCA's definitions also include quotes from Amartya Sen's works, including *Inequality Re-Examined* (Sen, 1992) as well as *Development as Freedom* (Sen, 1999).

References

Alkire, S. (2002). Dimensions of human development. *World Development*, 30(2), 181–205.

Alkire, S., and Deneulin, S. (2009). The human development and capability approach. In S. Deneulin and L. Shahani (eds), *An introduction to the human development and capability approach freedom and agency* (pp. 22–48). London: Earthscan.

Human Development and Capability Approach. (2010). *Briefing notes—Capability and functionings: Definition and justification.* Retrieved 9 June 2010 from http://www.capabilityapproach.com/pubs/HDCA_Briefing_Concepts.pdf

Legido-Quigley, H. (2004). *Applying the capability approach: An evaluation of the well-being of older people in the context of the HIV/AIDS epidemic.* A paper presented at the 4th International Conference on the Capability Approach: Enhancing Human Security, Pavia, Italy. Retrieved from http://cfs.unipv.it/ca2004/papers/Legido-Quigley.pdf

Mathai, M.V. (2003). Case studies: Observations on operationalizing Sen's capability approach. *Development.* Retrieved from http://cfs.unipv.it/sen/papers/Mathai.pdf

Max-Neef, M.A. (1991). *Human scale development: Conception, application and further reflections.* New York: Apex. Retrieved 20 February 2011 from http://www.max-neef.cl/download/Max-neef_Human_Scale_development.pdf

Sen, A.K. (1992). *Inequality re-examined.* Cambridge, MA: Harvard University Press.

———. (1999). *Development as freedom.* Oxford, UK: Oxford University Press.

11

Impact Evaluations: Ways to Get It Right—Tips for Achieving Impactful Impact Evaluations

N. Raghunathan, Siddhi Mankad, and Ravinder Kumar

Introduction

Evaluation is the process of determining merit, worth, or significance; an evaluation is a product of that process (Scriven, 2007). Evaluations measure what programs/organizations have achieved against the 'promise'. Impact evaluations (IE) measure changes in the well-being of beneficiaries or changes in 'quality of life'. In contrast with asking whether an intervention is doing the right thing or doing it in the right way, IE is about whether it has the right effects (Jones et al., 2009). IE also tries to address attribution, that is, the degree to which these changes can be attributed to the program. When attribution is difficult, IE can identify plausible contributions each actor makes to the achievement of higher-level outcomes and ultimate impact (Tall and Rugh, 2011, slide 77). To do so, IEs follow various designs, including comparing the differences in well-being between groups receiving program benefits and a counterfactual (a control group of people who do not receive the 'treatment'), and the degree of change in the well-being of the beneficiary group over time—before and after program implementation. IE can follow different models and frameworks. The appropriateness and quality of models and processes in designing and implementing an IE determine its quality and usefulness.

This chapter, based on the experiences of Catalyst Management Services Pvt. Ltd.[1] (CMS) in conducting IEs, suggests how a rigorous process in planning, designing, and implementing IEs can help achieve impactful IEs. It describes the potential obstacles for which evaluators need to be prepared and shows how a deeper knowledge of the programmatic context and complexities helps evaluators and other practitioners design better IEs. It not only reflects on the prerequisites of well-conducted IE but also examines influential factors specific to each phase of the evaluation. We argue that excellent designs combined with effective implementation allow IEs to have an impact that reaches beyond the program being evaluated.

Lessons are drawn from the four phases that an IE process goes through: **ideation**, **initiation**, **implementation**, and **impact**. These lessons cover the various stakeholders[2] who are involved (or should be involved) in the entire process. IE studies conducted by CMS are provided as good practice examples or experiences.

Ideation

Ideation is a critical stage of an IE, as it sets the foundation for the entire evaluation. It is at this stage that the 'degree of impact of IE' is decided and the key questions being asked by the evaluation are identified and agreed upon.

IEs are usually commissioned by donors or program implementers. There are two methods used to initiate IEs. In the first method (Type 1), funders or implementers call for proposals, which specify the design to a large extent, prior to selection of the evaluation agency. Funding for the IE is assured, within specified design boundaries. The second method (Type 2) is where the evaluation begins on a blank slate. The evaluation agency develops the design in collaboration with the funders and other key stakeholders. Together, they explore funding requirements and sources for the evaluation. The processes and outcomes of each of these initiation methods differ, as do the experiences and lessons learned.

At the ideation stage, funders' expectations and the reason for the IE are explored. The reasons for commissioning IEs vary and can be related to assessment of differences in impact of strategies across different geographies and target groups, assessment of the degree to which the program has contributed to identified changes, comparison between the program and other similar interventions, and assessment of the cost-benefit of the program. Obviously, these expectations should guide the choice of methods employed. It is possible for a mismatch between expectations and methodology to lead to a situation where the IE is largely academic and is not utilized for its intended purpose.

One Type 2 IE we were involved in evaluated the impact of an integrated livelihoods strategy of a large microfinance company. The microfinance organization promotes sustainable livelihoods for the rural poor and women (among others) by providing integrated financial and technical assistance. The organization developed an integrated model in response to the knowledge that credit alone has a limited impact on livelihoods and productivity. The evaluation assessed the impact of the integrated model using ex post and recall methodologies with a mixed-methods design. In this evaluation, we led the client team through a 'pains and gains' analysis of different options for the methodology. The intent was to have the organization understand the benefits and pitfalls of each methodology in relation to the specific purpose of that IE. After reviewing all the options, the organization felt that the gains from using a randomized control trial (RCT) would not be commensurate with the costs because control areas would have to be monitored and even small changes in the project design would affect the rigour of the evaluation. The organization decided that a qualitative design would better address its needs from the IE point of view. By discussing the options in detail, the organization was able to zero in on a methodology that best suited its requirement and was well within its resources and timelines.

Research questions are identified based on commissioners' expectations. Pin-pointing one or two critical research questions that focus on impact can lead to good choice of methodology, a reasonable estimation of the resource envelope and timeframe, and consequently, near successful, if not fully successful, meeting of the expectations.

In Type 2 evaluations, where designs are not specified, the evaluation agency has the opportunity to dialogue with the funders and implementers and explore their expectations. It shares options for methodology, clearly explaining the benefits and limitations of each option. Together, the evaluation agency and funder weigh the resource needs and cost implications associated with each methodology. Wherever appropriate, evaluation agencies should create opportunities to influence policy-makers and program designers through their research. Detailed analysis at this stage will facilitate decision-making and provide clarity of purpose among all stakeholders.

However, even in Type 1 IEs, where the design is defined beforehand, the evaluation agency has the responsibility to explore the expectations and assess congruence between the suggested design and the outcome expectations. A mismatch needs to be communicated to the funder, and either the methodology or the expectations need to be reviewed and modified.

One Type 1 IE commissioned to CMS by the State Planning Commission of one of the states in Northern India was to study the impact of agricultural interventions in tribal areas of the state. The objective of the evaluation was to understand and assess the impact and sustainability of agricultural interventions in the state, document the best practices, identify lessons learned, and provide recommendations for improving tribal area agricultural interventions. The evaluation covered 200 villages in 24 blocks in 12 districts representing eight agro-climatic zones. The evaluation used both qualitative and quantitative methods. It covered 4,007 households and included 50 focus group discussions and interviews with key informants at both state and field levels. In this evaluation, we realized that stakeholders from different government departments had very different expectations of the exercise, and therefore, an evaluation reference group, which brought all stakeholders together, became extremely important. Use of techniques such as 'pains and gains' analysis and expectation and resource matching support informed choice.

A clear threat to effective IE arises when, during the process of negotiation, evaluation agencies add up the expectations of different stakeholders and make the evaluation a potentially unwieldy exercise. The IE should have relevant and specific impact questions and the terms of reference (TOR) can be used to outline the key elements of purpose, scope, process, and products. TORs should be treated not just as the basis of the contractual arrangement with the evaluator but as a scope-of-work document to be developed through series of careful deliberations and negotiations. **LESSON 1:** *Buy-in by the commissioner of the evaluation/funder for the IE is critical and can be facilitated through the informed choice of a research design that best addresses the expectations within the available resources.*

Rigour and Practicality

RCT[3] methodologies are considered the 'gold standard' by many in the evaluation field. As explained by the Abdul Latif Jameel Poverty Action Lab, 'Randomized Evaluations are part of a larger set of evaluations called Impact Evaluations. Randomized evaluations are often deemed the gold standard of impact evaluation, because they consistently produce the most accurate results.' What RCT and quasi-experimental designs essentially do is provide an understanding of 'what works' and 'to what extent' by identifying a counterfactual and comparing these results or outcomes with those of the treatment group, so that the gap between the two can be understood as the effect of the intervention and causality can be established.

As noted in a paper published by the Overseas Development Institute (Jones et al., 2009), counterfactual is just one among many types of causality. Generative causality, for example, involves identifying underlying processes that lead to change, and a configurational approach to causality is where outcomes seem to follow from a fruitful combination of attributes (Pawson, 2002). There are many practitioners in the evaluation field who have highlighted how RCT has limited or no applicability in diverse and complex situations typical of development interventions. Carlos Barahona of University of Reading, UK (2010, p. 11) notes:

> Under a well-designed and carefully conducted RCT, where contamination is known to be negligible, issuing inferential causality statements is not difficult because the experimenter will control everything else apart from the treatment; any bias would have been removed by the randomization process, and the variable of analysis is known to be a reliable indicator of

the effect of the treatment. This requires the experiment to be conducted under very special conditions. However, as argued earlier, the difficulties in controlling the conditions under which development interventions are carried out are such that the ability of RCTs to provide a standard ('gold' or otherwise) that justifies causality statements is left on shaky ground.

The most technically rigorous methodology may not always be the best or most appropriate methodology due to a number of technical, ethical, and financial reasons, outlined as follows.

- *Technical:* RCT tests the 'theory of change', which specifies the long-term goals of a program, how they will be reached, and how progress will be measured. For an RCT to work, the program components have to be fixed throughout the program's life cycle. Often program implementation is process oriented and implementers add, delete, and modify components in the course of implementation. Initiatives that allow flexibility in design may not be able to employ the RCT methodology for IE. Other prerequisites for the RCT methodology that may be limiting include the need to have a minimum number of samples and a skilled team of multidisciplinary people. Other challenges include that an RCT starts when the program does and is operational through the program life cycle. Evaluations are often planned after a program starts, and if the program is unable to accommodate the evaluation timelines, RCT will not be a suitable option. Similarly, the RCT methodology requirement of 'non-contamination' of control samples might not be practical in many cases. Finally, the associated demands on implementers of an RCT may be beyond the capacity of the program.
- *Ethical:* RCTs can generate discussion on the ethics of providing benefits to a particular group while denying them to another. Identification of treatment and control samples raises the ethical question—should the research decide who gets the benefit of the program and who doesn't? Sometimes these considerations mean RCT is not the right approach. At other times the program is intended to roll out in some areas before others or there are no adequate resources to roll out the program in all areas immediately, so an RCT can be a good option.

- *Political:* Individuals who wield power in the program areas may dictate who benefits from the program, based on their own vested interest rather than on a scientific sampling or random assignments. Such interference would compromise the rigour of the design.
- *Financial:* RCTs require large funding investments for engaging technical experts and covering large sample sizes and multiple phases over time and so on. If funding is limited, the methodology may not be a good fit.

Quality and Availability of Data—A Big Issue

The availability of quality data needed to design an IE is crucial for methodologies like RCT and quasi-experimental designs. Yet data are not always available, or, if available, may not be credible. For instance, one evaluation we were involved in evaluated a large-scale program by a civil society organization (CSO) to improve the quality of student learning at the primary level in government schools in one of the states in South India. The objective of the IE was to assess the effect of the program on intermediate outcomes, such as community involvement in schools, school enrolment and retention, and learning achievement. An experimental design (RCT) was used for this IE, with three typologies of treatment and control areas, covering 720 schools across the state, over a period of four years with eight rounds of data collection. In this evaluation we needed data on where schools were located to design the IE of the schooling program evaluation, but it took time to get these data from the government, which delayed the start of the program.

In another evaluation, an international funding agency partnered with a corporation in the sugar sector to provide comprehensive extension services to 2,000 sugarcane farmers in Northern India to enhance farm productivity. The evaluation uses a mixed-method approach to assess and describe the impact. The quantitative component addresses the kind of impact (using crop-cutting experiments and household surveys) and who benefited and to what degree; the qualitative component explains how the impact was achieved and the contributing and limiting factors. In this evaluation, secondary data on sugarcane productivity were of poor quality and reliability. These problems can be subverted if identified at the ideation stage, for example, expanding the timelines and costs of sourcing credible data through secondary and primary methods. If this is not possible, the design will have to use whatever data are available and clearly cite this as one of the limitations of the exercise.

LESSON 2: *There is a need to have a balance between excellence and relevance in terms of methodologies; openness to a plurality of approaches is essential.*

Quantitative and questionnaire-based tools may at times reveal the degree and direction of change but may not always explain the reasons for change. Process evaluation can potentially examine the reasons for change; however, process evaluation may remain outside the ambit of an IE. Process monitoring can fill in some gaps in this regard. In the evaluation we carried out with the State Planning Commission, factor analysis was attempted through focus group discussions. However, that had limited utility in the absence of reliable process-monitoring data. While the availability of a good management information system (MIS) helped in the evaluation of the microfinance company's livelihood strategy, the validity of the information available was still far from what is essential and desirable.

IEs should include multidimensional sense making, which, to a large extent, can explain the social complexity surrounding socio-economic development programs being evaluated (Snowden, 2005). As Snowden notes, IE can follow two approaches simultaneously—a structured and ordered approach based on planned outcomes, and an unordered, emergent approach focused on starting conditions, expressed as barriers, attractors, and identities.

Extending the Snowden's argument, one can say that IEs should not be simplistic in their conception and execution and should to look at more human and less mechanical aspects. Therefore, the commissioners of IEs need to understand and capture social complexity. That understanding should be reflected at the ideation stage, when the IE TOR is being framed.

LESSON 3: Look for hybridization of methods that allow better understanding of social complexities and realities that cannot be explained through one- or two-dimensional enquiry; convince commissioners of evaluations to incorporate multidimensional sense-making processes.

Initiation (Design)

During the initiation stage, the blue print for the IE is drawn. The investment of time and effort at this stage sets a strong foundation for quality implementation of the IE.

Team Mobilization and Participation

In many evaluations, the evaluation agency and program implementers are not involved in ideation and enter at the initiation stage, where the IE design gets developed. Joint design development is an opportunity for all stakeholders to understand and appreciate all points of view.

The process followed in designing the IE of the schooling program is a case in point on good 'matchmaking' for IE. Instead of asking agencies to collaborate and bid for the study, the foundation brought together different universities and non-governmental organizations and presented the project and its expectations for the IE. The agencies discussed what they could bring to the study, based on the identified collaborations. It was an opportunity to get to know a number of organizations, consider how they could align with each other, and, finally, mobilize the best possible team to steer the design of an IE based on agreed expectations and common philosophy.

However, many commissioners of evaluations would rather keep implementers away from the entire IE process. Though IE can be conducted independently without implementer participation, this comes at a great cost, since the value of the implementer's experience while designing the study is lost and their ownership in the process remains low.

A combination of skills is needed to conduct an effective IE. In the case of Type 1 evaluations, we can identify requisite skills through a microscopic examination of the TOR and of the basics required to accomplish a successful IE. In Type 2 evaluations, like the public trust example described above, a process of matchmaking contributes to establishing the right consortium of organizations (picked for their skills) that can deliver the IE product effectively. In both typologies, the collaborators should jointly develop the proposal for the IE. Since the implementer is usually a new addition to the team at this stage, the processes followed during ideation need to be repeated to include the implementer's experiences and perspectives. Major changes can happen in the design framework with the inclusion of implementer's experiences—such as access to districts, sample selection, adapting to the context of the study region, and so on.

LESSON 4: *Good 'matchmaking' is critical to ensure good intentional design and implementation.*

Simplifying IE Language

Terms such as RCT, regression discontinuity, contribution analysis, theory of change, empowerment index, and so on can be quite overwhelming to non-evaluators. For example, many recipients of evaluations understand randomization and random sampling to be the same thing. The evaluation agency and commissioners of evaluations have a responsibility to explain the terms used in evaluation design and to ensure that implementers understand the subtle differences between the terms so that they can contribute to the process of developing a sound design. Technical terms need to be clearly explained, with examples wherever appropriate.

Time and expert resources are the two important prerequisites of a high-quality evaluation design proposal that would be acceptable to all stakeholders. Pre-proposal activities—such as field visits and sharing and debating issues—contribute to the design process. Involving people with expertise in different areas (designing IE methodologies, domain experts, field experts, etc.) brings credibility and robustness to the design. Furthermore, involvement of stakeholders who are affected by the evaluations is a *sine qua non* during the initiation of evaluation, as it can build understanding and ownership of the process itself, while bringing additional rich perspectives to the design. Investment in these initial processes fetches returns by smoothing the way for, and ensuring the quality of, subsequent processes. Watchful patience among the commissioners of evaluations, therefore, can impart rigour to the design that will contribute to achieving the objectives of the IE.

In the evaluation with the State Planning Commission described earlier, the initiation process was rushed because timelines were tight and the involvement of various concerned ministries could not be secured in time. When the ministries all finally came together at the presentation of the evaluation findings, they were clearly not on the same page in terms of understanding the relevance of the design and the quality of the processes that went in implementing the IE. So while the evaluation brought out policy-relevant findings and observations, the chances of these being incorporated in policy discourse were diminished—partly because the initiation process was rushed and partly because the political context was poorly managed during the evaluation. We are not suggesting that political management should be within the scope of evaluators who wish to inform and influence through the evidence base (IFs by their very intent have a political element); nonetheless, more awareness and sensitivity towards these issues help in making IEs useful.

LESSON 5: *Watchful patience among commissioners of evaluations improves the possibility of achieving the purpose of IE, while the converse is also true, as a rush at the initiation stage can 'spoil the party' during the presentation of results.*

Restricting Flexibility of Program Design

Often implementers are enthusiastic to start the program and are impatient with having to wait for the IE design to be finalized; they get upset with the IE process. The funders and evaluation agency need to be sensitive to such situations and keep implementers informed and involved in the IE process to assure their participation and acceptance.

Impact evaluators and implementers are often at loggerheads on how the program should run during the IE. Some impact evaluators subscribe to a fidelity-based approach, which dictates that the program not deviate from its stated design. Implementers, on the other hand, may feel that the addition, modification, or removal of components happens as field contexts change and knowledge for improved implementation is generated. They may want the flexibility to be able to implement the changes and have to be convinced to maintain fidelity to the project design during the project period. For example, in the IE of a large-scale schooling program, the non-governmental organization running the program planned to introduce cluster resource centres (CRCs), which were not part of the original design, in the third year of the project. The CRCs would undertake teacher training, which in turn would affect the final learning outcomes. The degree to which the CRCs contributed to change in learning outcomes would be difficult to measure, since there was no baseline. The IE design had to be modified mid-way to accommodate this change, extending its timeline by a year.

LESSON 6: *In the case of RCTs, managing the tension of rigour with program implementation requires adjustments by both evaluators and implementers.* Impact evaluators need to resist the urge to change the project to fit a desirable design. The project drives the evaluation design rather than the evaluation design driving the project.

Involving Policy-makers

Involving policy-makers is also useful at the ideation and initiation stage. Policy-makers have their own interests in the study, which may be addressed in ways other than just robust design. If the design can incorporate their needs, they are more likely to consider the findings as evidence for policy modification or change when the time comes.

The IE of the agricultural interventions in tribal areas described earlier was commissioned by the State Planning Commission in one of poorest states in India, but the agricultural initiatives being evaluated were implemented through the Agriculture Department, which also develops the agriculture policy. The involvement of the Agriculture Department was low because of this divergence between commissioning and implementation responsibilities, resulting in a lower acceptance of the findings by the department. In contrast, in the schooling program evaluation, the Project Director was closely involved in developing the design and all his queries and needs were accommodated. This led to a high level of satisfaction with the outcomes of the IE and the findings being incorporated into policy dialogue.

Implementation

Rigour in the ideation and initiation stages of the IE design needs to be carried through to the implementation stage. The resource agency and implementer are the key players during this phase, yet the funders, policy-makers, and external experts involved in the design need to remain informed and provide guidance as required. Success in the implementation of IE findings rides on comprehensive planning for internal validity parameters. Some of these parameters (which are presented as threats to internal validity) and the relevant strategies that can be used to address them are described as follows.

- **Ambiguous temporal precedence**: In most IEs, clearly identifying the timing of impacts is challenging especially when activities are continued over long periods of time. In the evaluation with the State Planning Commission, it was difficult to isolate the impacts that had happened only over the past five years, as agriculture interventions by the government have existed in tribal areas for a much longer time. Without a clear baseline, assessing impacts becomes a difficult and controversial exercise. Similarly, in many evaluations of NGO programs, we have found that due to continuing long-term funding in a particular area, it is impossible to decipher impacts of certain interventions within a particular timeframe. In such situations, certain methodologies, like regression discontinuity design (RDD),[4] have strong internal validity. In addition, impact evaluators can look at a range of time-series-analysis-based methods (like story line, time-series analysis) that enhance better understanding of outcomes vis-à-vis the timeframe in which they happened. However, the time lag between the trigger and the actualization of change may still make it difficult to avoid temporal ambiguity completely, making it the task of impact evaluators to assess the attribution of change to a particular project or intervention.

- **Inappropriate proxy indicators:** Proxy indicators are used when it is difficult to find a measurable proxy for the impact indicators. For example, the use of income as a proxy for welfare or economic condition is fraught with problems related to both its adequacy and measurement. In circumstances like this, better internal validity can be obtained by using an empowerment framework or a well-being index to measure the impacts. Furthermore, a mixed-methods design with strong reliance on qualitative datasets can ameliorate the situation.

We developed an empowerment index for the IE of a large-scale civil society program in Northern and Eastern India that aims to reduce gaps between socially excluded communities and the rest of the population by increasing the uptake of entitlements by socially excluded groups in a large number of India's poorest districts. We also used the Progress out of Poverty Index and the Multidimensional Poverty Index as a measure of the economic status of the sample households.

- **Unreliable respondent memory or deliberate distortion**: In this instance, internal validity of IE is jeopardized due to deliberate distortion and/or fading respondent memory. This would clearly indicate a need to conduct a pilot before a full-scale survey is carried out to understand how widespread the problem is and to identify an appropriate response to address the anomaly.
- **Disorganized data protocols and data management**: Towards the beginning of the implementation stage, the resource agency needs to keep a close watch on the veracity of the data on which the design was founded—especially for data available from the public domain. The study team needs to review the data coming from the field frequently so that calibrations to the design, if needed, can be made early on. All the necessary government approvals need to be sought before field data collection can commence. The lowest cadre in the government needs permission letters from superior officers before consenting to data collection within their jurisdiction. A set-up team, which visits the region ahead of the main data collection team, secures all permissions and takes care of logistics enabling the field team to enter into the area without any challenges.

In many studies, there tends to be a greater focus on field data collection than on other stages in the implementation process on the assumption that this is the most difficult stage of implementation and that once data collection quality is assured, quality outputs will follow. Studies can crumble on the back of such assumptions. Data management can pose many challenges to quality issues and should be tightly managed. Preferably, the data entry should be centralized to enable easy supervision. Stepwise data entry and cleaning checks need to be undertaken, including

i.   field-level checks by the field quality assurance officer, to ensure that data formats are complete and legible,

ii. tracking forms by coding and entering data formats into registers/
     formats as they are given to teams and received at the data office,
iii. using data entry software that has validations for fields,
iv. ascertaining the quality of the data entry with double data entry
     or ensuring that a portion (10–20 per cent) of the data entry
     back-checks are made by the data manager,
v.   generating and checking the first set of tables for inconsistent data
     and outliers to nip any data-entry issues in the bud and to pre-
     vent issues from blowing up into large and unmanageable pro-
     portions, and
vi. addressing questions that remain or emerge at the time of analysis
     by going back to the original questionnaires.

- **Design-specific and non-sampling errors:** Though some evaluators advocate standardization, a degree of flexibility may need to be
  built into tools to accommodate the local context. In the absence
  of such flexibility, information that is critical to understanding and
  measuring impact may be lost. Pre-testing data collection tools
  can help evaluators identify and incorporate field contexts before
  finalization. In addition, keeping the tools flexible enough to be
  able to collect new information in subsequent rounds is also an
  option. Process monitoring needs to be incorporated into design
  to allow the design assumption to be monitored constantly. The
  resource agency collects detailed data from the implementers on
  the activities being implemented, the dates of implementation, the
  difference between the treatment and control samples, and so on.
  Process monitoring is important to understanding the change taking place and the drivers of that change.

In studies with treatment and control samples, where there is a high
level of top-down sample selection, shadow samples need to be identified to accommodate 'missing' or 'absent' samples.

- **Maintaining motivation:** For the field data collection work,
  the field team needs to be constantly motivated so that energy
  is maintained over the period of the IE. Developing daily plans,
  with end-of-the-day reflections, is one way to maintain motivation. In addition, morning, mid-day, and end-of-the-day reviews

reported to the project office assure quality control. Field teams are paired, and the members of each pair should be rotated every three days. This allows for cross-learning between teams and also cross-checking for quality.

LESSON 7: Better IEs require consideration of and adherence to internal validity parameters.

Impact

Sandison (2005) captures various uses of IEs, including instrumental use, conceptual use, legitimization use, and ritual use. Instrumental use involves direct implementation of findings and recommendations to help decide whether to continue, terminate, expand, or modify policies or programs. Conceptual use involves evaluations providing new ideas and concepts. Process use involves learning on the part of people and management involved. Legitimization use involves corroborating a decision or understanding. Ritual use serves a purely symbolic purpose.

Ensuring that uses are not solely ritual or around legitimization involves clarity, strategic thinking, and 'political economy'[5] skills on the part of the evaluators or those who have a stake in making IEs work. These skills are even more important when contextual factors like political dynamics, the need to protect organizational funding, and credibility play a role in catalysing utilization of IEs. Essentially, an impact evaluator's role does not finish with the evaluation. Evidence is necessary but may not be a sufficient condition for change resulting from IEs.

In the evaluation with the State Planning Commission, CMS was mandated to deliver the evaluation report with one-time sharing of the evaluation findings and recommendations. We were not mandated to continue to engage with the State Planning Commission, the Agriculture Department, the Tribal Welfare Department, or any other department. The realization that we had a larger responsibility, given that we were handling a policy-relevant subject, drove us to conduct at least three specific engagements to present the evaluation findings to relevant stakeholders and to suggest an alternative to the existing model of agriculture extension. In fact, the State Planning Commission asked us to demonstrate the alternative model in the field, resulting in another stream of work for a CMS sister organization. Similarly, in the evaluation of the livelihoods project, a series of communication mechanisms were developed so that the organization (recipient of evaluation) and the sector as a whole could benefit from the results of the interventions (brought out by the evaluation) in terms of future strategies related to livelihoods finance. Developing mechanisms for communication or feedback loops once the IE exercise is completed enhances the visibility of the evaluation and its implications for better programing, strategies, and policies.

Strong evidence needs to be backed by strong engagement processes with key stakeholders, which can tip the scale towards moving the evidence to policy implementation. IE studies provide the opportunity to go well beyond an exercise of learning, to provide evidence to influence policy. Though difficult, the involvement of key stakeholders needs to be mapped and sought, since this has a bearing on their involvement and support in the policy advocacy process. Given varied stakes, this is likely to be a challenge. Some of our tips for making this update more likely are provided as follows:

- **Build a factor of safety in the design:** A common challenge in working with governments is that decision- and policy-makers often change over the period of the evaluation. Each person who occupies the decision-making position may have a different orientation to and expectation of the evaluation. For instance, some officials would prefer quantitative methods and others might be more inclined towards a qualitative inquiry. We encountered these diverse expectations in the evaluation with the State Planning Commission, wherein a particular department wanted a macro-analysis and perspective from the evaluation, while another department wanted a micro-analysis and perspective to enrich the policy process. Clearly, a factor of safety that accounts for a potential increase in resources and expertise needs to be built to accommodate such eventualities, preferably at the design phase.
- **Simplify communication:** The language used to share evidence needs to be simple and jargon-free, so that stakeholders can understand and appreciate the outcomes of the study and take forward recommendations and actions emerging from it.

- **Unpack implications of the evidence:** Understanding and teasing out the various implications of the evidence is a key activity at this phase of the study. There is a cost and effort involved in bringing the evidence forward for strategy modification and policy advocacy. The resource agencies need to unpack the implications of implementing the recommendations. Reflection on some key questions helps identify the implications of the evidence: Who will be affected with a change in policy? How will they be affected? What are the resource implications? Implementer and policy-makers need to be involved in these discussions, as they are in a position to respond to these questions.

- **Productize the strategies:** Finally, a 'product' that addresses the key developmental challenges and is well packaged accelerates adoption. For example, through the IE we could offer a prototype of the agriculture extension model to demonstrate how to provide demand-based agriculture services at the door step of the farmers that improved farmers' returns, making the findings particularly interesting to government stakeholders.

LESSON 8: *Impact evaluators have a larger responsibility that goes beyond doing the evaluations and translates into catalysing conditions to make the worthwhile utilization of evaluations eminently possible. For bringing change, evidence is necessary but not sufficient.*

Conclusion

The phrase 'use it or lose it' applies to IEs. IEs lose their relevance if they do not stir a debate, create chaos, disturb the equilibrium, stimulate thinking and action, or lead to any discursive changes or policy dialogue. IEs have the power to stir a debate and create short-term and lasting changes in development practice and policy. For more than a decade, we at CMS have been involved in a range of IEs in South Asia and have experienced all kinds of situations (and the associated emotions) from no-use IE to impactful IEs. This chapter is a synthesis of our experiences related to what makes IEs work and how IEs can be made to work.

Obviously, there are both endogenous and exogenous factors that influence the delivery of impactful IEs. The evaluators who understand cultural context, organizational dynamics, human psychology, and political economy, along with having the research and other skills to design and deliver the IEs well, have a better chance of success in achieving the purpose of IE.

Though these experiences cannot really be condensed into learnable tips, we have made a modest attempt to do so in this chapter. We have especially highlighted obstacles that we normally face in the ideation, initiation, implementation, and impact phases of IE. We have shared some of the tips related to how these obstacles can be surmounted and have drawn out nine lessons from the challenges that we encountered in doing IEs. These lessons are listed again below, and we welcome debate and further elaboration from the broader evaluation community.

- **LESSON 1:** Buy-in by the commissioner of the evaluation/funder for the IE is critical and can be facilitated through the informed choice of a research design that best addresses the expectations within the available resources.
- **LESSON 2:** There is a need to have a balance between excellence and relevance in terms of methodologies; openness to a plurality of approaches is essential.
- **LESSON 3:** Look for hybridization of methods that allow better understanding of social complexities and realities that cannot be explained through one- or two-dimensional enquiry; convince commissioners of evaluations to incorporate multidimensional 'sense-making' processes.
- **LESSON 4:** Good 'matchmaking' is critical to ensure good intentional design and implementation.
- **LESSON 5:** Watchful patience among commissioners of evaluations improves the possibility of achieving the purpose of IE, while the converse is also true, as a rush at the initiation stage can 'spoil the party' at presentation time.
- **LESSON 6:** In case of RCT, managing the tension of rigour with program implementation necessitates adjustments by both evaluators and implementers. Impact evaluators need to resist the urge to change the project to fit a desirable design. The project drives

the evaluation design rather than the evaluation design driving the project.

- **LESSON 7:** Better IEs require consideration of and adherence to internal validity parameters.

- **LESSON 8:** Impact evaluators have a larger responsibility that goes beyond doing the evaluations and translates into catalysing conditions to make the worthwhile utilization of evaluations eminently possible. For bringing change, evidence is necessary but not sufficient.

Notes

1. Catalyst Management Services Pvt. Ltd is a consulting firm working in social development. See http://cms.org.in
2. This article uses the following terms for key stakeholders: *resource agency* is the agency involved in the implementation of the IE and is likely to be a collaboration of agencies; *commissioner/funder* is the agency that funds the program and the IE; *implementer* is the agency that implements the program; *policy maker*, usually a government body, is responsible for making and implementing development policies; *advisors or experts* are external individuals brought on board at different phases of the study to provide their expertise towards quality improvements; *study team* includes all the agencies and individuals directly involved in conducting the IE and may include all or some of those mentioned above; and *field team* is the team mobilized by the resource agency to carry out field data collection and analysis.
3. RCT is generally the primary methodology used for the quantitative IE of a program in a randomized experiment. With RCT, 'treatment' and 'control' samples are selected randomly from all clusters covered by the program.
4. RDD is a quasi-experimental technique wherein assignment of treatment and control is not random. There is a known cut-off in treatment assignment (e.g., 33.3 per cent SC + ST + Muslim population and with more than 28.3 per cent poor population was taken as cut-off in RDD of a large civil society program in India). The continuity assumption formalizes the condition that subjects just above and below the cut-off are **comparable**—requiring them to have similar average potential outcomes when receiving treatment and those when not. RDD yields an unbiased estimate of treatment effect at the discontinuity (Roberts, 2010).
5. According to Wikipedia (*Political economy*), 'Political economy most commonly refers to interdisciplinary field drawing upon economics, law, and political science in explaining how political institutions, the political environment, and the economic system—capitalist, socialist, mixed—influence each other.'

References

Baker, J.L. (2000). *Evaluating the impact of development projects on poverty—A handbook for practitioners.* Washington, D.C.: World Bank Publications.

Bamberger, M., Rao, V., and Woolcock, M. (2010). *Using mixed methods in monitoring and evaluation: Experiences from international development* (World Bank Policy Research Working Paper Series). Washington, D.C.: World Bank.

Barahona, C. (2010). *Randomised control trials for the impact evaluation of development initiatives: A statistician's point of view* (Institutional Learning and Change Working Paper, No. 13). Rome: Institutional Learning and Change Initiative.

Deaton, A. (2010). Instruments, randomization, and learning about development. *Journal of Economic Literature*, 48(2), 424–55.

Fetterman, D. and Wandersman, A. (2007). Empowerment evaluation yesterday, today, and tomorrow. *American Journal of Evaluation*, 28(2), 179–98. Retrieved 11 June 2014 from http://www.davidfetterman.com/documents/EEyesterday.pdf

James, C. (2011). *Theory of change: A report commissioned by Comic Relief.* London, UK: Theory of Change. Retrieved from http://mande.co.uk/blog/wp-content/uploads/2012/03/2012-Comic-Relief-Theory-of-Change-Review-FINAL.pdf

Jones, N., Datta, A., and Jones, H. (2009). Knowledge, policy and power—Six dimensions of the knowledge–development policy interface, London: ODI.

Pawson, R. (2002). Evidence-based policy: The promise of realist synthesis. *Evaluation*, 8(3), 340–58.

Pawson, R. and Tilley, N. (1997). *Realist evaluation.* DPRN Thematic Meeting 2006 Report on Evaluation, University of Amsterdam, Netherlands.

Roberts, M.R. (2010). *Regression discontinuity design (RDD): Empirical methods* (PowerPoint slides). The Wharton School, University of Pennsylvania. Retrieved from http://www.google.ca/url?sa=t&rct=j&q=&esrc=s&source=web&cd=2&cad=rja&ved=0CCsQFjAB&url=http%3A%2F%2Ffinance.wharton.upenn.edu%2F~mrrobert%2Fteaching_files%2Ffin926%2FLecture%2520Slides%2FRDD.ppt&ei=x1V0UNrnJeq30AH7_oHIAQ&usg=AFQjCNFlotdCa97H3OSYXepp1r9N4_dLCg

Sandison, P. (2005). The utilisation of evaluations. In J. Mitchell (ed.), *ALNAP review of humanitarian action: Evaluation utilisation* (pp. 89–146). London: Active Learning Network in Accountability and Performance in Humanitarian Action. Retrieved from http://www.livestock-emergency.net/userfiles/file/common-standards/ALNAP-2006.pdf

Scriven, M. (2007). The logic of evaluation. In H.V. Hansen et al. (eds), *Dissensus and the search for common ground* (CD-ROM; pp. 1–16). Windsor, Ontario, Canada: OSSA.

Snowden, D.J. (2005). Multi-ontology sense making: A new simplicity in decision making. In R. Havenga (ed.), *Management Today Yearbook 2005*.

Stufflebeam, D.L. (1999). *Foundational models for 21st century program evaluation*. Kalamazoo, MI: The Evaluation Center, Western Michigan University.

Wikipedia. (n.d.). *Political economy*. Retrieved from http://en.wikipedia.org/wiki/Political_economy

12

Giving Voice: Making Evaluation Contextual for Marginalized Groups in South Asia

Nazmul Ahsan Kalimullah and Mojibur Rahman Doftori

Introduction

Evaluation is a yardstick for measuring the relevance, performance, efficiency, and impact of project's work against its stated objectives (Bakewell et al., 2003; Fetterman, 2005; Mertens, 2009). Its aim is to ensure accountability (to both project donors and users), improve performance, identify lessons that can be applied to other projects, and increase communication between different stakeholders. Within the evaluation community, it is agreed that participation of stakeholders in general and project users in particular is highly valuable in measuring project impact. Evaluators' perceptions about the broader relations within society, a particular development project, the change process, and reality are conditioned by their own social, economic, cultural, class, and power relations in their own community and in broader society.

In his excellent book *Development as Freedom*, economist and Nobel Prize winner Amartya Sen emphasized that 'expansion of freedom' is both a primary end and the principal means of development. According to Sen, '[d]evelopment consists of the removal of various types of unfreedoms that leave people with little choice and little opportunity for exercising their reasoned agency' (Sen, 1999, xii). As any given society has competing interests, the role of authentic development is to help the weak overcome the oppression of the strong to strengthen their own agency and dignity.

There is a considerable debate about good evaluation practices in South Asia, in particular whether the objective and value-neutral technocratic approach to evaluation—examining input, process, and output— can bring about a nuanced understanding of the impacts of development interventions in complex socio-economic and cultural contexts. In contrast, the more subjective and value-relative pluralist approach is seen as being more culturally sensitive and respectful of the different perceptions of reality in any given context (Bakewell et al., 2003). It is not the intention of the authors to debate the relative merits of each but rather to shed light on the usefulness of the pluralistic approaches in conducting effective evaluation in complex cultural contexts.

This chapter analyses the cultural contexts of South Asia and explores what pluralist approaches bring to the evaluation and development field in South Asia based on existing literature on evaluation in South Asia as well as on the authors' direct experiences in development research and project evaluations. The goal of this chapter is to shed light on the concepts of 'choice', 'agency', and 'distinct voice' as they relate to marginalized groups and their input into policy debate and the practice of evaluation and to contribute to furthering evaluation research and making evaluation more participatory, inclusive, and truly democratic.

Different Approaches to Evaluation

Based on the diverse views on how the development process should be monitored and evaluated, Bakewell et al. (2003, pp. 8–9) proposed two contrasting approaches: the technocratic approach and the pluralist approach (see Table 12.1). The technocratic approach considers that the right inputs (i.e., right resources, science, and technology) will provide the solutions to all human problems and their progress can be evaluated using mechanisms that are objective and value neutral The pluralist approach is based on the pluralistic view that different perceptions of reality should be treated with respect and valued. This means that there are no absolute or objective criteria for evaluation that can be set in advance by external development planners or evaluators based on their own value judgments. It also calls for the incorporation of a wide range of stakeholders' opinions and perceptions (including those of target groups) and does not depend exclusively on the views of project management and evaluators.

Table 12.1
Differences between Technocratic and Pluralist Evaluation Approaches

Technocratic	Pluralistic
Mechanistic	Holistic
Objective	Partially subjective
Value neutral	Value relative
Rigid	Flexible
Exclusive	Inclusive
Quantitative	Qualitative

Source: Adapted from Bakewell et al. (2003).

Pluralist approaches to evaluation are more flexible and inclusive in terms of incorporating diverse opinions. Empowerment and transformative evaluation are two examples of pluralist approaches to evaluation. Proponents of empowerment evaluation say that it places a focus on community ownership, inclusion, democratic participation, social justice, community knowledge, and evidence-based strategy in evaluation (Fetterman, 2005). Empowerment evaluation calls for evaluators to facilitate active community participation in the development and evaluation of projects, that is, helping people help themselves. Donna Mertens (2009) introduced the transformative paradigm and approach to evaluation to address the issue of people pushed to the margins of society throughout history and to bring their knowledge and voices into the world of research and evaluation. Mertens' approach is derived primarily from her own work with deaf people and their experiences with sexual abuse and court access, with parents of deaf and hard-to-reach children, and with minority group women. With this approach, evaluators work as partners with the 'voiceless' to increase social justice, human rights, and social change by incorporating their perspectives in evaluation work.

This approach does not assign blame to the 'victims'/excluded groups and considers target groups and communities as resilient and as having power to make change in a supportive social context. The evaluators take into consideration the power structures that perpetuate social inequities and work as advocates to address issues that arise from power imbalances, discrimination, and oppression. The transformative evaluation critically examines the assumptions that historically have guided research and evaluation studies and puts evaluators in the role of instruments of social change.

The role of Mertens' evaluators resonates with the role ascribed to educators by the Brazilian educator Paulo Freire (1970, 1990, 1998). Freire advocated that knowledge must be sympathetic to the disadvantaged groups and encouraged 'dialogue' between educators and learners to unveil 'opportunities for hope' for the latter. Although Freire called for transformative education in a different time and ideological context in Latin America, his view of educators as those who supported the counterhegemonic struggle to make education a tool to affirm the unrealized potentials of the oppressed groups is similar to the role ascribed to evaluators by Mertens. She sees evaluators as those who value the capacity of target (i.e., marginalized) groups and provide spaces for them to reclaim individual dignity and social possibilities. In hierarchic social, cultural, and political contexts, such as those in South Asia, pluralist approaches to evaluation are more inclusive than other approaches in recognizing and valuing the experiences and voices of marginalized groups. In this way they open up a door for claiming or reclaiming voice.

For example, in their evaluation of an HIV/AIDS program in Bangladesh, Nepal, and Indonesia, targeting males having sex with males (MSM), Coghlan et al. (2008) found it challenging to identify and contact members of this mostly covert (by choice and necessity) group within the different social and cultural milieus of South and Southeast Asia. They found that giving participants greater ownership of and investment in evaluation motivated them to support the evaluation work. Addressing key stakeholder involvement and ownership had similar results in an HIV/AIDS awareness program in a Cambodian village where a monk at the local pagoda was uncooperative with the team promoting HIV/AIDS awareness in the village. Looking more closely at the situation, evaluators found that the monk had been left out of the decision-making process when it came to planning important activities in the village. When the team realized the problem, it apologized and the monk immediately became cooperative (Jayakaran, 2008).

Relevance of Pluralist Approaches to Evaluation in South Asia

Theories of development originated in the Western Europe and were exported to the non-Western world so that developing countries could follow Western development patterns and emulate industrialized or modern societies' political and social institutions. Since the mid-1940s, developing countries have been following different development models and several East and Southeast Asian countries are catching up to the West in terms of becoming societies based on mass consumption (Martinussen, 1997). Beyond that, countries such as China, India, and Brazil have succeeded in creating state institutions strong enough to support state-led development through industrialization. However, a large portion of their population has no access to the benefits of development interventions. Many developing countries in Asia, Africa, and Latin America face the 'strong society-weak state' syndrome, and their public institutions and institutions of representative democracy are too weak and fragile to reach the majority of their citizens (Migdal, 1988).

For the majority of the population in South Asian countries, the state is an unfamiliar institution with little impact or involvement in their lives; this alienation is even more pronounced for the poor and those belonging to cultural minority groups. Because of the hierarchic worldviews established and maintained by historical and cultural forces, oppressed and marginalized groups get less space in state-led development agendas and interventions. Historical and cultural forces have shaped state- and nation-building processes, educational opportunities, worldview, group identity, and social hierarchy in South Asia, creating a unique region.

The challenges in evaluation in the region are similar to the challenges in education. Different education systems in the region have different roots and links—including religious, colonial, and development aid organizations—which shape the mindsets of the students in each group. The predominantly colonial roots of the education systems in South Asia created a 'gentleman' class of educated people who are Western in tastes, opinions, morals, and intellect and detached from everyday reality of common people. This class of people is detached from or may have contempt for manual and technical work and the people who do it. They are represented predominantly in the arenas of policy-making and the implementation of development programs. As a result, the voices of ordinary people hardly reach the policy level, as they do not have the power or opportunity to compete and contest the views of those who are connected to the decision- and policy-makers in development.

The existing, and some would argue culturally biased, education system does not necessarily fit with the social and economic needs of the rural and urban poor. It is male-biased and does not promote equity and democratic citizenship (Doftori, 2004). Because of the weaknesses of the prevailing educational systems in South Asian countries, there is a need to reform education systems so that educated people do not become uprooted from their culture and can respect their own roots, cultures, values, and other members of society, irrespective of their economic, social, or cultural backgrounds.

In similar way, there is a need to rethink the role of evaluators to include incorporating the perspectives of the poor and marginalized groups. As in many other societies, poor, marginalized, and cultural minority groups in South Asia lack a sense of 'self-worth' as persons within the context of broader society because of poverty, lower status, and in many cases hopelessness. Developing a sense of autonomy, hope, and/or self-worth among typically marginalized groups—such as persons with disabilities, untouchables, women victims of trafficking and prostitution, street children, and child labourers—is a big achievement for any development intervention. From this point of view, evaluation methods require appropriate methods and tools to give the poor, the marginalized, and the culturally oppressed a voice. Because of the special cultural contexts of South Asian countries, pluralist approaches such as empowerment evaluation and transformative evaluation can be used to make evaluation more contextually relevant. The adoption of pluralist methods can make evaluation and intervention planning more inclusive and democratic by making 'agency' of target groups count, irrespective of the group's or the individual's economic, social, and/or cultural background.

Agency, Facilitation, and Self-initiative

Doftori's doctoral dissertation on education for marginalized children (2004) and the evaluative work on disabled people's self-initiatives for development in Bangladesh by Kalimullah and de Klerk (2008) and Kalimullah and Islam (2010) are cases that demonstrate the importance and relevance of pluralist/transformative approaches to research and evaluation, particularly in South Asia.

Children, Poverty, and Access

Based on his fieldwork with disadvantaged children in Bangladesh and Nepal, Doftori (2004) challenged the predominant thesis that poverty is the most important determining factor in children's participation in child labour activities in South Asia. He found that though poverty has impacts on children's participation in schools, it cannot totally block children's access to education. In fact, the study found that poverty should not be a significant barrier to the education of child labourers in developing countries. In his study, Doftori looked at the role of non-governmental organizations (NGOs) in the education of child labourers. He found that child labourers involved with the NGO schools and education projects were able to combine their work and education, despite family poverty, largely unfavourable household and school environments, and broader cultural norms that see work as the only option for children from poorer households. In the findings, Doftori argues that the underlying cause of child labour is not poverty itself; rather, it is the unequal distribution of resources within a country, a society, and among households. This inequality is further supported by social and cultural norms regarding childhood, children's agency, citizenship rights, needs, and welfare and is aggravated by less relevant and low-quality education.

In this study, Doftori used a range of qualitative research methods that allowed him to tap into and tease out the contextual, cultural, and individual influences and outcomes related to the NGO's educational programs. In particular, he looked at the role of children, their perceptions of themselves, and the role of adults in their lives. He found that

- children in South Asian cultures are never accorded with an identity of their own, and they remain an object of their parents' wishes and family needs.
- there is general sense of children being 'owned' by their parents in South Asia and the autonomy and/or agency of children is considered an outrageous concept.
- cultural respect for seniors gives the adults of South Asia authority over children. Parents may demand labour from their children; employers can take advantages of labour of children who are considered as innocent, docile, and less troublesome. In most cases, child labourers in the study were deployed in work and their work and income controlled by their parents.
- the opinions of girls in the study challenged the 'romantic view' across South Asian cultures that families are a cohesive and sharing unit of solidarity. Patriarchal social norms put girls and women in South Asia under tremendous unpaid workloads, give them low visibility, and are less likely to value investments in their education and development. Which raises a serious question, 'Do parents or community always represent the best interest of children?'

While conducting research on children, a researcher needs to listen to the perspectives of children to be able to conduct authentic research. The researcher needs to picture children's everyday lives and their aspirations and dreams and incorporate their voices, being sympathetic to their causes. This makes the researcher an advocate for the rights of marginalized children, and the research work participatory and authentic.

Using this approach Doftori was able to tap into children's perceptions and found that

- children under NGO education and skill development programs went through an uphill struggle and negotiation with their own family members, community, employers, and teachers to assert their 'choice' and 'agency' and feel empowered within themselves.

- the life stories of children manifested that poverty and hardships were not significant barriers to the education of child labourers. Most of them combined education, skill development, and work in innovative ways and contributed their families in better ways with the proactive support of NGOs. This enhanced their morale as contributing members of the family and society.

- children under the study learnt reading, writing, and numeric skills in NGO schools, along with social consciousness on issues of health care, first aid, nutrition, family planning, civic responsibilities, and so on. These had immediate effects on their 'self-confidence' and capability to handle day-to-day affairs better and escape from exploitative social relations.

- the role of NGOs in education for disadvantaged children gave children a sense of being 'somebody' in the society. Impacts of education cannot be measured solely on the basis of input and output, as education also has long-term benefits for students that cannot be measured by short-term cost-benefit analysis.

- NGO schools have increased students' 'confidence', 'capability', and 'choice to act' in society. The changes in attitude have positive effects not only on children themselves but also on the future generations.

The study on education and skill development and disadvantaged children required the researcher to be sympathetic to contexts and causes as well as to understand children's realities at home, community, work, and school to draw an authentic and representative picture of the impact. Within the given context, the researcher had to play the dual role of researcher as well as advocate for child rights (Doftori, 2004; Holmes, 1998). Value neutrality within this context can be termed as unfair and cruel to the lives of those children in especially difficult circumstances. Within this special context, research methodology should focus more on the emotional side of disadvantaged children.

Disability and Self-determination

Kalimullah and de Klerk (2008) and Kalimullah and Islam (2010) evaluated the impact of the Persons with Disabilities' Self-initiative to Development (PSID) project in Bangladesh. The PSID is a consumer-driven, rights-based, holistic approach that empowers persons with all types of disabilities. They focused on the self-initiatives of disabled people themselves under Bangladesh Protibandhi Kallyan Somity (BPKS), an NGO working for and organized by disabled people. They assessed the social impact, institutional development, and economic and financial sustainability of the programs.

Persons with disabilities are at the margins of society in Bangladesh and totally excluded from mainstream development projects and programs including education, health care, income generation, and social security. As a result, many live a life of seclusion and exclusion, ashamed to express themselves in the social context of stigma associated with being disabled. Many live simply by begging. They also have problems of accessibility in public places, as policy planners care little about their causes.

The PSID approach supports disabled people's organizations to assist disabled persons access to basic services such as health, education, government allowances, access to government and NGO training and development programs, and access to financial services provided by government banks, social welfare departments, and microfinance institutions. The program also aims to develop the self-confidence and self-esteem of its members through group formation, leadership training, awareness of disability issues and basic rights, microcredit and income generation activities, and equal participation of disabled persons in social and economic life.

Disabled persons' self-initiative and self-organization provided a central role in addressing the needs of disabled persons. These projects addressed their basic needs (assistive devices, therapy, referrals), self-confidence building and self-organization (individual and organizational capacity building), and economic inclusion (income generation activities, training, loans).

The evaluation team acknowledged that the team members had to be sympathetic and play an activist role to be able to understand how the program significantly changed the disabled persons' perception of self and life. As individuals, they became disabled at different stages of their life, experienced different types of disability, and had to go through their own unique experiences of despair and adjustment. The PSID intervention revolutionized the worldviews of persons with disabilities. With the arrival of the PSID approach, persons with disabilities developed a sense of self-worth and gained more respect from parents, other family members, and the community. Now disabled children are sent to school and begging is not an option. Parents do not neglect their disabled family members and, under the project, have begun to take their opinions seriously as they have become contributing family members. Groups' members conduct weekly meetings and write meeting minutes on their own, with no or little support from project staff. They make plans for earning their livelihoods themselves; they choose their partners in marriage and participate in local government activities through their own organizations.

Before the start of the program, many of the members depended completely on their families and their families did not expect them to contribute financially or to become self-reliant. Through joining the disabled peoples' organizations, they were able to get capacity-building training, coupled with advocacy, motivational, and skill development training, which helped them gain self-confidence. This self-confidence was enhanced by the support and encouragement of the other members in the group and by the attitudinal changes in their families and the wider community. The projects have also promoted the mobilization of savings among the group members for building up their own capital and provided training and support for pursuing income-generating activities.

The evaluations of these projects show that under the right facilitative environment, disabled people can be productive citizens, just like anyone else. The problems lie not with disabled people themselves but with the social and cultural norms and institutions that have constructed a notion of disability that is more isolating and harmful than the disability itself. The evaluators of disability projects, like the project workers, need to understand and focus on the strengths and resilience of disabled people, instead of on preconceived ideas about their inability as disabled persons. They should also take a political stand, strengthen the position of disabled people, and draw an authentic picture of disabled people's development.

Lessons Learnt and Conclusion

Based on the results of the work by Doftori, Kalimullah, and de Klerk, and Kalimullah and Islam, it can be argued that the proactive role played by researchers/evaluators to give voice to the most disadvantaged groups can play a key role in making evaluation broad-based and contextual and, hence, relevant and effective in terms of development goals. Acknowledging marginalized children, persons with disabilities, or others as individuals with 'agency' is the first step towards giving them a voice in research or evaluation work. Being sensitive to the living conditions, aspirations, and struggles of marginalized groups is the first step towards a more pluralist approach to evaluation, through which evaluators can examine both the economic and the non-material gains—such as a sense of autonomy, agency, and self-worth; hope for the future; and intergenerational impacts—achieved in development projects/programs. Evaluators need to have a sympathetic attitude and give moral support to disadvantaged groups who are in Sisyphean struggles against all the structural and social odds to reclaim their autonomy, dignity, and social possibility through facilitated self-initiatives. Pluralist evaluation approaches lead to a further nuanced understanding of development projects.

Pluralist approaches to evaluation are highly relevant not only for child labourers and people with disabilities but also for other disadvantaged groups such as women, tribal/indigenous groups, cultural minority groups, victims of sexual abuse, untouchable groups, and many other groups in South Asia. In fact, comments of some evaluators on a research report based on technocratic approach are worth mentioning. The Asian

Development Bank's 2001 evaluation report on rural credit assistance in a number of South Asian countries stated,

> Traditional rural credit projects with their focus on growth are effective in encouraging increased production and productivity, but less effective in reducing poverty and disparities in income because they were not primarily designed to address poverty reduction directly. A more focused approach on poorer clients would need to be adopted to have credible impact on poverty reduction. Such an approach would require a participatory process of beneficiaries and other stakeholders to clearly identify the poor in terms of incidence, locality, priority, and needs.

This indicates that the credit operations of the Asian Development Bank need to be redesigned to address poverty reduction and that evaluators need to target poorer clients and look at their particular context to make evaluations credible and effective. This provides a clear justification for the use of pluralist approaches in project/program evaluation in the wider context of poverty and income disparity.

The pluralist approach to evaluation aims to make project evaluation and development planning and practices more contextual, ethical, and humane to reclaim citizenship rights of the most disadvantaged groups in South Asia. To portray an authentic picture of the heroic struggles of disadvantaged groups, evaluators require sympathy and compassion, as well as appropriate methods and tools. The hopes, aspirations, and struggles of the people at the margins of society are not less valid than traditional indicators of economic and social development. If and when the pluralist approaches suggested by this chapter are implemented together with other approaches, they will make evaluation and development planning and interventions more inclusive, more authentic, and more democratic.

This approach works well in the context of deep social inequality—it amplifies the voices and recognizes the agency of the poor and most vulnerable groups and contributes to furthering the objectives of development. Within the context of South Asian region, which is culturally hierarchic, this approach is extremely relevant and appropriate.[1] However, it has its potential limitations. The activist role of evaluators is permissible as long as there is deep inequality supported by cultural norms and as long as human dignity is under challenge.

Note

1. Such an approach is less applicable in comparatively less hierarchic social contexts. In such contexts, triangulation of data can reduce the risk of data being biased and can be a used for quality of information in an evaluation. To ensure reliability of data, findings from different sources can be cross-checked. For triangulation, Roche (Roche, 1999, cited in Bakewell et al., 2003) has suggested using three different perspectives in evaluation, that is, using different sources of information, using different methods of data collection, and using different people to collect data.

References

Asian Development Bank. (2001). *Impact evaluation study on ADB's rural credit assistance in Bangladesh, People's Republic of China, Indonesia, Nepal, Philippines, Sri Lanka, and Thailand*. Manila, Philippines: ADB.

Bakewell, O., Adams, J., and Pratt, B. (2003). *Sharpening the development process: A practical guide to monitoring and evaluation*. Oxford, UK: International NGO Training and Research Centre.

Coghlan, A.T., Girault, P., and Prybylski, D. (2008). Participatory and mix-method evaluation of MSM HIV/AIDS programs in Bangladesh, Nepal, and Indonesia. In B. Williams and M. Sankar (eds), *Evaluation South Asia* (pp. 35–46). Kathmandu, Nepal: UNICEF.

Doftori, M.R. (2004). *Education and child labour in developing countries: A study on the role of non-governmental organizations in Bangladesh and Nepal*. Helsinki, Finland: Helsinki University Press.

Fetterman, D.M. (2005). A window into the heart and soul of empowerment evaluation: Looking through the lens of empowerment evaluation principles. In D.M. Fetterman and A. Wandersman (eds), *Empowerment evaluation principles in practice* (pp. 1–26). New York: Guilford.

Freire, P. (1970). Cultural action for freedom. *Harvard Educational Review*, 68(4), 1998, 471–521.

———. (1990). *Pedagogy of the oppressed*. London: Penguin Books.

———. (1998). *Pedagogy of hope: Reliving pedagogy of the oppressed*. New York: Continuum.

Holmes, R.M. (1998). *Fieldwork with children*. London: SAGE Publications.

Jayakaran, R. (2008). New participatory tools for measuring attitude, behavior, perception, and change. In B. Williams and M. Sankar (eds), *Evaluation South Asia* (pp. 47–60). Kathmandu, Nepal: UNICEF.

Kalimullah, N.A. and de Klerk, T. (2008). *Encompassing all: Impact study of the PSID programme of BPKS*. Dhaka, Bangladesh: BPKS.

Kalimullah, N.A. and Islam, S.K. (2010). *Final evaluation of persons with disabilities self-initiatives to development (PSID) project in Chittagong*. Dhaka, Bangladesh: BPKS.

Martinussen, J. (1997). *Society, state, and market: A guide to competing theories of development*. London: Zed Books.

Mertens, D. (2009). *Transformative research and evaluation*. New York: Guilford.

Migdal, J.S. (1988). *Strong societies and weak states: State-society relations and state capabilities in the third world*. Princeton, NJ: Princeton University Press.

Roche (1999), cited in Bakewell, O., Adams, J., & Pratt, B. (2003). *Sharpening the development process: A practical guide to monitoring and evaluation*. Oxford: International NGO Training and Research Centre.

Sen, A. (1999). *Development as freedom*. New York: Oxford University Press.

13

Voices from the Field

Ethel Méndez

'The evaluation context in South Asia is changing,' said Manas Bhattacharyya (see Chapter 7), a development professional, during an interview about his experience as an evaluator in the region (personal communication, 16 May 2011). His opinion is not isolated. Between August and September of 2010, more than 130 South Asian evaluation stakeholders—including evaluators, researchers, academics, and representatives from non-governmental organizations (NGOs), government, and donor organizations—gathered in meetings organized by the Community of Evaluators (CoE)[1] in Kathmandu, Mumbai, Chennai, and Dhaka to reflect on the state of evaluation in South Asia. Their conclusions portray a strengthening field that is plagued with power imbalances and technical and theoretical challenges. They speak about opportunities and about how to improve evaluation in South Asia. Their opinions matter. They have shaped regional events such as the Evaluation Conclave, which drew more than 300 evaluators from around the globe in 2010, and the second evaluation conference held in the same city in April 2011. Their voices continue to shape the evaluation context in the region and have reached donors and evaluation forums internationally.

However, if their opinion is changing the field, what exactly are they saying? What is their take on the state of development evaluation in South Asia? Does it need to change? If so, how? This chapter seeks to answer these questions. It draws on documents from CoE meetings, papers written by its members, and interviews with South Asian evaluators to convey the voices from the field.

This chapter is divided into two sections. The first section discusses stakeholders' views on the state of the evaluation field in the region. The second section provides an overview of suggestions for future directions for evaluation in South Asia shared at regional CoE events held in 2010.

The State of Development Evaluation

Evaluation in South Asia spans a variety of development areas, from food security and climate change to health and gender issues. Despite the variety of domains, evaluators have identified prominent features that characterize the field. They comment on evaluation's learning and accountability purposes, on the fact that it is a donor-led exercise, and on prominent debates around methods. They also reflect on the need for improving evaluation use and quality and for creating more spaces for dialogue and sharing.

Learning and Accountability

Evaluation consultant Veronica Magar (see Chapter 5) states, 'evaluation matters because it is about learning and about the transformative impact it can have' (personal communication, 24 August 2011). Like Magar, many evaluators in the region see evaluation as a necessary learning exercise in project management, one that 'has the potential to facilitate deeper insights into development processes, improving programs and policies' (CoE Bangladesh Chapter, 2010, p. 1.). Bhattacharyya adds that evaluation matters in South Asia because improvements in development work would translate into improvements in the lives of millions of people living in poverty and exclusion (personal communication, 16 May 2011).

Despite the strong focus on learning, evaluators agree that the predominant view of evaluation in South Asia is as a tool used only for accountability. While evaluators understand the value of accountability, they argue that such a focus, *without a learning lens*, has created the perception of evaluation as a 'threatening exercise; [used to] to close down or disengage with the projects; [a] fault finding exercise' (CoE Chennai Region, 2010, p. 2). Evaluation is also perceived as a 'ritual, [a] part of the project cycle, and a mandatory word which does not help in any stimulation or synergy' (CoE Chennai Region, 2010, p. 2). Similarly, evaluators noted that they are perceived as 'interlopers' and 'quick-fixers' and that their attitudes, experiences, and credibility are often overlooked.

> For a lot of people evaluation means that someone will come and police you. I think that is why it is not in our culture. They think it is only about accountability and transparency, but it should go beyond that. . . . I think evaluation can be very helpful in our context, if only we develop a positive culture around it. (Ram Chandra Khanal, personal communication, 14 September 2011)

Donor-led Evaluation

Evaluators in the region agree that donors and developed countries still drive evaluation practice, namely that 'donors . . . set the objectives, scope, tone, and when to have [evaluations]' (CoE Chennai Region, 2010, p. 1). Evaluation plans are ratified with the evaluators and the groups to be evaluated after they have been designed, which creates difficulties when 'evaluators have to compromise on methodology and its rigour due to [design] limitations of time and resources' (Solomon, 2010, p. 4).

> [The evaluation scenario] has shifted from the logical demand in the project necessitating for an evaluation to an artificially created situation where the evaluants are forced into the 'evaluation' as a mandatory activity. (CoE Evaluation Conclave participant [Solomon, 2010, p. 4])

The predominant view is that evaluations are commissioned to comply with donor demands and to ensure accountability, which is often linked to continuity of funding. These two facts have led some evaluation stakeholders to explain attitudes toward evaluation with the phrase 'Not that I did it for my learning, but you did it and let me see what I could learn from it' (Solomon, 2010, p. 2). This attitude toward evaluation is seen as detrimental, for it emphasizes donor needs over learning and removes ownership of the evaluation process from the evaluated group. Evaluators' depiction of the evaluation scenario as 'fund focused, not context specific, culturally irrelevant, and insensitive' (CoE Chennai Region, 2010, p. 3) speaks of the challenges they see in donor-driven evaluation. The fact that donors and donor interests drive evaluation practice has also led to the exclusion of key stakeholders at different phases in the evaluation process, resulting power asymmetries. Evaluators in South Asia say this happens too often, particularly in summative evaluations where implementing agencies are brought in after funders have decided to evaluate. Formative evaluations tend to follow the project cycle and, therefore, allow the implementing agency to be engaged at an early stage (CoE Chennai Region, 2010). A related challenge is that 'evaluators are never involved in goal setting or strategy development stage of programs' (Solomon, 2010, p. 3). This results in poorly defined program objectives and theories of change and/or indicators that make it hard to assess the program's achievements.

> Terminology like 'participatory evaluation' and 'partnership' has become just jargon which is understood insufficiently, misinterpreted, and misused. (CoE Evaluation Conclave participant [Solomon, 2010, p. 4])

Another level of exclusion occurs for members of communities or groups that benefit from the programs. In these cases, evaluators sometimes 'take the role of the power holder' (Solomon, 2010, p. 3). Evaluators and stakeholders participating in CoE regional meetings in Mumbai noted that community members and intermediaries are hardly involved in planning and finalization of an evaluation, which could have implications on the degree of ownership they have of the process and of the evaluation results (CoE, 2010).

However, some evaluators, like Khilesh Chaturvedi (see Chapter 7) from the Association for Stimulating Know How (ASK), say there is evidence that donors and commissioning agencies are becoming more open to different approaches to initiating, leading, and ensuring participation in evaluations. The opening comment by Bhattacharyya on the changing context of evaluation relates specifically to this point, as he perceives a more inclusive, receptive approach by commissioning agencies (personal communication, 16 May 2011). Such a change could offer a great opportunity for evaluators in the region to influence the field's future.

Evaluation Methods

There is a vibrant debate about quantitative and qualitative methods in the region. Quantitative data are often seen as apolitical and myopic, while qualitative data are criticized for being highly subjective. There is also the perception that quantitative methods are preferable to qualitative ones. Researchers Ratna M. Sudarshan and Divya Sharma (in press) explain, 'numbers are often more effective in advocacy than narrative ... discussion and case studies become supplements to the data generated through a survey, responding to the demand for quantification stemming from the implementer/donor (or both).' Preference for quantitative methods is a concern for some evaluators who warn that the human then becomes a 'number' (Solomon, 2010, p. 2).

> Evaluation practice in South Asia has been fairly unimaginative. This needs to change, so that better evaluation can take place. Being creative is a first step to improving evaluation practice. (Suneeta Singh and Sangita Dasgupta, personal communication, 23 June 2011)

Suneeta Singh and Sangita Dasgupta from Amaltas (see Chapter 8), a consulting and research organization in New Delhi, suggest that more creativity in methods is needed to improve the evaluation field. They note, 'evaluators must describe the research question clearly and simply and then be very creative in how they create the tools to answer that question' (personal communication, 23 June 2011).

Similarly, Zaveri (see Chapter 4) goes beyond suggesting new tools and methods and raises the idea that they need to be contextually relevant. To exemplify this need, she narrates her experience applying the Stanford–Binet intelligence test to children in the region. Zaveri noticed that the children repeatedly got a question about patterns wrong. Intrigued, she redesigned the question to test the same principle but replaced the patterns provided in the standard test with patterns familiar to the children, such as patterns found in the mats they sat on. The children were then able to answer the question correctly. Zaveri notes that this is a case where a misunderstanding of context could result in misinformed findings (personal communication, 7 June 2011). Like Zaveri, others such as Solomon (see Chapter 6) and Nazmul Ahsan Kalimullah (see Chapter 12)—a professor from Bangladesh—speak of the need to contextualize the tools and methods used, whether by creating new ones or simply by using languages understood by the communities where they are applied (personal conversation, 6 June 2011).

Evaluation Use

Evaluation use is also an area of concern for South Asian evaluators. They hold that 'the evaluation findings and reports have limited dissemination, stay within the donor and the evaluands, and are used/misused selectively' (Solomon, 2010, p. 2). The attitude assumed by commissioning agencies, which evaluators refer to as 'patent- like', coupled with exclusion of certain stakeholders during the evaluation process, leads to at least two scenarios that compromise use. In one scenario, the commissioning agency or 'patent holder' might not be the best user of the evaluation findings, and failure to transmit results to the appropriate users leads to no use or a misuse of findings.

In a second scenario, where the commissioning agency does not assume a 'patent' attitude and disseminates findings adequately, the implementing agency or community members may not see the relevance or value in implementing changes derived from a process conducted without their active participation or that they do not fully understand. Again, use is compromised. For evaluators working in the development field, like Bhattacharyya, no use or misuse of evaluations has significant consequences; it becomes a missed opportunity to improve the performance of an initiative that could have a significant positive effect on people's lives.

Some evaluators, like Dr Pal, former Chief Executive Officer of the Programme Evaluation Organization (PEO) at the Planning Commission, Government of India, speaks to the need to sensitize planners, policymakers, and administrators on the importance of evaluation use in order to build the field. He notes, 'sensitization . . . about the usefulness of evaluation . . . is necessary to transform the current superficial demand for evaluation into an effective demand so that these actors realize the importance of creating an enabling environment for developing domestic evaluation capacity' (personal communication, 15 September 2011).

Quality of Evaluation

In his introductory message at the Regional Meeting on Evaluation Practices and Challenges in Bangladesh, Khairul Islam, a founding member of the CoE, pointed out that quality remains a persistent gap in evaluation (CoE Bangladesh Chapter, 2010). Evaluators in the region agree and associate poor quality with low evaluation capacities in the region. In fact, they hold that low local evaluation capacities have led donors to import evaluators, most often to lead evaluations. The reasons for low capacity are diverse, but many point to inadequate and insufficient evaluation training.

> Capacity building on evaluation is not a priority of government or funders. (CoE, 2010, p. 2.)

> Crucial at this juncture is capacity enhancement of evaluators. (CoE, 2010, p. 2.)

Almost all evaluators interviewed pointed to capacity building as an important, if not the most important, activity to improve evaluation. However, there is diversity of opinions on how and on what to build that capacity. Zaveri notes, 'I think it is important to use several approaches for capacity building . . . if we want to bring more adaptation, innovation, and hopefully theory building' (personal communication, 7 June 2011). In terms of approaches, the Teaching Evaluation in South Asia project[2] has developed a diploma-granting curriculum on evaluation, which will be delivered at various universities in the region. Others, like Solomon and Zaveri, emphasize their experience as mentors in a Utilization-focused Evaluation (UFE) project in India and suggest mentoring as an effective mechanism for capacity building. On the content of potential trainings, Chaturvedi sees the need for skills and methods training while Ram Chandra Khanal (see Chapter 10), an evaluator from Nepal, suggests a greater focus on developing capacities on evaluation theory. Despite the general low capacity, it is worth noting that evaluators also sense a change from informal and less rigorous practice to one that is highly professional and expert.

The quality of evaluation is also compromised by the poor quality of data in South Asia. 'Authenticity is always problematic in the data collection, collation, processing, correlating to absolute number and documentation' (Solomon, 2010, p. 3). Practitioners in the region rely on government sources and academic statistics that often do not tell the full story. Data collected by community-based organizations, on the other hand, are questioned for their validity, as 'it becomes difficult to identify and value it or [to] isolate the emotions attached' (CoE Chennai Region,

2010, p. 2). To cope with data issues, evaluators sometimes end up modifying or redesigning the proposed methodologies.

Another deficiency in evaluation quality is that evaluations do not question the development premises upon which programs are built. More specifically, 'the evaluation scope and its implementation hardly dwells on and checks the root causes of the issues on which project or program is built; the reason for the deprivation, grassroots complexities and the relevance of the problem to the current situation' (CoE Chennai Region, 2010, p. 2). In a forthcoming article, Katherine Hay (see Chapter 3), former Senior Program Specialist at the International Development Research Centre (IDRC) based in New Delhi, suggests that different approaches to evaluation, such as applying a feminist lens, can tease out and challenge iniquitous discourses underlying programs or projects. The Institute of Social Studies Trust (ISST) in New Delhi launched a project in December 2011 to explore feminist and other similar approaches that can help evaluators address this quality concern.

Spaces for Dialogue and Sharing

Evaluator Abu Hanif notes that 'there is currently no visible platform providing space for interaction and exchange of views for knowledge sharing in the region. As a result, there is limited reflection, convergence, and research on evaluation taking place' (CoE Bangladesh Chapter, 2010, p. 1). He explains that the CoE emerged in response to that situation: as a platform to bring together evaluators for dialogue and sharing. Since its creation, the CoE has worked to engage evaluation stakeholders and improve evaluation practice, but members agree that more needs to be done to engage more practitioners in a more meaningful way. They note that more exchange groups, platforms, and evaluation associations need to emerge to check or challenge practices, improve dissemination, promote good practices, and open spaces for exchange between regional and international evaluation experts.

Looking Ahead

Based on the review of their context and their own experiences, evaluators have started to develop an image of what evaluation practice should look like in South Asia. The CoE has played a critical role in bringing together the voices of evaluators who were previously working in isolation. They understand that they have significant work ahead, but together they have developed a vision for the field. Below are some of the comments and suggestions shared at the 2010 Evaluation Conclave held in Bangalore (Solomon, 2010), which provide a glimpse of their collective thinking about the future direction of evaluation in South Asia.

- Evaluation should focus on the bottom-up learning, knowledge, methods, achievements, critical gaps, and a futuristic road map. It should take cognizance of the traditional wisdom, people-centric knowledge, social fabrics, and nativity. There should be inclusiveness and social accountability.

- Evaluations should focus and escalate to address the larger programs/projects and macro-policy issues: evaluating large government programs like the Mahatma Gandhi National Rural Employment Guarantee (MNREG) in India, or evaluating the overall impact, the development role, and the interventions of the internationally funded NGOs in the country.

- [There is a] need to desist from following the government approach of evaluating its programs, which has the overtone of auditing. . . . Rather, the government should learn the evaluation perception, methods, and approaches set by the other actors like the Community of Evaluators (CoE). But ensure that the evaluation is not done as a fashionable activity copied from the West.

- The evaluation should be the collective responsibility of the donor, the evaluants, and the evaluators; the collective search and onus is on all the three stakeholders.

- The evaluators should know the domain, field, culture, and people who are to be evaluated. He/she should understand the context, vision, and mission of the organization before undertaking evaluation.

- The evaluation should seek clarifications on the development perspectives, the strategic options, the ideological alignment, the social change process, and the future directions. [There is a] need for a framework to define weightages for process versus impact.

- [There is a need to improve] implementation of the review findings into the decision-making and USE for the improvement, the effectiveness of the project/program, and the institution.

Evaluators in South Asia believe that 'evaluations lead to drastic changes' (CoE Chennai Region, 2010, p. 2) and are committed to working—both individually and collectively—to ensure that evaluation practice continues to move toward the vision they described. Their reflection on the state of the evaluation field identifies many challenges, but they understand every challenge is an opportunity for developing potential solutions and for change. More important, their engagement in the reflection process and subsequent events and forums is evidence of their strong commitment to ensure that change happens.

Notes

1. Constituted in October 2008, the CoE is a platform that provides space for interaction and exchange among evaluators in South Asia. The goal of the CoE is to promote and enhance the quality of the theory and practice of evaluation in South Asia and to contribute to the same, particularly from a South Asian perspective, globally. Its current members come from Afghanistan, Bangladesh, India, Nepal, Pakistan, and Sri Lanka.
2. This IDRC-sponsored project aims at strengthening evaluation training in South Asia by developing a diploma-granting evaluation curriculum that will be offered at several universities in the region.

References

CoE. (2010). *Evaluation Conclave 2010: Making evaluation matter. Regional events and multiple voices: Road map for a change*. New Delhi, India: CoE.

CoE Bangladesh Chapter. (2010). *Report of the regional meeting on evaluation practices and challenges in Bangladesh*. Dhaka, Bangladesh: CoE.

CoE Chennai Region. (2010). *Brief report—synthesis*. Chennai Region Meeting—Evaluation Conclave—CoE. Chennai, India: CoE.

Solomon, C. (2010). *A synthesis: Regional events*. Evaluation Conclave 2010—CoE. Bangalore, India: CoE.

Sudarshan, R. M. and Sharma, D. (in press). Gendering evaluations—Reflections on the role of the evaluator in enabling a participatory process. *Indian Journal of Gender Studies*.

About the Editors and Contributors

Editors

Katherine Eve Hay leads the monitoring, learning, and evaluation function for the Bill & Melinda Gates Foundation in India. This leadership role involves decision-making on evaluations, fostering outcome-focused investments, and promoting evidence-based programming. Katherine is the strategic lead on foundation evaluations of programmes in both Bihar and Uttar Pradesh, with decision-making responsibilities for evaluation design, strengthening grantee organizations' monitoring and evaluation (ME) systems, and use of real-time monitoring data and evaluation findings. Her responsibilities include ensuring the technical and pragmatic quality of the foundation's evaluation work in India, using evidence for decision-making, and ensuring an engagement model that supports foundation grantees and programme officers to design robust, outcome-driven grants. Katherine brings a strong gender and equity focus to her work. She is a member of the Adolescent Girls working group at the Gates Foundation and has focused extensively on women's empowerment and gender equity throughout her career. Katherine has written on women's empowerment, feminist evaluation, and evaluation capacity building. Prior to joining the Gates Foundation, she worked at the International Development Research Centre in New Delhi. Katherine has supported many funders and organizations in setting up gender- and equity-oriented evaluations and systems. She has recently agreed to serve on the joint UN Women Global Evaluation Committee.

Shubh Kumar-Range is currently leading the gender and food security integration in agricultural policy for United States Agency for International

Development/Volunteers in Overseas Cooperative Assistance (USAID/ VOCA's) support to the Government of Ethiopia's Agricultural Growth Program. She has been actively involved in the Community of Evaluators for South Asia and its strategic development since 2008. She has conducted a large number of strategic, policy, and programme evaluations focused largely on poverty, nutrition, and food security. Earlier, between 1978 and 1995, she conducted path-breaking research with the International Food Policy Research Institute, establishing the significance of women's income and their role in decision-making for improving household welfare parameters, including food security and child nutrition. She has written and published extensively on these issues, and many of her writings have been used as reference material in leading universities around the world, including the Kennedy School of Government at Harvard University.

Contributors

Manas Bhattacharyya, a development professional with over 22 years of experience working with grassroots groups in child development, child labour, and health and nutrition projects—has, over the past 7.5 years, been involved in monitoring and evaluation, organization development activities, and issue-based studies.

Khilesh Chaturvedi, a founding member of Association for Stimulating Know How (ASK) with over 23 years of experience in the development sector, has expertise spanning organizational development, strategic planning, project development, project management, participatory approaches, and social developmental evaluation and research.

Sangita Dasgupta, a sociologist, has over a decade of experience with gender, maternal and child health, adolescent sexual and reproductive health, HIV/AIDS, and nutrition projects; she has managed programmes and has conducted research and evaluation. She has worked with several organizations including Amaltas, MSG Strategic Alliance, CARE and CINI among others.

Mojibur Rahman Doftori has focused on child labour, Education for All (EFA), the role of civil society organizations (CSOs) in education sector development, governance and elections, and Poverty Reduction Strategic Papers (PRSPs). He is also a freelance researcher with a PhD and post-doctoral work from the universities of Helsinki and Tampere in Finland.

Sarah Earl is Director of Program Research and Development at the YMCA of Greater Toronto. She is responsible for the strategy to build evaluation into its youth leadership programmes using developmental and participatory approaches. Sarah previously worked with IDRC on developing innovative approaches like outcome mapping and managing projects to develop evaluation theory and practice in the global South such as building an evaluation network in the Middle East and North Africa.

Nazmul Ahsan Kalimullah is teaching Public Administration since 1984 in the University of Dhaka, Bangladesh. He got his BSS(Hons) and MSS in public administration from the University of Dhaka. He completed MSocSc and earned a PhD from the University of Birmingham, UK, in development administration. He has completed his postdoctoral research in development studies from the University of Bath, UK. He is a life member of SLEvA and a member of CoE. He is also acting as the MD of CoE, Bangladesh.

Anuska Kalita works for the ICICI Foundation for Inclusive Growth— Centre for Child Health and Nutrition. She has an interest in community health workers, nutrition, public health systems, governance, and developing local research capacities. She has a degree in psychology and a master's in development, with a specialization in health.

Ram Chandra Khanal is a development professional from Nepal working on sustainable agriculture, biodiversity, natural resource management, and climate change. He has worked for the International Union for the Conservation of Nature (IUCN) and the United Kingdom's Department for International Development (DFID).

Ravinder Kumar holds a degree in physics, chemistry, and mathematics, and a postgraduate degree in forestry management. With over 14 years of experience in social development, he has expertise in monitoring and evaluation, research, and organizational development across a number of focus areas, including livelihoods, agriculture, private sector models, and natural resources management.

Veronica Magar, an independent consultant with previous experience of working with CARE, holds a master's in public health, a master's in Latin American studies, and a doctoral degree in public health and is the founder of REACH (Research for Action and Change).

Siddhi Mankad is a development professional with postgraduate degree in rural management. She has over 16 years of experience in research and evaluation, particularly Qualitative and Mixed Method Research methodologies, with particular expertise related to health, education, disaster risk reduction, social protection and livelihoods with postgraduate degree in rural management.

Ethel Méndez is an advisor to the Honorary Ministry of Health's HIV/AIDS/STI Program on monitoring evaluation. She wrote the Ministry's 2010–2012HIV/AIDS monitoring report and is working on developing monitoring plan for national prioritized indicators. She has led studies on the surveillance information system for most at-risk populations and needs assessment for the implementation of specialized services for Garifuna communities—a Honduran ethnic community—and for people living with HIV/AIDS. She is a member of the Honduran evaluation professional society, REEDHPRESS, where she helped organize regional events in Central America. Prior to her current role, Ethel worked for the International Development Research Centre, India, where she was involved in strategic evaluation on research excellence and became a part of the group that explored contributions of feminist theory to evaluation. She is the co-ordinator of a volume about feminist evaluation in South Asia and is a master's in public and non-profit management.

Pradeep Narayanan, a development professional who has worked for the Government of India and is currently at Praxis Institute for Participatory Practices, holds an MA in development studies.

N. Raghunathan, an agricultural engineer with postgraduate degree in rural management, has over 20 years of experience in research and evaluation in the social development sector, with particular expertise related to livelihoods, health, education, and natural resources management.

Y. Dayanand Singh is trained as a social worker and has worked for the Government of India, Amaltas and various multilateral organizations; he has experience working in HIV/AIDS, health, micro-finance, rural development, and with grassroots and self-help groups.

Suneeta Singh is the CEO of Amaltas, a research and consulting organization based in New Delhi. Trained as a medical doctor, Dr Singh has had extensive experience in the policy and strategy space, having worked previously at the World Bank, Department for International Development, UK and the Government of India. Her interests are broad, ranging from encompassing public health, evaluation, social systems, public–private partnerships for development and sustainable solutions.

Chelladurai Solomon is an independent consultant with postgraduate degrees in sociology, rural policy and planning, and business management and with over 17 years of experience in monitoring, evaluation, and training.

Sonal Zaveri, a PhD, specializes in participatory, gender and equity-focused evaluation with a strong emphasis on use. She is the founder member and Secretary of the Community of Evaluators South Asia. Zaveri is also an advisor to the feminist evaluation network in India and an International Advisor with the Child-to-Child Trust, Institute of Education, London. Sonal writes on the intersection of evaluation with context, vulnerability and empowerment.

Index